Handbook of Human Resource Information Systems

Handbook of Human Resource Information Systems

Reshaping the
Human Resource Function
with Technology

Alfred J. Walker

McGraw-Hill, Inc.

New York St. Louis San Francisco Auckland Bogotá
Caracas Lisbon London Madrid Mexico Milan
Montreal New Delhi Paris San Juan São Paulo
Singapore Sydney Tokyo Toronto

Library of Congress Cataloging-in-Publication Data

Walker, Alfred J.
   Handbook of human resource information systems : reshaping
the human resource function with technology / Alfred J. Walker.
      p.   cm.
   Includes index.
   ISBN 0-07-067815-4
   1. Personnel management—Data processing. 2. Management
information systems. 3. Information storage and retrieval systems—
Personnel management. I. Title.
HF5549.W288 1992
658.3′0285—dc20   92-24327
                                       CIP

 This book is printed on recycled, acid-free paper containing a minimum of 50% recycled de
inked fiber.

   3 4 5 6 7 8 9 0 DOC/DOC 9 8 7 6 5 4

ISBN   0-07-067815-4

*The sponsoring editor for this book was Betsy N. Brown, the editing supervisor
was Marion B. Castellucci, and the production supervisor was Donald F.
Schmidt. This book was set in Baskerville. It was composed by McGraw-Hill's
Professional Book Group composition unit.*

Printed and bound by R. R. Donnelley & Sons Company.

To Heather

Contents

Part 2. Bringing the Vision to Life: Principles and Practices of the Development Cycle

Foreword

Al Walker has finally given us the premier guide for designing human resource information systems. We've seen books and articles on the functions required for an effective HRIS—reporting, recruitment support, benefits calculation data—but this book has a higher goal. It shows us new ways of thinking about HRIS. It helps us elevate the capabilities of our systems to be something more than "back office record keepers." Instead, it brings those systems to the forefront for users of all levels.

The decentralization trends in IS today—fueled by the marriage of the desktop and the mainframe—warrant changes in the way we deploy and manage human resource systems. Essentially, we need to empower the HR professional to communicate openly with other users and employees. We need to give managers and decision makers access to the information they need to advise and guide the work force. We need to enable users to manipulate the software themselves, without requiring technical assistance. And we need to replace mundane tasks with technology so HR professionals can focus on more important, and often more interesting, objectives.

Walker's broad knowledge of HRIS history provides a foundation for understanding the agents that have molded the systems of today and for learning from the wrong turns we have taken. He draws on the mistakes of the past to illustrate the requirements of the future. Then he shows us the impact of technology on human resources in that future.

First-hand experience with world-class organizations and a complete knowledge of business needs make Walker a master of methodology. The development approach he outlines here addresses a wide range of implementation issues, from needs analysis to disaster recovery to costs.

More importantly, he simplifies and translates his methodology into one that all users, from beginners to veteran HR professionals, can readily understand. His flair for bottomline, no-nonsense terms makes us clearly see that we can all apply his project management principles to build systems that "extend the reach" of today's HR offerings.

Much like learning a new language, this guide teaches us to think about HRIS technology in different, broader terms. In the end, we'll be able to communicate with a whole new group of people and operate effectively in a whole new corporate culture. No longer will we have to rely on legacy systems that can't provide accurate, timely information and that leave us a decade or two behind the times.

So read on. You'll find that you'll use this handbook again and again as a tool for applying technology to manage your company's most valuable asset—your employees.

DAVE DUFFIELD
President and CEO
PeopleSoft, Inc.

Preface

A basic premise of this book is that human resource information systems (HRIS) are in their infancy in most organizations where they exist at all, but that they can and probably will become the central business technology of successful organizations in the twenty-first century. The critical issues faced by American organizations operating in a global economy are, to a growing extent, human resource management issues. And the information and automated processes needed to manage human resources effectively are simply not available to most organizations today. For example:

- Most human resource (HR) departments are devoting between 40 and 60 percent of their efforts to administering their HR plans—activities which can (and should) be transferred to technology, thereby freeing up the HR staff to perform higher-value work.

- Line managers who are already using sophisticated computer tools in their work cannot gain access to the records on their own employees.

- In the average American organization, as much as 40 percent of total compensation cost goes to benefits. Yet the average employee continues to know very little about the value or cost of the benefits package—such as what it will take to finance their retirement years.

- Organizations today operate, increasingly, in a global economy with virtually unlimited technology transfer, a fact that has changed forever the meaning of "the available labor force." This book—or a daily newspaper, for that matter—could be written in Cannes, set in type in Puerto Rico, edited in London, and printed simultaneously on presses throughout the world—wherever the publisher finds the most effective human resources to do each job.

- Jobs in the growing service industries, increasingly, come down to customer service. Whether the organization is selling cheeseburgers in Chelsea or accounting in Akron, the quality of customer service represents the key business differentiator, or competitive edge, if one exists. In the past, production-line workers could be effective without speaking English if they could communicate with the foreman; today most employees must be able to communicate with the customer.

- Jobs in all industries at all levels are part of the worldwide "mechanization of work." New skills and qualifications for computerized jobs are essential if the promise of productivity improvement is to be realized; yet new employee qualifications in the United States, at least, are tumbling at unprecedented rates.

What is still needed within the organization are better methods of informing management about employees and other workforce participants. Although automated personnel systems have been in use in major corporations for over 25 years, they still have not lived up to their promise of granting instant access to employee records or detailed skills and knowledge banks to permit better job placement, to put the right person in the right job at the right time. Most of the systems deployed over the years have been back-office record keepers, there primarily to track salaries and benefits and to ensure that the payroll is handled correctly. Nowhere in these systems does one find the objective of helping line managers meet their sales or customer service goals. The next wave of systems must change that orientation. The HRIS of tomorrow, if it is truly to help the organization meet its profit or service goals, must go beyond the traditional human resource record-keeping functions and deliver to line managers and the employees, as well as to everyone in human resources, the necessary information and administrative assistance and in a much more cost-effective manner.

Many of the ideas and principles expressed in this book have been developed in the course of my work with major corporations over the past 10 years or so, both at AT&T and at Towers Perrin. The clients include but are not limited to such companies as American Express, BASF, Coca-Cola, Dun & Bradstreet, Exxon, GTE, Kmart, Marriott, Ontario Hydro, 3M, Sears Roebuck, Turner, and Xerox. These companies, like many others, want to reshape the human resources functions both to help them become more effective by transferring activities to technology and to help line managers and employees communicate more directly with each other and to participate more freely, and knowledgeably, in company programs.

The technology of the future will enable human resource people to act more as business advisors and consultants to the business units and at the same time enable and empower line management to carry out their functions more easily. Today's systems and the attendant support functions in HR administration, HRIS, IS and finance organizations must change in order for this to happen. It is hoped that this book will help that change occur.

A few words about the organization of this book may be useful to the HR managers and HRIS professionals for whom it is written, not all of whom have the same needs or interests. Although certain themes and principles are treated as constant—such as that the HRIS team must change the work, not merely automate existing procedures—the book encompasses a range of viewpoints and methodologies that are generally relevant to four stages of HRIS: planning, development, management, and cost justification.

The first three chapters present "the vision"—what we mean by an extended HRIS that can become the central information and decision-support system in the organization—as well as historical background and some "principles" learned over the years. The history is important, I think, because it not only identifies the mistakes and shortcomings of the past, but it also shows what HR and HRIS managers have been *trying* to accomplish for nearly three decades, and the reasons why they've been only moderately successful. The lessons of this particular history are not all negative. In many cases, they show the durability and continuing importance of certain key human resource management objectives, such as the identification of the right person for the right job at the right time and at the right cost.

The second of the five parts of this book deals with the development cycle, from a methodology for analyzing business needs for an extended HRIS through work-flow analysis, the identification of critical success factors, influences on HRIS architecture, and some special concerns of multinational organizations. It is hoped that HRIS professionals planning a new system will read these chapters in sequence, because they begin with the macro level of organizationwide needs analysis, focus in Chapter 5 on the all-important task of reengineering work before automation, define a methodology for isolating make-or-break business issues that should drive HRIS development, and show how all of this influences systems design.

For readers who already have a "perfect" HRIS that will serve their organization's needs into the next millennium, skip the first eight chapters and begin with Chapter 9. Sarcasm aside, no book on HRIS development can be complete without some information about how to manage the system, because in this field it is axiomatic that implementation never ends. Effective HRIS management begins in the development cycle—with early user involvement and provision for accuracy—but no HRIS runs itself thereafter.

The fourth part discusses HRIS cost justification, and HR managers and HRIS project leaders in some organizations may decide to start here. At times, getting the budget resources needed to realize your "vision"—and being able to identify costs and benefits in dollars-and-cents terms—may seem to have first priority. As discussed throughout this book, however, the application of HRIS technology to existing HR practices and procedures—simply doing things faster, more voluminously, or at lower cost—is a short-sighted goal. More needs to happen than that to justify a major investment in HRIS, and these are, to me, the first things to consider.

The final part discusses where we will go from here. HRIS in your organization's future will need a new type of management, the subject of Chapter 13, and should anticipate some of the changes emerging in HR management and technology in the years ahead, the subject of the final chapter.

There are many people who helped make this book possible, and I would like to express my appreciation to them. First, there are my clients who have helped me understand the critical issues facing them and through this understanding crystalize and organize my thoughts over the years. It was they who were tolerant enough to listen to my ideas and methodologies, and believe in me and my approach sufficiently to adopt them. Then there are my colleagues at Towers Perrin, who not only put up with me on business trips and meetings but helped sharpen my focus and offered suggestions and improvements, especially Jim Battisti, Joe Bender, Chuck Harshyne, and Frank Tetz. In addition, there are others in the HR information management consulting field and the Human Resources System Professionals organization who have given me support and encouragement for my work, such as Mark Miller, Ren Nardoni, Ly Seamans, and Randy Velez.

And lastly, in preparing the manuscript, my thanks to Beverly Britt, who patiently went through version after version without complaint; and to John Monaghan, who remains a good friend and supporter and who worked with me in organizing the material to make it more understandable and readable.

ALFRED J. WALKER

Handbook of Human Resource Information Systems

PART 1

The Vision

**HRIS as the Primary Delivery
Vehicle for Human Resource
Services in the Future**

1
How and Why We've Arrived at a New Beginning

The history of human resource information system (HRIS) development in the United States is a great deal more than a trip down memory lane for those of us who have been engaged in this field for the last quarter-century or so. There's nothing very nostalgic about the wars we've lost (or failed to win), the objectives that turned out to be unattainable, the unintelligible marching orders, or the "enemies" we fought without conviction with weapons that were never quite all we hoped they'd be. In HRIS, it's a lot more fun to look forward than to look back, even for those of us who feel we've "won" a few battles over the years, and who have some "successful" HRIS projects in our résumés.

The job of creating a computerized system dealing with people and jobs—one that scores of differently motivated users can use for scores of different reasons—is in itself a Herculean task. If all the HRIS developers in the world today had started when I did (back in the late 1960s), and if all of us had

- Today's technology and the resources to use it,
- An unchanging regulatory environment for 30 years,
- The same human resource (HR) programs and policies to automate,
- A demographically homogeneous, unchanging workforce,
- The full support of top management, and
- Similar, and constant, strategic objectives,

we still would not have created a "perfect" human resource system. The fact that *none* of the above conditions has remained the same over the years—and most are still changing at a rate that deters any author from talking about "new technology" or "today's most critical issues"—helps explain why the evolution of HRIS in this country as been an "unnatural history," fraught with false starts, half-realized efficiencies, and a highly checkered pattern of "success" stories.

Still there are compelling reasons for knowing this history, especially for those of us engaged in creating the HR system we "should have had all along." The reasons relate largely to the reasons for HRIS development and use: business-based goals of efficiency and management effectiveness that have evolved as the HR function has grown and diversified, the business environment has changed, new demands have emerged for information about "people" skills and talents, and the employment exchange itself has become increasingly complex.

Surprisingly, many of the business reasons for having a HRIS—the issues human resource managers and systems professionals wrestled with in the technological "stone age" of the 1960s and 1970s—are just as relevant today as they were then. One might assume that advanced technology changed everything, and that nothing managers did or thought before the last few years matters much. Worse, someone planning or developing a HRIS of the future—complete with voice-activated access, distributed processing, advanced languages, scanning capabilities, telecommunications links, and the rest—might assume that technology *by itself* would solve all of the problems associated with the increasingly demanding job of human resource management. A look at the history of HRIS development and use over the past 20 or 30 years belies such assumptions, and provides, I believe, some of the key insights needed to assure that today's—and tomorrow's—technology is fully exploited in the service of human resource management objectives.

In the first place, the business managers and systems managers of the past were no fools. Although personnel was one of the last functions to be computerized in most organizations, there were (and continue to be) reasons for this that have nothing to do with technological capabilities. The basic subject matter of a HRIS—people—represents the most volatile, variable, individually complex, multiply interrelated set of factors ever covered by a computerized information system. And yet the early sponsors and developers of HR systems were sure that it *should* be done, and the business reasons for doing so drove development of systems that may have been technological dinosaurs by today's standards, but that were usually created for the "right reasons," and that can instruct us today as we enter the "candy store" of technological possibilities available as we approach the next millennium.

Another important perspective that emerges from a review of the history of HRIS is an improved understanding of how available technology has shaped so many of the human resource systems we have today. Systems developers in this field have always been constrained by a technology (particularly software applications) that has been a few steps behind the needs of enlightened human resource managers—whether we're talking about the punched cards of the 1950s, the flat file data structures of the 1960s, the mainframe-dependent systems of the 1970s, or the uncontrolled microcomputer proliferation of the 1980s. As a result, HR management needs have often been compromised by the limits of available technology. As will be discussed in Chapter 5, processes and procedures were often automated without first analyzing them for possible improvement: The available technology was simply not flexible enough or comprehensive enough to be shaped to business and HR management needs, so the needs were fitted to the technology. This has changed, of course, as a result of today's technological possibilities. But the thinking of many HRIS developers too often remains mired in the attitudes of the past.

Other lessons of the history of HRIS emerge from a review of the forces—technological, legislative, economic, HR functional, and business based—that have shaped the HRIS evolution through three fairly distinct eras:

1. *Forerunners:* the early packaged systems, and the defining characteristics of systems dedicated to personnel management

2. *Early evolution,* including the forces of technology in shaping HRIS work, management objectives as they emerged in the 1960s and 1970s, and the "10 most common mistakes" made by systems developers of the time

3. *The micro era,* beginning around 1980 and continuing today, including what today's database technology, distributed processing, and other technological advances have meant in terms of achieving the goals of a new human resource management agenda

Although this overall history of the evolution of HRIS may not exactly parallel the history of HRIS in the reader's own organization—some companies never had a HRIS until the microcomputer era—the lessons that emerge from a review of this history are broadly applicable. As will be discussed in Chapter 13, the manager responsible for creating technology to match today's business needs should take nothing for granted about how the existing system works, what it does, who uses it, or what it should do. The reasons for an existing system's characteristics should always be examined from a fresh perspective, and one way to gain this perspective is to understand the thinking and environment that led to what we have today.

Put another way, tens of thousands of human resource and HRIS professionals today have never worked without computerized systems. Virtually every organization in America with more than a few hundred employees, and most in the other developed nations around the world, uses some level of computerization to help with personnel or payroll management. And yet we may have only scratched the surface in terms of putting this technology to work in the service of human resource management. Some of the reasons why, and food for thought for those of us who are committed to the development of strategically relevant, optimally efficient, effective human resource systems, emerges from a review of how the field got to where it is today.

The Forerunners; Historical Evolution of HRIS; Regulatory, Technical, and Functional Issues That Have Shaped Systems

Human resource systems in the United States trace their beginnings to two primary sources, skills inventory systems and payroll systems. Skills inventory systems, developed in the late 1950s, became the rudiments of what we think of today as human resource systems—systems to provide management with access to information about work and workers. Payroll systems, as will be seen, were "just there" at the beginning. Although these were basically "production" systems rather than systems designed to produce management information, payroll systems did provide automated data about employees, and often served as the starting point for personnel system development.

Defense Contractors' Skills Systems

Skills systems were developed by defense contractors, who found themselves growing in size and having difficulty bidding on government contracts because they could not easily keep track of the specialties of their engineering and technical staffs. The contracts often called upon the bidders to present the résumés of their key technical talents with their proposals. In response to this requirement, defense firms such as Lockheed, General Dynamics, and McDonnell Douglas developed coding schemes based on standard government occupational classifications for the primary work of their organizations, and specifically the qualifications of the staff to be assigned to the work for which they would be bidding.

In the competitive arena, project staff strength and experience were key. To collect the needed data, contractors summarized the skills terms in a data collection booklet, distributed it to their technical and critical support staffs, and asked that they select the areas in which they had expertise. These skill terms were often transferred onto edge-notched (McBee) cards, and later to punched cards, along with the background and education of the employees. This file was subsequently used as a basis for producing the résumés of the staff who could be assigned to work on the contract if the company was awarded the business.

Personnel department employees in these companies recognized the potential of the skills systems to help with job staffing. When they adapted the coding schemes and punched-card formats for internal use, these skills systems were incorporated into the manual operations of the personnel function, and became one of the predecessors of a full personnel system.

Payroll Systems "Already There"

Payroll systems, the second of the two primary sources of human resource systems, were automated in most companies about the same time, in the mid- to late 1950s, though some large employers used them earlier. Since they were part of the finance and accounting area, the payroll applications were usually automated when punched cards and electronic accounting machinery (EAM) were introduced. The accounting and payroll methods had been in the process of mechanization since the 1930s and 1940s (and even earlier if we include mechanical and electrical calculators).

In the 1940s and early 1950s, tabulating equipment, sorters, accumulators, and plugboard wiring were introduced. With these advances, column totals were automatically calculated, data quickly assembled and cross-tabulated, and new data fields computed. Card decks were the basic storage media. New data input, such as the employee's time for the week, was transferred to 80-column card input and then introduced into the payroll sequence. A new set of 80-column cards was produced after sorting, manipulation, and calculation. Paychecks were then printed from these updated sets of cards. Multiple accumulating registers were used, all under the control of a prewired board. As noted above, the systems used in the 1950s relied on punched cards (or punched paper tape) as the primary input and master file medium, with the cards carrying the employee's name and employee number as key identifiers. The rate of pay, department number, location number, pay frequency, shift code, and perhaps an indication of whether the employee was hourly or salaried would also be on the card.

These machines were not really computers as we know them today, as they had no stored program control. They did make life easier, however, especially for employers requiring large payroll processing.

Impact of Technology: First "Breakthrough"

Simultaneously with skills and payroll automation, great advances were being made on the technical front. Prior to 1953, only the government and some technical laboratories and universities had computers. The computers of those days utilized thousands of vacuum tubes, required major air conditioners, large maintenance staffs, and actually had very few capabilities. In 1959, transistorized computers were introduced, significantly reducing costs and physical size, and permitting enhanced capabilities. This was a landmark breakthrough. By the early 1960s, with the introduction of the 1401 model and later the System/360 line, IBM and other manufacturers significantly advanced business computing by putting computer technology into the realm of affordability. At the same time, computer software began to attract attention, because computers obviously did not exist just for their own sake but to help solve problems.

Stored program control concepts, symbolic languages, operating systems, and utilities were introduced. This enabled a much larger instruction set to be employed by the user as well as permitting a variety of input devices to be used. Also, the notion of defining sets of operations to the computer was developed. Procedure-oriented languages were perfected to instruct the computer, and these were introduced into the marketplace. Commercial business applications, not just scientific ones, could now be cost-effectively handled by computers.

These advances in turn enabled payroll and human resource work to advance. Since the accounting procedures and steps were already laid out in tabular, punched-card formats, they became a natural choice for transfer to the newer, bigger computers. It was clear that with the increased capacity of these machines, other traditional aspects of business, such as finance and marketing, could now profit from some of the benefits of computerization. It was hoped that personnel departments could as well, if their applications were based on payroll systems that already contained several key items of information, such as employee name, rate of pay, department number, and the like. Thus, some companies began using payroll data to produce headcount reports and wage analyses.

Impact of Early Employment Regulation

But it took a bigger push to get beyond mere headcount reporting, and federal compliance was one of the major reasons hastening the computerization of personnel systems. Just as the Fair Labor Standards Act of 1934 and subsequent amendments on work hours helped provide the impetus for time clocks, payroll systems, and other related technology, a series of employment laws and regulations in the 1960s and 1970s gave employers a "business reason" for automating the personnel department. The first was the Equal Pay Act of 1963. The primary thrust of this legislation was to ensure equality in pay between men and women for work that is substantially equal. Compliance was impossible without data and statistics. It took a good deal of information about job content, where people worked, pay levels (starting pay, increases, etc.) and more, and it quickly showed the inadequacy of a card-based system tagged on to payroll, which did not have the sophistication needed.

Title VII of The Civil Rights Act of 1964 became the major piece of employment legislation for the American worker up to that time. It forbade discrimination in employment, housing, education, and other areas and showed that the government was interested in attaining equality for all citizens regardless of race, sex, color, or creed. Further, it set forth steps to remedy these deficiencies in later amendments.

For businesses, Title VII established the Equal Employment Opportunity Commission (EEOC) and brought a new need for discipline to personnel processes. It also set forth record-keeping rules and requirements for employees of more than 25 (later 15) or more employees. With the companion legislation Executive Orders #11246 (1964) and Revised Order #4 (1972), the concept of "affirmative action" was introduced. These created requirements for calculating "availability," setting goals and targets, producing utilization reports, and deriving workforce analyses. This extent of government intervention in personnel matters was new and caused many American firms to begin to seriously monitor their workforce in order to comply with the record-keeping requirements. For larger companies, computerization was the proper way to handle this problem. Most firms first met these needs by adding the needed data elements to their payroll systems, if they could, since the payroll database was already in machine-readable form. "Tacking" on a race and sex code fell within the range of normal enhancement to the payroll master, allowing employers to produce at least the EEO-1 report, which had to be filed annually.

Economic and Business Impacts

During the mid-1960s the workplace was also becoming much more complex. New products were being brought to market with increasing frequency; sales were growing; plants were expanding or being built; and as a result the organizations themselves grew and changed. New departments and jobs were created, which led to new demands on the personnel department. Jobs had to be evaluated and slated in the appropriate grades, with salary ranges agreed upon by all concerned. And of course the incumbents had to be rated for performance appraisal and salary increase purposes.

The larger the companies grew, the more time consuming these tasks became. And although management was not pleased, the personnel function had to add to staff in order to cope with the increased administrative load, and the growing numbers of forms and records. The employment function, wages and salaries, benefits, and payroll functions all were being especially hard hit by the increased work load. Up to this time these sections had no other recourse but to add people. However, there was some help on the horizon.

Birth of Packaged Personnel Systems

Sensing an opportunity for a computerized approach to job matching, a new company was formed in May 1965 by several individuals who worked at IBM. The new company, Information Science Incorporated (known as "InSci") was to be the first purveyor of automated personnel systems. Their first product, PICS (Personnel Information Communication System), used the concepts of skills systems. InSci's objective with this software was to fill employers' open jobs by matching the jobs with applicable résumés codified by the submitter — in this case people seeking employment. InSci would be the outside staffing agency augmenting corporate headhunters and internal staffing groups.

The first InSci system never became the success its creators had hoped for. What did happen, though, was that employers seeking relief from their personnel records nightmare began to approach InSci with the idea of building a customized personnel system to help meet their specific personnel needs, which were broader than just staffing. InSci responded by building a number of customized personnel systems, and in 1970 came out with HRS II, a mainframe-based system designed for banks and the first packaged personnel information system.

At about the same time, other vendors and a number of large organizations, including AT&T, were working on dedicated personnel systems. In this period, the characteristics of a "true" personnel system, which are briefly summarized in Figure 1-1, were generally agreed upon by both vendors and companies developing their own HR systems internally.

Personnel System as Defined in the Late 1960's

A "true" personnel system (a system that is not just appended to payroll) has the following characteristics:

1. It is used to solve personnel's needs, not just payroll's. That is the system is developed primarily for the Personnel Department's use, to solve personnel—not financial-problems.
2. It is multifunctional in that it handles or addresses user needs in more than one personnel area. In other words, it is not limited to one function such as benefits, or employment, or wage and salary administration.
3. It utilizes the five basic concepts underlying human resource systems [These concepts are expanded upon in A. J. Walker *HRIS Development—A Project Team Guide to Developing an Effective Personnel Information System*, Van Nostrand Reinhold, New York, 1982 (contact author for copy).]
   - A database with definitions specified for data elements
   - A method of data update and entry
   - Ad-hoc retrieval techniques
   - A human resource information center to assist with administration
   - A data quality focus

These concepts bring methodology to the development and operation of personnel systems. As objectives, they provide an approach and structure for the work, and they necessarily involve procedures, users, and systems professionals.

Figure 1-1. Characteristics of "true" personnel systems.

Forces in the Early Evaluation of HRIS; Objectives and Mistakes of the Past

Some of the situations those of use who created our own human resource systems in the late 1960s and early 1970s went through — and why we made the effort — may be instructive to today's HRIS developers and managers. As noted earlier, the business managers and HR directors of the time were not fools — They knew what they wanted, for the most part, but they were under pressure from a number of sources and were severely limited by the state of the technology at the time.

As the reader reviews this discussion, covering employee profiles, early systems architecture, HRIS management requirements, and a changing environment, one important thing that *hasn't* changed should be kept in mind: Human resource management has always been one of the most difficult subjects to computerize — but solutions have usually been found. Many of the problems and constraints you encounter today, especially if they are essentially technical, have a way of being overtaken by time and events. But the management issues involved — getting the right data to the right people at the right time, in cost-effective, useful form — have not changed as the primary shapers of HR systems objectives.

First Challenge: Employee Profiles

Once they were defined as separate systems, early personnel systems were usually able to maintain data in several categories:

- *Descriptive, personal data* about each employee, such as name, address, date of birth, race, sex, etc., to help with basic statistics, headcount control, and demographic needs.

- *Organizational data,* such as the department and organization (cost center) code identifying the group to which the employee reports. Also, the job number and job title were kept, with pay ranges and grades, if the personnel system was sophisticated enough to utilize table concepts and if pay grades were tied to job codes. Physical location codes and descriptions of the exact location where the employee worked were also maintained.

- *Wage and salary data* sufficient for salary administration, union contracts, and clerical wage progression plans. Performance appraisal data, annual salary, compa-ratios (relationship of salary to the range midpoint), and the like were kept.

- *Employment information* regarding schools attended, prior work experience, military status, and any special skills and abilities the employee possessed.

- *Continuous work history data,* with entries for every job, salary, work location change, or department change/transfer.

The concept of work history was a major difference between early personnel and payroll systems. Since payroll systems were interested primarily in the current rate of pay, systems lacked the ability to provide sufficient historical data for analysis. More, the HRIS was supposed to provide users with information with which to make decisions, whereas the payroll system was an operational system whose objective was to pay employees and account for the pay. This is still basically true today, although the systems are becoming much more closely linked, and at times are parts of the same system (see Chapter 7).

The continuous work history information generated by the early systems recorded and saved the data about each change as it occurred. Therefore, users were able to produce a computerized employee profile or work history record. This profile was the equivalent of an employee service record card or SRC.

For many employers the SRC was the official record of an employee's employment status, earnings, and length of service. It was prepared manually and generally maintained by a centralized clerical unit. It was the source of information for staffing decisions, pension calculations, group insurance, performance appraisal history, and verification of employment. But the SRC was usually not used to record time and attendance data, and therefore could not be used to back up a weekly or monthly pay record. Because it was at the very heart of the employee record-keeping function, it became one of the targets of elimination for the early personnel systems. Eliminating the clerical expense associated with the maintenance of SRCs also helped justify the cost of the new system.

Most of the companies that installed early personnel systems in the 1960s had an SRC or a similarly structured document. There was an area at the top of the card for employee name, employee number, and basic data such as date of birth and home address. The bottom half of the card was devoted to a chronological record of rates of pay and changes in job and organization. Depending on the company, there were entries for schools attended and any skills or specialties.

Since these were the official and in most cases the only place in the company where these records were kept, they were located in a secure place and were never allowed to leave the file room. Data was transcribed or photocopied for use by others. The clerical unit responsible for maintenance was on the distribution lists for all forms that could provide pertinent information. Hence, new hire forms (so they could begin a new card), changes to employee status, changes to pay rates, terminations, etc., were all routed through the unit. The unit usually became the final repository for the signed forms themselves, as it also maintained the complete employee files — referred to as personnel files, personnel folders, or employee records.

In these records, originals (or copies) of all official documents were preserved in order to authenticate or verify any particular claim or personnel issue. Original employment application forms, diplomas, authorized increases in salary, performance appraisals, etc., were filed in these records. They were the employee's "papers," or depiction of the employee to the company, and were (and still are to a great degree) used during the job selection process or when employees changed units or changed jobs. These records were extremely important to an employee's career, since they became an integral part of the personnel processes. The information in these records was reviewed by supervisors and, rightly or wrongly, opinions of the employee were formed or at least influenced by them. Many of these records are now subject to privacy laws in some states and in the public sector. Rules allow for employee review and make provision for update if records are incorrect. Obviously, there can be many erroneous, out-of-date, or incomplete entries which employees feel the need to correct, and most are now permitted to do so.

Systems developers in the 1960s who had to deal with these users of employee records often had great difficulty in getting management's approval for projects that would replace the files. The difficulty stemmed from the belief that it was acceptable to replicate the SRCs and other employee records with the computerized employee profile. But how could a computer file or database substitute for all the different types of data in the employee records? These records, users argued, were the foundation and repository of the history of an employee's career with the company, and they felt that all data contained in the files would have to be automated, all with new, shaky security systems. Further, attempting to computerize everything in those folders conjured up an Orwellian "Big Brother" image in some managers' minds. Putting appraisals, potential ratings, supervisors' comments, etc., in the early personnel systems was viewed with much skepticism. Thus, when such projects were approved, it was usually only to automate the basic data in the SRC as a first step.

Next came inroads on paperwork elimination. Studies in the late

1960s showed that most mid- to large-size companies used from 300 to 500 separate documents to store and maintain information about employees. These forms ranged from employment inquiry or application forms to insurance enrollment forms, pension projection estimates, name changes, address changes, and pay change forms, in addition to attendance records. Among these were unofficial or "bootleg" forms as well as company-sanctioned forms, and informal documents were widely used to supplement standard forms. For example, a company would have an SRC which was the official record of an employee's total career history, and in addition the line functions would often have their own version of the form to add additional items or explain a change in more detail.

Since there was no good method for accessing the centralized SRCs or employee folders on a regular basis, the local supervisor, division management, local personnel organizations, and other intermediate layers of management kept their own copies of records and forms. In the users' eyes, there were always valid reasons for these extra forms and processes.

Opportunities for improvements were obvious to the systems designers. They could automate the central files, thereby eliminating the expense (or at least a great deal of the expense) of the upkeep of SRCs and employee folders. This would also help reduce the extra cost of record keeping due to the duplication of files and records maintained by other groups. These extra files all took time to maintain and post, and this expense could be reduced if there was a uniform method of producing the data *once* and then making copies as needed. The employee profile filled the bill, they thought.

About this time it was felt that additional saving could result from utilizing the employee profile as an input document as well as a display document. The various input vehicles to the central files—the employee status change forms, name change forms, address change forms, and the like—were rendered obsolete by the new, computerized method of using the profile form as a multipurpose device. These forms were (and often still are) referred to as "turnaround documents," since they are more than a mere report or display vehicle, but are also an input device. These forms had space on the bottom for all the necessary signatures and approval levels, so a copy could be filed in the employee's folder as official, approved data.

Limits of Database Structure

The systems developed in the late 1960s for the most part used magnetic tape as their primary storage medium, because of its cost effectiveness and versatility. They employed either fixed-length records or a fixed-length portion for the basic employee master files which stored the employee information, followed by a variable-length section for work history. The fixed-length area of the master file was physically segmented or apportioned into data fields which corresponded to the data items themselves. For example, the unique identifier for an employee was very often his or her social security number, which would reside in data field #1, and would be physically found on the tape or record positions 001–009. Similarly, the employee's last name might follow in data field #2, positions 010–024, assuming that 15 characters were allocated to this item. The task of defining the characteristics of the data—such as the length of the fields, the edits if any, and other such specifications—was critical, since the programmers had to know precisely where the data was to reside, how to edit it, and what to do with each character of data—i.e., overlay the data, calculate new salary, etc. This was important because they had to write programs to accept incoming data changes, usually keyed onto 80-column cards or magnetic tape, and apply those changes to the master file. If the incoming data passed all the edits, it was then accepted into the system and was then applied to the new master file. This meant a set of specifications had to be generated that included detail of how to handle all data and combinations of changes.

The old master file was usually not destroyed or overwritten. Rather, a new copy was generated containing the old or previous data plus the new information. Usually this process was performed in a sequential manner starting with the employee with the lowest employee number or social security number and ending with the employee who had the highest number. Or, if the master file was organized by company or division, the data update program would begin with the employee who had the lowest social security number in the first company (or division), and then go to the next employee in the first organization, not proceeding to the next company until all employee changes to all employees in that company had been applied. If there were no changes to an employee's record, the update program simply copied the old record onto the new master file.

Obviously, this type of processing depended on the data being in the proper sequence—usually low to high—on a similar field (e.g., social security number). The program would search for a match and apply the changes. If no match was found, an error report was generated.

User access and report generation access to these sequentially based systems was usually performed utilizing the same principle, i.e.; a set of conditions was presented to the master file and it was "stepped through," record by record, looking for matches to the data. For example, to produce a salary report which displayed departments, names, and base salaries, the programs would examine the master files for the key data fields and then sort the master file (or an extract file) into as close to the final report sequence as could be obtained—in the above case, perhaps name within salary (high to low sequence within department.) The configuration of the data in the master file was extremely important in these systems, because the commonly used file organization available to programmers at that time was sequential. This meant that the file had to be resorted and resequenced for each and every report. This was an expensive undertaking, because sorting required the use of core memory, which was limited even in the largest computers.

The same was true for ad-hoc retrieval programs. These on-demand reports were usually single requests, answering questions not covered by fixed reports, usually regarding a discrete employee subpopulation. They often would dictate a sort sequence which changed from request to request, and, as a result, require hefty computer time.

Early Use of Tables.   In these early systems, then, a good deal of computer time, in both main memory and peripheral devices, was spent preparing the data for update or presentation, not in performing calculations. One of the techniques which helped with the file structure and the organization of the data itself was the use of table files. A forerunner of relational systems, tables enabled the system designers to develop subsets of information pertaining to groups of people which could be logically and physically associated. When a change occurred to a piece of information, it could be updated in the table record without going through the entire master file and updating the information for each of the employees who were affected. For example, a change to the pay range for a particular salary grade could be made without individually altering each of the employee records in that grade. At the next update, the new data would be associated with the employees in that particular pay range and the link-up made during the update process. If the systems were on-line, as they generally are today, the changed data would be available to be matched to the employee record immediately. However, the systems in the late 1960s used mostly batch update methods, and as long as the changes were made first to the table files, the data was as current as it could be under those conditions.

Table files also helped with standardization and consistency throughout the database. In the pay-range example, there is a greater chance for error if we change the pay range individually than if the system updates the records under program control; with individual updating, inevitably, someone would be overlooked, or a change would be rejected by the edits, or the wrong employee would be changed. Updating the records en masse is a much quicker, safer and more efficient method of altering the database.

Report Writing Added Flexibility. Report-generating programs were another significant feature often found in these systems. The ability of users to produce their own one-of-a-kind reports, or to go to a dedicated resource to do so, enabled users to all but bypass the programming department to extract data, and was a major help. Normally, to produce a report, user specifications would have to be drawn up for the programmer, stating the output desired, the population, the desired calculations, and the like. This was a time-consuming and distracting activity, since the data processing group felt their time was better spent building new systems or enhancing current systems to improve their operation. The ad hocs, or special requests, were also usually fairly urgent in nature and frequently involved special mixes of data from different files, e.g., employee master file plus recruiting files. And they were often requested by senior management, which put a high level of priority into the picture. This combination of factors encouraged both programmers and users to search for a method by which these requests could be satisfied in a more cost-effective manner. The report generators enabled parameters to be input at the time of the request, and these generalized programs could vary the arithmetic operations and display data in a number of formats. As these systems advanced, capabilities such as report and column headings became easier to manipulate, as did the output media and the number of master files the programs could handle with a single request. They also utilized English-language statements to query the database and put restrictions on the number of searchable or sorted items removed.

Early HRIC Organizations. The ability to produce their own reports became so attractive to personnel users that it often became the primary reason to establish a separate group—the Personnel Information Center, also referred to as a Human Resource Information Center (HRIC) when the term "personnel" was replaced by "human resources." The HRIC performed retrieval and later other specialized data processing activities within the personnel department on an ongoing basis, and grew to oversee all human resource information activities.

The establishment of the HRIC in the 1970s legitimized the computerization of human resource data and focused efforts on the extraction and retrieval of information. It also provided a home for the production of systems specifications work. By necessity it required a special type of manager. Since the retrieval activity was brought about by the creation and installation of the HRIS in the first place, it naturally was added to the duties of the HRIC supervisor or systems analyst, especially if the position was not yet a managerial job. The scope of work in the HRIC crossed most of the functions in HR, and as a result the staff became very familiar with a range of activities. The qualifications for the job at the time were fairly unique. The incumbent had to be able to operate the computers and extract data, either via CRT devices (as terminals were referred to then) or via fixed reports, audit reports, or by using the generalized reporting tools. In order to properly understand the user's request and to be able to satisfy it as closely as possible, the HRIC staff also had to understand the business of personnel, as well as that of the company itself. They also had to fully understand the data content, i.e., the data definitions and code structures of the database, and be able to extract the managers or the marketing department. In essence, they had to have a fairly good grounding in all three areas— HR, EDP, and company operations.

Early Systems Integration Efforts. As these early HR systems were designed and developed, several objectives began to emerge, which covered both the technical and organizational aspects of their installation and operation. These goals became clear guidelines by which to judge the soundness of the approach design used by the implementers, as well as to evaluate the vendor products which were being brought to the marketplace in the late 1960s and early 1970s. Among these objectives were:

- *A simplified method for user input,* built and designed around computer-produced documents which were used to display the current data on the database and update the data.

- *A consolidated, single database* of accurate current and historical information regarding the population (usually employees) for whom the organization had record-keeping responsibility.

- *A full set of reports, displays, and retrieval tools* to enable users to access the database and produce the desired reports and statistics. The reports could be standard periodic reports, audit reports, control reports which the systems produced on a preset schedule or on an as-needed basis through parameter-based reports, or a generalized, ad-hoc retrieval program which could bypass the need for time-consuming and costly programming.

- *Establishment of data administration* to oversee the management and control of the system's development and operation. This generally took the form of a dedicated organization whose responsibility it was to handle the design and development as well as the ongoing administration of the system, including data input, table maintenance, scheduling and operation of the update cycle, specification of interfaces, and production of reports and analyses.

- *An awareness of the need for data integrity and quality,* which included the idea of data item ownership by the data users as well as utilizing better editing and auditing tools to assist in the task of keeping the database as accurate as possible.

As these concepts became accepted in the field and as systems designers became more aware of the need for more applications to handle the growth and complexity of user needs, HRIS developers became concerned with the lack of standardization and uniformity among data files. Since their payroll system was most likely in place when the first HRIS was built and installed, there were at least two different systems being used. And, as time went on, there were Equal Employment Opportunity (EEO) subsystems, benefits systems to handle annuitant files, relocation systems, and so forth. These in turn had their own databases, and unless there was a very strong push for uniformity, the data fields, reports, profiles, and displays were different. Users at that time, as a rule, did not think that there was any major problem with these differences. They were solving their problems and satisfying their need for information. In fact, management information specialists encouraged this, in a way, since user needs were being met one by one and they were at least involved with the user in the specification and development process. The name field was just as the user desired it, as was the home address field, etc. It did not seem to matter that this information was in a different format from the payroll, HRIS, or other HR data. There was little or no reason to compare the data with other databases or to combine it on reports—or so was thought at the time—and when there was, the MIS people could always write a custom-designed program to handle the need.

Things change, however, and it did not take long for users to discover that when you have different databases with the same data elements, the data will inevitably differ, and they wanted to know why, and what could be done about it. The reasons, of course, include the fact that the data update vehicles were generally different—that is, there were different source documents (often for the same employee), or the timing of the updates was different, or there were different edit criteria. All of these reasons, and more, contributed to variances in quality and accuracy, as well as nonuniformity of the data across databases.

These variances also put a burden on users, in that they had to learn and operate different systems if they used more than one, and many personnel users did. This meant training users in the vagaries and idiosyncracies of the screens, reports, codes, and definitions of the elements—no small task for a nontechnical user base. The nonuniformity and the proliferation of systems also meant that the MIS organization had to maintain the various systems, and this put an increased burden on the programming staffs since they had also to remember and document these differences in order to keep the systems running. With the turnover of staff and scarcity of good talent, it became an arduous task for programmers to "babysit" the growing number of HR systems. As a result, it became increasingly clear that something needed to be done about the nonstandard nature of these data sets, applications, and systems.

These problems fell to the HRIC manager and the MIS areas for solution, since they affected both users and programming groups. To help achieve greater integration, users needed to put some of their differences aside and agree to adopt similar data conventions and usage patterns from a data input and display standpoint—for example, a standard "last name, first name, middle name" format for name data, and a similarly configured home address block for both the employment department and the benefits function.

Lack of standards and system proliferation brought problems to data processing as well. If the systems were connected, it was normally by interfaces rather than true integration. Interfacing generally means transferring data from one system to another by generating an output file of transactions from one database and then accepting that file as an input file to the second database. This intermediate file was usually treated like any other input to the receiving system, and as a result data could be accepted by the edit or rejected. Therefore, with each interface there was an edit and transaction log to be generated and "proved in"; data errors to be traced down and fixed; and control totals and balances to be reconciled. This was fairly intense clerical activity, which could be eliminated by better system integration. In the 1970s, though integration was not yet an objective, most believed there would be less work if systems could be more fully integrated. That is, if systems were somehow joined better technically, there would be less need for many separate inputs, outputs, edits, and interfaces. The number of update programs could also be reduced if a single input could cause an update in two or more systems. System maintenance would be substantially lessened by reducing the number of program modules, steps, and functions.

Systems integration finally became a major objective of most HRIC staffs in the 1980s. In fact, a new specialty arose—"systems integrator"—as vendors became aware of user dissatisfaction with existing products. It is ironic that the whole problem arose in the first place because vendors tried to increase their own sales by not providing any direct method of transferring data between their own and other vendors' devices. The result was that in the 1960s and 1970s there was often no easy method to transferring data from one vendor's mainframe or minicomputer (this was before PCs) to another. The intermediate file, or interface, was a virtual necessity. So systems integration involved more than just the MIS department rewriting the applications into a more encompassing system. The integration effort was often dependent on the computer vendors as well, to provide utilities to enable data to pass between systems. Often these vendors had to alter their file structures, operating systems, and internal machine code to permit this exchange.

More Legislation, More Work for HRIS

During the 1970s, new legislation affecting personnel continued to pour out of Washington. In 1974 Congress passed the Employee Retirement Income Security Act (ERISA), also known as the Pension Reform Act, which defined certain rules and obligations surrounding pension plan structures, plan rules, funding, and administration. It also established the Pension Benefit Guaranty Corporation (PBGC), which guaranteed certain minimum benefit amounts to be payable to any qualified participants covered by ERISA. Vesting schedules were defined under ERISA along with fiduciary responsibilities; plan eligibilities in terms of length of employment and years of service were also spelled out in detail. Also, certain reports now had to be filed with the government, and an annual fee paid to the PBGC. All in all, the legislation introduced a new level of complexity to the pension record-keeping process.

A similarly imposing piece of legislation was the Occupational Health and Safety Act (OSHA) of 1970. Enacted primarily to force employers to maintain a safe and healthy workplace, it established on-site inspections and also called for records to be kept on an annual basis. Further, it set up standards for the classification of accidents and injuries, and set fines and penalties for failure to comply.

These and other pieces of legislation, including state and local laws, coupled with the business changes which companies were facing in the 1970s and the need for information about the business itself, were sufficient incentive for virtually all large employers to automate at least some parts of personnel management.

When "Personnel" Grew up to Become HR

In the 1970s and early 1980s, the personnel function was being further transformed into the Human Resources Department. The number of functions and services offered grew: relocation, management development, organizational analysis, employee testing, and others were added or significantly enhanced during this time. Areas such as job evaluation and compensation became increasingly technical and created new job specialties. With these changes and added HR duties, even mid-size companies (those with from 1000 to 4000 employees) found that they could justify a HRIS. These companies could operate on a mid-size computer and did not necessarily need the power of a mainframe, because their HR functions were relatively small and it was not too difficult to change methods to adapt to a commercial product. In some cases time-sharing products were utilized. These could be installed quickly and did not vie for programmers' time or computer resources. Time-sharing systems were expensive, though, and many users migrated their applications off time-sharing during the late 1980s in an effort to cut costs.

Difficult Times: Some Early Mistakes of HRIS Development

During the late 1970s and early 1980s, many personnel users began to feel the limitations of computer systems and the system development process, especially in their inability to automate the number of complexities in a given area. For example, in employment, which at first glance seems rather straightforward, a series of complex tasks and processes need to be specified if they are to be automated, including activities such as setting up and recording campus recruiting visits, scheduling medical examinations, keeping track of home relocation expenses, and the like. Users have to be precise with terminology, and policies need to be examined for such basics as "when is an applicant an applicant" (and not just someone who happens to be in the neighborhood), and how to interpret the provisions of affirmative action regulations. Further, the integration needed between external employment activities and internal transfer and staffing processes must be understood and agreed upon. When systems analysts came to grips with these various processes and activities, they usually found them to be quite a bit larger and more intricate than anyone had imagined, or budgeted for. As a result, the scope of systems in the 1970s expanded greatly for many companies, and HRIS development projects took years to complete if they even were brought to completion. Some were simply halted after a period of time or were abandoned. These were very difficult times for those involved in these projects. What appeared so simple — HR work — turned out to be (and still is) one of the most difficult areas to quantify and computerize.

Some of the more common reasons why systems projects failed in those days (and sometimes still do) are:*

Ten Most Common Mistakes of HRIS Development

1. Being all things to all people – all at once.
2. No personnel expertise on project team.
3. Separate systems increase vulnerability to errors.
4. Avoid superfluous complexity: Resist demand for reports.
5. Insufficient or waning management support.
6. Design by committee.
7. Technical marvels fail if not user-oriented.
8. Loose project control.
9. Promising force reductions: savings that don't occur.
10. Building when you can buy.

Privacy Issues Also Influenced Design

In the late 1970s there was also serious concern with maintaining and protecting an individual's privacy in an increasingly computerized world. The integration of data brought about the potential for misuse, as it became easier to transfer data from one organization to another. The concept of an employee's (or data subject's) right to privacy was legislated in many states after in-depth examination of this area by the Privacy Protection Study Commission. Many of the principles regarding the protection of privacy were adopted by companies installing HR systems at that time, since it was either mandated at the state level or it made good business sense to offer the protection recommended by the commission.

*Reprinted from Alfred Walker's article which appeared in *Personnel Administrator*, July 1980. "The 10 Most Common Mistakes in Developing Computer-Based Personnel Systems and How to Avoid Them."

Today's (and Tomorrow's) HRIS Technology; Micros/LANs and Their Impact on the Way Human Resources Are Managed; Integration; Front-End Technology; Open Architecture; Expert Systems

In the early 1980s, the landscape of computer technology changed forever with the introduction of the microcomputer, or personal computer (PC). The PC had a dramatic impact on the human resources field for it offered some relief for the problems of a fast-changing set of requirements in a difficult-to-standardize field. The relief came in several ways. First, micro-based systems were a lot less expensive than mainframe or minicomputer systems; second, they could be installed in a matter of months rather than years; third, they could be maintained by the user, i.e., the HR department, directly; fourth, they were easy to modify; and fifth, they were easy to use, with "pretty" screens and formats, and with hooks to spreadsheets, word processing packages, and graphical display programs. They were a release from the mainframe "data jails."

When PCs first came on the market, HR applications usually had to be built by the purchaser/user directly, as there often were no trained PC programmers in MIS. In fact, use of PCs was actually banned in some companies. When they weren't forbidden outright, MIS often imposed standards on their purchase and use, in an effort to regulate the number and variety of microprocessors.

Lest the systems organizations be characterized as ogres, let me say in their defense that there were (and remain today) some real problems with ungoverned PC usage—especially in human resources work. Justifiable MIS concerns were many as PC usage spread. These concerns included little or no provision for backup or recovery of the data should the machine malfunction or the user fail to make a copy; or the entire system failed; or the data were stolen. Also, system developers (users) often failed to document the system or provide any knowledge of its use, so there was no easy way to train someone else in its use. And, of course, at this time systems often were not integrated and relied on duplicate input, which was not only expensive but invariably led to inconsistent or outdated data or data in multiple systems which did not match.

The revolution was not to be reversed, however, and MIS resistance gradually gave way to reluctant acquiescence to providing assistance. One way was the establishment of end-user support groups. These functions were usually resident within the MIS area (or IS organization, as it became known in the 1980s) and were often geographically situated with clients. These organizations assisted end users in the use of PC tools such as Lotus 1-2-3 and word processing programs, as well as database products such as dBASE and Paradox. Also, some of the more "user friendly" products being offered on the mainframe and PC platform, such as RAMIS, FOCUS, SAS, and the like, were supported. Some vestiges of these support groups remain today, but as users themselves became more conversant with the technology and software products become easier to use, the need for these groups has diminished.

In larger organizations, connectivity of the various microcomputers to the mainframe became an even larger issue. Users were not delighted that in some cases they had to have side-by-side terminals, one to access the mainframe where the payroll/personnel data were entered and was resident, and the other a PC where the data were downloaded. Not only was this cumbersome, it was expensive. And there were the attendant problems of duplicate conventions and access protocols, data standards, support, and the like. Why could they not have direct access to the data from the PCs, where the platform and architecture was such that the data could be more easily manipulated, passed into spreadsheets or word processing packages, and analyzed as desired? Further, why couldn't they tie the PCs together into networks, so that one user could access another's database or application?

As it turned out, they could, although solving the technical problems was no small task. Even with these problems, the PCs were in many instances connected. During the late 1980s there was a strong push toward building such computer networks—with and without the mainframe as an integral part of the design. The networks were generally classified as either local area networks (LANs) or wide area networks (WANs), depending on the type of physical wiring and telecommunications systems used, the number of users, the distance, and the use of file servers and other factors.

Users in human resources, however, were somewhat slower than other groups to fully embrace networks, for several reasons—almost all of which began with economics.

First, in large companies a mainframe-based application was generally already in place, which was providing some functionality and related benefits to the user population. Adding another type of system on top of the current application had to be proven feasible and the project cost-justified.

A second reason was the lack of available applications. In the mid-1980s, when networking was emerging, very few real human resource applications could be purchased commercially. There were a growing number of applications for stand-alone PC operation, but few could also be networked. So the use of networks often implied custom programming, and with scarce programming and systems resources, it again became difficult to justify the cost. And even if a network were installed, transference of functionality from the mainframe to the PC network remained an obstacle.

A further reason, which has plagued human resources since the introduction of computer technology, was the lack of understanding of the potential that automation (in this case networking) offered to users. Most HR professionals were just not as computer literate as their brothers or sisters in finance, production, or engineering. As a result, they could not persuade their management to invest in this area. It actually took a new generation of employees entering the workforce—a group much more familiar with computers and their capabilities—to get behind networking as a concept and to get such projects moving.

Another reason it took a while to establish networks was the technical problems of installation. End users were not accustomed to the seemingly endless succession of difficulties encountered such as downtime, incompatible hardware, lost data files, abrupt stoppages of keyboards, and new releases and versions to be installed. These were not IS workers who lived with such problems on a daily basis; these were HR users who had little technical training and low tolerance for paving new ground.

The end result was that there was a reluctance to try the new systems when they became available, especially when the message spread that LANs were still a bit shaky and not as reliable as a mainframe or a non-networked PC.

Regardless of the problems with networking, the move to distributed processing in human resources picked up momentum during the 1980s. Distributed systems were not a new concept by any means. Vendors such as Digital Equipment, Hewlett-Packard, and others had been successful with this technology in order entry, process control, and finance for some time. Human resources was still fairly centralized at the beginning of the 1980s, but as the HR function itself began to be decentralized to meet changing business demands, there came a demand to decentralize HR systems as well. And whether or not the distributed data concept was articulated as such in those days, the implication was clear to HRIS designers. The old models of a central database with a single edit and update program would most likely not work too much longer. In fact, with the move to more market-driven businesses with smaller workforces operating in different competitive areas, users were demanding a matching flexibility in their HR systems.

The Changing Business Environment
of the 1980s

Throughout the 1980s the business scene was rife with mergers, acquisitions, spin-offs, new ventures, and business failures, as companies were adapting to global competition and shrinking profit margins. All of this had a direct impact on HR systems, as the plans, policies, employment records, and data on the workers in these companies had to be reassessed and altered. As a result of market shifts and responses, the organizations themselves were going through massive upheavals. Millions of workers were to face layoffs as a result of the changes. Round after round of downsizing and force adjustments took place, and the work that remained in these companies had to be done by fewer people. In many cases there were offsetting gains in productivity and infusions of new capital and equipment to help with the work. But often there was not, with such results as longer work hours, higher levels of stress, and shocked and jaded workers. These shocks were felt especially in middle-management and white-collar areas, often the targets of cost-reduction programs. Managers were "de-layered," organizations flattened, spans of control increased, and often salaries frozen and merit salary increases cut back. Managers who were declared surplus were often given termination pay or an outplacement package, which often included adjustments to the pension or profit-sharing plan. These changes were usually not factored into the work load of the HR staff, or the HRIS staff either, and caused a nightmare of late hours dealing with unpleasant situations, as the settlements and adjustments had to be handled in a one-by-one fashion—often manually, since the HRIS programs on mainframe could not be changed quickly enough.

The organizations which came out of these changes very often had a new set of workers with new bosses—not necessarily new to the company but new to the department. There was a learning period to go through which the HRIS system often could help with by producing an organizational chart, headcount totals, and employee profiles for the new manager; but just as frequently could not, since it was often unclear "who actually reported to whom." Organizational charts built on the hierarchical format did not always apply. And the concept of skip-level or peer-to-peer reporting relationships could not be depicted easily with the available systems.

Moreover, the skills and abilities of the workers were often not as sharply defined as they had been when they were first collected in HR systems during the 1970s and early 1980s. And now, in the mid- to late 1980s, with companies attempting to put together new work teams which could be more customer-focused and attentive to demand, there was a higher premium on such data. The new bosses wanted to know who was good at what—the strengths and weaknesses of the workers in their organizations. Not an unreasonable request, but one very few HR systems could satisfy. During this turbulent timeframe the impetus for change from the legislative front was as active as it had been in the 1970s, especially in the area of employee benefits. Capital Hill was busy, and round after round of major new legislation affected group insurance and the administration of pension plans, causing massive reprogramming and redesign of HR and payroll systems. One result was that work was again diverted from helping management to keeping pace with regulation.

Still More HR Legislation

Major pieces of legislation included the Omnibus Budget Reconciliation Act (OBRA), the Consolidated Omnibus Budget Reform Act (COBRA); the Tax Equalization and Finance Readjustment Act (TEFRA); and the most troublesome of all, the Tax Reform Act of 1986 followed by a series of Technical Correction Acts. All of these and many Department of Labor and Internal Revenue Service rulings created problems in the design and administration of employee benefit plans. Other major pieces of legislation during the 1980s with impacts on the HR function included amendments to the Age Discrimination in Employment Act (ADEA) and the Immigration Reform and Control Act (IRCA). Legislation continues into the 1990s with the 1990 Americans with Disabilities Act (ADA), effective in 1992, which added further needs for data. In a very direct way, tax issues and Washington's spending habits had a bearing on the employment picture, since the income government derives from employers and employees depends in part on the taxability of benefits. Congressional committees and budget advisors, as a result, began putting increasingly stringent definitions and limits upon the benefits to be derived from these plans. These tax code proposals arose as a result of revenue shortfalls as well as changes needed to strengthen provisions of ERISA and related legislation. Some changes were required due to liabilities faced by PBGC as a result of underfunding by some employers, for example.

The tax reformers put tremendous pressure upon employers to review eligibility provisions, participation rates, formulas, vesting schedules, plan payout rates, and definitions for almost all qualified plans. New restrictions on loans and withdrawals were also introduced. Certain aspects of the Tax Reform Act were to extend the concept of discrimination testing begun with 401(k) plans with "highly compensated employee" definitions and actual deferral percentages (ADP) to other qualified and group plans, but that feature (Section 89) was later retracted after an outcry from employers.

The complexities descending in the 1980s upon the payroll department as a result of these and other factors cannot be minimized. The budget trouble in Washington spread to the states, and new tax levies down to county and local municipalities became commonplace. Also, with changes and improvements in banking systems, the popularity of direct deposit of pay spread, as did the features that many credit unions and financial institutions offered, and which employees desired. Added to this came changes in taxable pay; to the definition of calendar year versus fiscal year; new bonus and incentive payments—and the inadequacies of the existing payroll system became obvious.

Workforce 2000 Trends

Changes to the workplace itself were just as dramatic, highlighted in such studies as *Workforce 2000,* published jointly by the Hudson Institute and Towers Perrin.* It described the changing nature of American workers—our gender, ethnic background, education, literacy, birthdate, age, and income level—with the many implications that such changes bode for employers and the management team. For example, the percentage of the American workforce who are women is expected to rise from 42 percent in 1980 to 49 percent in the year 2000, and one of the fastest-growing groups among women are those with preschool-age children—implying a growing need for child care, alternative work hour schedules, and similar programs. The "cultural diversity" of the American workforce means different things to different organizations, but demographic trends say that 57 percent of the total workforce growth between 1986 and 2000 will be made up of Hispanics, Blacks, Asian-Americans, and other minorities. And the training implications of data showing severe skills shortages in the years ahead—as the labor force shrinks in both absolute numbers and basic skills levels, at the same time that jobs are becoming more demanding—seem insurmountable for many individual employers. In the early 1990s, one New York bank was reporting that it interviewed 40 applicants to find *one* who could be trained for a teller's position.

Overwhelming Complexity of Benefits

Another problem for HRIS teams during the 1980s was an inability to handle the demands of flexible benefit plans. Moving to a full flexible

---

Source: Towers Perrin and American Productivity Center Survey of Top U.S. Corporations, 1986.

benefit system under Section 125 provisions brought many data problems to the forefront: for example, computation of a credit pool if credits are to be used; the flexible spending account feature; the problems of annual enrollment of the workforce within finite periods of time; how to handle life event changes during the year; and the reporting and controls needed to monitor the plan. All of these posed new challenges to HRIS designers. Often, plan features were not finalized until a month or two before enrollment was to begin. So it was not uncommon for companies to turn to third-party administrators to handle this area, at least until the necessary changes could be made to the internal systems.

Another area where extensive changes were required to HR systems in the 1980s was savings and investment plans administration. Due to the relatively expensive nature of defined-benefit plans and the many protective devices imposed on them by the federal government, companies began shifting the emphasis of some plans to that of a defined-contribution plan. These plans specify a fixed rate of contribution by the employer (and generally the employee), whereas under a defined-benefit plan the final benefit is specified according to a formula, and the employee usually does not make a voluntary contribution.

One effect of the shift to defined-contribution plans has been a more immediate administrative load on the benefits group and the HRIS team, as plan contributions are made each pay cycle and investments are priced at least quarterly. Also, statements showing the established investment choices have to be presented periodically to the employees, along with provisions for loans, withdrawals, and voluntary contributions. All in all, benefits has become a troublesome field in which many payroll and benefit managers are wondering whether they are in human resources or banking. As a result, many employers have turned to outside record keepers for administration.

The 1980s also brought to the forefront problems of rising medical-care costs. Medical costs skyrocketed during this decade: Annual costs increased about 15 to 20 percent in each of the 10 years of the 1980s. Employee wellness plans, health maintenance organizations (HMOs), managed-care initiatives, preadmission tests, and second opinions were tried, along with other attempts to limit expenses. Some helped; some met with little or no success. Preferred-provider programs were established by some employers in an attempt to steer their employees into medical channels where the costs were more reasonable. Use of employee-paid deductibles were rare in 1980, but by 1989 they were almost universal.

Demands for demographic data regarding the workforce and their dependents grew as plan designers, consultants, and carriers searched for solutions. HR systems often lacked the data required to predict claims adequately, since the claims experience, medical background, overall health, and lifestyles of employees and household members were not normally collected. Even if some of the data were captured in machine-readable form, the information was often maintained in separate databases because of confidentiality and privacy considerations. Therefore, extensive programming was usually required to make the information available for analysis.

The incidence of drug treatment and use of health plans to pay psychiatric and related mental health costs also added to the problem. Also, Americans were living longer and wanted more medical treatment.

Pressures on HR/HRIS at the Start of the 1990s

Changes on the business side, of course, brought demands for new HR programs such as training and development, compensation, staffing and selection, among others. Pressures on HR staffs were growing to meet these line management needs, and the ability of most HR departments to satisfy the needs was sorely tested. HR staffs needed the skills to assess the need for a new HR program, to develop a program to meet those needs, and then to install the program and modify it as required to be successful in the field. In the past, HR work had often required little creativity, and truly innovative professionals were rarely drawn to the field. Now, however, the plans and programs being asked for might include a new competitive sales incentive program, division-level management succession plans, employee involvement and productivity programs, merit appraisal plans which emphasize pay for performance, or a mid-career program, and most HR staffs did not have the ability to produce them. Further, adding HR staff to help was not an option.

Suffice it to say that in the 1980s, senior line management was not satisfied with the HR function's inability to cope with the increase in demand from their operating units. They demanded better-quality programs from their staff groups even while the size and budgets of these groups were being tightly controlled. Surveys taken by Towers Perrin during that time confirmed senior management's dissatisfaction with the HR function and set forth criteria for a successful HR activity:

CEO Comments Regarding the Human Resource Function

- Function too reactive

- Have record-keeping mentality
- Not positioned to intervene
- Not knowledgeable about the business

*CEOs Want the HR Function to Move in
New Directions:*

- Support line operations
- Contain costs
- Improve quality of services
- Upgrade professionalism of the staff
- Take a leadership role

The chief executives wanted to revamp the HR function, which along with finance were the two most critical staff functions. In a nutshell, they wanted HR management to focus on the more value-added activities they could perform, and to get away from records and administration. By concentrating on the analysis of business needs, the CEOs knew that the HR staff would help make the entire organization more effective.

The issues facing most U.S. employers in the 1980s were truly compelling ones. We have discussed several of them, such as the needs to be cost competitive and flexible. In our work at Towers Perrin, we listed the 10 most pressing HR issues in 1985–1986 as follows:

Top 10 HR Issues of the 1980s

1. Containment of benefit costs – primarily medical care

2. Development of future management talent succession planning and executive development

3. Redesign of compensation programs – variable pay, incentives, bonuses, stock

4. Changes in labor relationships – unions as partners, not necessarily enemies/antagonists

5. Organizational changes – mergers, acquisitions, new functions, markets

6. Changes in staffing levels – downsizing, delayering, productivity push

7. Legislative and regulatory change – benefits, tax reform, environmental impacts

8. Improvement of employee communications — getting business and HR messages to employees and listening to them

9. Management of technological changes — introducing new technology in the business and in HR

10. Upgrading the HR functions — strengthening the department to become a business partner

The HR function of the late 1980s was thus in a good deal of difficulty. They were in trouble from a mission standpoint — i.e., their goals were not as well aligned with corporate priorities as senior management desired — and they were in a dilemma from not being able to focus or shift resources to meet this need. Their staffs and computer budgets were locked into a seemingly bottomless pit of legislative-driven and management-desired benefits, payroll, and tax changes. Every person was working longer hours, and there was always more to do. And the application of HR systems did not seem to help. In fact, HRIS was soaking up a bigger and bigger percentage of the HR budget — with little to show in return. No wonder that, in surveys and client meetings, the HRIS staff was often viewed as part of the problem and not seen as being able to assist with the work load or to reorient the HR staff to work on management's agenda. The HRIS, payroll, benefits, and IS group, it seemed to many, had in a sense drawn a line between themselves and the rest of HR. The feeling was that the only work worth doing was that which was legislatively mandated. Washington, D.C., was in essence dictating the HRIS agenda, and users felt they had no other choice. They were caught up in the undertow as well.

This attitude changed somewhat under the Bush administration, when the Section 89 provision of the 1986 Tax Reform Act was finally withdrawn. For the first time in perhaps 15 years (1974 ERISA through tax reform 1986 implementation 1987–1989), there appeared to be a respite from major legislation in the benefits/payroll area. Perhaps, HR designers hoped, this would mean an ability to examine the true business priorities and finally apply some technology to the other HR issues.

This was just what happened in many of the larger companies. In the HRIS strategy studies conducted in the early 1990s it came as no surprise to find that there was a widening gap between user needs, such as those cited above, and HRIS delivery capabilities — still largely back-office oriented. Also, there were major advances in computer-based technology, which other business areas had been utilizing but which were nowhere to be seen in an HRIS application, above and beyond networking and database technologies. These included voice-response and voice-activated systems, scanning and other remote devices; imaging, CD-ROM; inference engines and other knowledge-based systems; and other advances. And some HRIS managers were distressed to find that in many companies, users had gone ahead and installed new technology or applications on their own, since their needs were not being met by the centralized HRIS group.

In the early 1990s, the picture emerged of an HR systems development function coming home from the battlefront, finally released from government service, to find the hometown had not stood still in their absence. The bad news was that they were tied up for so long in such service; the good news is that the users are, for the most part, happy to see them and anxious to put them to work.

2
Extending the Reach of HRIS

A Business-Based Planning Perspective for Long-Range Systems Implementation

The overall theme of this book, reshaping the human resource function with technology, starts with the basic principle or goal of extending the reach of human resource information systems. Extending the reach of HRIS is a concept with a number of critical ramifications for systems planners and human resource managers responsible for managing business-based human resource programs and policies. Extending the reach helps shape human resource work.

Most important, the underlying premise of extending HRIS is the growth and continued expansion of human resource management as a vital business function, a role that is increasingly pivotal in determining organizational success and survival. Where HR management goes, so must go HR systems, to provide the information and automated processes needed to manage work and workers. And where is HR management headed?

- For companies that require increasingly specialized, industry-specific or company-specific skills and talents, the acquisition, retention, and development of these critical human resources—especially technical skills—is a make-or-break issue.

- For organizations in which employee costs represent 40 to 50 percent of operating costs—more in some service-providing organizations—

the management and control of benefits, pay, and other employment costs is essential to survival.

- For companies that compete in a global economy—as a multinational employer or in competition with products or services marketed across national boundaries in a global marketplace—the human resource information needed to compete effectively has taken on new scope and diversity.

- For all organizations in which the performance and productivity of the workforce has a bearing on the achievement of business goals and objectives, the information needed to identify and improve people-work relationships is a central business need of the years ahead.

That's the general picture, which each employer can fill in with the details of specific organizational human resource management needs and the need for systems to support HR's business-based goals. Chapter 4 presents a methodology for identifying these specific needs.

Before proceeding we will explore some other ways in which the HRIS can be extended:

- *Extension to line managers,* potentially including the collection and distribution of new kinds of operational information about work and workers, information links with all locations enterprise-wide, and HRIS features that provide line managers and team leaders with the self-sufficiency they need to be independent users of HRIS data and processes

- *Extension beyond regular employees,* to incorporate data about the "phantom" or contingent workforce of part-timers, temporaries, contract employees, and others who may be part of the business, as well as business partners, clients, service providers, and major customers

- *Extension to all employees as users,* in systems that permit use by all or most of the employee population, to improve benefits communication and reduce the costs of benefits administration, allow employees to change their data, communicate policies and procedures effectively, identify critical attitudes and perceptions, and provide networks for intracompany sharing of information and knowledge

- *Extension beyond and further into traditional HR functions,* to include companywide training and performance support, traditionally separate payroll processing, operational planning and management, and marketing, as well as deeper penetration into the processes inherent in these applications

In each of these extensions of HRIS, a single word is applicable to the future requirements of the HRIS database, data collection methodologies, the HRIS user community, systems integration, and the ease of use of the planned HRIS. The word is the same one used by labor leader Samuel Gompers when a congressional committee asked "What does labor want?" Gompers said, "More," letting it go at that.

Fortunately, today's new and emerging HRIS technology permits a strategic planning perspective based on the idea of "more." But here we mean a greater percentage of focused, pertinent knowledge about a subject—the right information needed—not just an increased supply of data. For example, we can have increasingly large and complex databases in microcomputer-based systems that match the capacity of mainframe systems of the 1970s and 1980s, and midrange and mainframe systems or networked microprocessors whose total capacity is virtually limitless. All employees at all locations can potentially be HRIS users, as tumbling equipment costs and new telecommunications technology continue to spread the reach of systems. And the systems can be as easily used as automatic teller machines (ATMs), given the power at the disposal of today's designers to simplify access and processes at the user interface.

Reaching Line Managers with Operational Data at All Locations

What is the proper organizational location of human resource management functions and the availability of HRIS data and processes to support these functions? The answer to this question may be different for each organization—and different for different functions within the same organization—but a growing number of leading organizations are deciding that human resource management needs to occur where the work of the organization is being performed—not just at staff headquarters. This decentralization of HR management—and the systems that support it—occurs when:

- A plant manager in Skokie can use HRIS models to work out an optimal flexitime schedule for production workers

- A regional sales manager can compare the performance of her sales reps with those in other regions, and relate variance to training or other HR factors

- A project manager or team leader in San Francisco can identify a candidate slate of qualified engineers at other locations, and start the transfer process on-line

On a more mundane level, what do line managers such as these really know about the human resources they are responsible for managing? Do they have complete job histories, educational records, and other job-related information? What are their strengths, weaknesses, and job interests? Or is all this data and access to it confined to human resource managers at headquarters?

In the earliest days of HRIS, characterized by laboriously developed and maintained mainframe systems that could only be used directly by technically qualified HRIS or data processing staffers, line managers seeking human resource information locally or enterprise-wide were understandably ill-served by HR systems. The best they could hope for were annual profiles of their employees, and monthly or quarterly printouts designed by people hundreds of miles away—physically and sometimes intellectually.

Today's technology, as discussed in Chapter 7, has removed the technical obstacles to extending the reach of HRIS to line managers. In planning systems that will most effectively achieve organizational goals through such extension, however, three key characteristics deserve advance attention: (1) a focus on operational data that line managers can use; (2) delivery systems that reach all locations; and (3) line managers' self-sufficiency in using such systems, without staff help.

Delivering Operational HR Information to Line Managers

Perhaps the most important type of HRIS extension that will characterize successful human resource systems in the years ahead—a change mandated by more complex business requirements and made possible by new and emerging technology—is the provision of HR-related operational information to line managers "in the trenches" of organizational work. Some of this data is information that has always been available to senior management and human resource functional managers, some is information that may previously have been available only to staff functions such as engineering or operations research, and some is likely to be "new" data about people and jobs, information made possible by the expanded capacities of information systems. In all cases, the key thrust will be the delivery of data, mechanized analytical capabilities, and work-related operational information to managers and supervisors down the line, information that is both locally relevant and at times corporatewide.

Bureaucratic approaches and paper-driven processes cannot be transferred directly to the line: They must first be reengineered, that is, streamlined and examined for work elimination (see Chapter 5). Moving low-value-added work to the line just makes matters worse. Depending on the nature of the business and business objectives, any or all of the following types of HR-related information and access to the underlying work processes and functions now controlled by HR can and should be made available to line managers:

- Individual data on the people in the department or at the location, including demographic data, employment history, qualifications, career plans, and training and development completed or needed

- Data about contractors, consultants, part-timers, and temporaries

- Information about people's time-off patterns and desired work and location preferences

- Individual information about others in the organization who might be available for job reassignment or redeployment (and a new staffing process for efficiently filling jobs and making changes in job assignment)

- Operational data about the workforce itself—such as optimal staffing packages, workforce size, productivity ratios, work measurement factors, and resource allocations—both within the line manager's organization and in similar work organizationwide, or even industrywide in some cases

- Such data as needed to support new and varied compensation plans, such as gain sharing and skill-based pay

- Short-term operational and long-term strategic goals and objectives— from seasonal production schedules to new projects, changes in customer orders, and long-term technological change—to help managers plan and manage the workforce

- Information fed from other systems, such as time and attendance data, payroll, applicant data from an applicant tracking system, training records from the career development system, cost data from accounting, and so on

- Environmental data with impacts on the human resources managed by the line manager, supervisor, or team leaders such as salary surveys, skills shortages, new employment legislation, demographic trends, or reblock competitors' compensation policies, retirement trends, and changing attitudes and values of workers

In many cases, the extension of this information to line managers will follow closely upon the "expansion" of data available in the more comprehensive HRIS and help empower line managers to discharge their people responsibilities. For example, job analysis data that more fully identifies the specific requirements, performance measurements, and other characteristics of positions—a key characteristic of position-driven HR systems, which are typically more data-intensive than traditional one-job, one-person databases—may simply not have been available at any level in the past.

In other cases, information made available to line managers in an extended HRIS represents data that have always been available to HR functional managers or staff managers. The extension to supervisors and managers directly responsible for the successful performance of work—worldwide in some cases, as discussed below—provides line managers with more information about the people they manage, and puts this information in the context of regional, national, global, or industrywide data and trends.

The impacts of this on-site availability of operational HR data—apart from the obvious benefits of getting to know one's people better—can be suggested by a few hypothetical questions line managers might ask:

- Is the work now being done by my people needed? Can it be altered to provide better service?

- Can two jobs be handled by the same individual? Will that lower costs and provide similar or better results?

- What skills would that take, and who has the skills to do both jobs in my organization or in other locations?

- What has been the company's experience when these two jobs were merged, in terms of production and costs? Any customer service or labor turnover impact?

- How does the job change when it is merged with another position? What technology is needed? What changes in work flow or relationships to other work will be required?

The effective delivery of operational and other data to line managers in the HRIS of the future will also be conditioned by two other characteristics: the ubiquity or "globalization" of human resource data and HRIS automation; and line managers' freedom from systems professionals, or ability to use the HRIS or a specific application self-sufficiently, without help from the HRIS organization or from MIS.

The Global HRIS: Extending the Reach to Other Organizations and Locations

Another key aspect of extending the reach of human resource management and the systems that support it is essentially organizational and geographic in nature. Nationally and multinationally, HR data and automated processes need to be available to all departments, locations, and establishments if the HRIS is to be fully utilized in companywide operations. The power of new and emerging technology has made this "globalization" of HRIS technically and economically feasible, and the advantages of using one system to manage human resources in all business units in all locations offers compelling reasons for this approach in the increasingly competitive global economy.

In general, these advantages may be characterized as flowing in two directions: (1) from centralized staff operations where resident human resource management skills, overall business strategies, and coordinated HR management practices can be delivered to all locations; and (2) from all locations back to centralized staff operations for analysis, review, and management interventions that may be needed to assure companywide control and the optimal use of all resources.

A key advantage of the outward flow of HRIS data and capabilities is the ability to "leverage" increasingly specialized human resource management skills and knowledge throughout the organization, to locations that may not be large enough to support on-site human resource managers and professionals. One of the main trends over the years when the "Industrial Relations" or "Personnel Department" was becoming "Human Resources" has been its spreading, increasingly specialized fragmentation into a series of highly demanding disciplines: salary administration, benefits management, equal employment opportunity assurance, recruitment, pension planning, training, job analysis, HR planning—these and other human resource management functions are each performed within a different set of professional standards, and require up-to-date knowledge and function-specific skills.

A problem emerged in the 1970s and 1980s when companies added staff to these areas in order to keep up with the demand for their services. This led to more and more employees in staff departments, at headquarters or divisional levels, with, unfortunately, a much higher price tag.

These large staff groups often become isolated from line operations and in many companies began dictating to the line how to run the business. The HR function was one of these groups, and the HRIS in turn became a mandated system forced on departments and divisions from corporate headquarters. In such companies, there was only one way to do business: the corporate way.

With the newer method of operating, with more flexible and decentralized units a well-designed HRIS can provide a means of distributing and leveraging centrally located expertise to all locations in a more consistent, acceptable, and cost-effective way. Such systems not only provide data, they provide procedures and knowledge. This is a further way of reshaping HR work. Whether technically an "expert system" or not, an HRIS application that provides a standard format for, say, enrollment in a benefits plan, can incorporate a wealth of specialized information and guidance for the use of line managers and others with no previous benefits knowledge or experience. Through system edits that prevent incorrect entries or omissions, on-line help that explains each step in the benefits enrollment, on-line access to reference material on company policies such as eligibility requirements, and the standardization of enrollment procedures, the system can in effect handle some of the roles of a specialist and be a "benefits manager" at each site. When advanced expert systems technology is part of the HRIS, even the most complex procedures can be assisted by users, such as selection and enrollment in a "tailor-made" flexible benefits program unique to one individual while being consistent with corporate benefits policies.

Just as technology can extend the reach of the HRIS and HR management expertise to all locations—providing specialized knowledge without HR staffing costs, for example—data and procedures that originate at all locations linked by the HRIS can be centrally managed and controlled by the "global system." A few examples with clear advantages depending on the need and desirability to have similar rules applied are:

- Applicant tracking systems can provide immediate data regarding job applicants at all employment locations, identifying qualified candidates who might be needed elsewhere in the organization, or simply assuring that minimal employment criteria are being met at all locations.

- Operating data such as productivity and employment cost information can be immediately available for review and analysis, permitting prompt management response to changing conditions in distant locations.

- Governance and oversight can be exercised over all human resource programs at all locations, from EEO requirements of a companywide affirmative action plan to benefits eligibility rules, assuring that the business objectives of companywide HR programs and policies are not endangered by local variance.

Not only will the plans and procedures be more consistent across the company, but the standardization will result in lower cost of delivery.

Self-Sufficiency: Key Factor in Line Managers' HRIS Use

Another characteristic of human resource systems for line managers that will define their value in many organizations is line managers' self-sufficiency in using the system. In many cases, the key to the success of a HRIS as a widely used decision-support tool, or the success of an application designed for total organizational participation across all locations and business units, will depend on the ubiquity of direct interaction with the system — without the intervention of HRIS staffers, MIS programmers, or other technical personnel.

The design of systems that can be used directly by nontechnical managers and professionals has been made possible by technological advances that simplify data access, provide more on-line help and ease of use at the user interface, and distribute the power of large systems to microcomputers throughout the organization. The increased capacity of computer programs and hardware that has characterized the microprocessor revolution will continue — with more and more capacity and power in smaller and smaller packages. In many cases, systems designers are using this increased capacity to add ease of use to computer systems, such as graphical user interfaces (GUI) and "windows"-like features that are making access to the HRIS in these companies as simple as using an ATM at the bank. In fact, the systems are sometimes joined to gain access to cash management or loan features.

The availability of technology, in itself, will not be the driving force behind HRIS applications that permit total self-sufficiency of nontechnical users. More often, successful applications will be driven by the functional *reasons* behind HRIS access or use, not just the mere existence of user-friendly systems or the presence of a microcomputer on the desk. This means that the work itself will change; the line manager will be able to complete a function or work process that was heretofore under HR control. The process itself will change (see Chapter 5), and therefore technology will become the *enabler* but not the entire reason for the change. Empowerment, effectiveness, and efficiency will be some direct reasons.

For example, relational database management systems, first introduced in HR systems in 1979, have been a major technological breakthrough for nontechnical users. By permitting ad-hoc or one-time searches of the database by virtually any data element or combination of data elements — such as employees with a certain skill in a given region — relational technology helps obviate the need for programming by technical specialists. Managers don't need to know where the data resides or how to create the instructions needed to find it: They just ask, using simple, English-language queries.

Reaching Beyond the Regular Workforce to Temporary and Part-Time Employees, Business Partners, Suppliers, and Major Customers

Another new constituency for both human resource management and the systems that support human resource management is the range of people who might be called the contingent or "phantom workforce," people and functions that are not regular employees or part of the internal organization but are in fact "part of the business." They include, for example:

- Temporary and part-time employees, including some who may be employees of an outside agency responsible for the administration of pay and benefits but who may need access to certain company information as training courses

- Rehired pensioners, who may be receiving pension checks from the company

- Business partners, such as insurance agencies and their employees

- Key suppliers and service providers and the people who work for them

- Major customers, especially when they represent a critical client base

The reasons for knowing about the people and jobs in this diverse extraorganizational universe are the same as the reasons for knowing about regular employees and what people do within the organization: They are part of the business, and they have an impact on costs, product or service quality, and the achievement of other organizational objectives.

Too often, organizations with a vital stake in the quality of work and workers who function outside the regular payroll or beyond the boundaries of the organization chart have a tendency to overlook the importance of human resource management in these areas. In many cases, it is not a matter of developing a human resource system capable of collecting data or providing information; rather, the idea of extending human resource management practices and policies to extra organizational people and jobs has not taken hold, leaving a gap in human resource management that can at times be disastrous.

At times the quality of services provided by outside organizations has a direct bearing on internal human resources. For example, when an outside organization is under contract to provide training, the effectiveness and quality of this training will have a direct impact on those who are sent to the training organization. Questions to which you might want to know the answers include trainer qualifications, course content, turnover rates among trainers, differences in locations, and so on. Is your outside training organization taking a "cookie-cutter" approach to training, assuming that all accountants are alike or that computer skills are generic? Or is their training appropriate to your organizational values and needs, such as ethical considerations in accountancy, or the special skills needed to use your heavily customized computer software?

A primary reason for the existence of a HRIS is to provide information needed to assure the continuing performance of employees. But should "employees" be constricted to those on whom you file W-2 forms? People who work full-time as temporary employees of outside agencies, and part-timers who are not in the regular payroll system, are often critical human resources to the organization. Whether they are secretarial temps or engineers hired to work on a short-term project— or leased employees whose pay and benefits are handled by an employee leasing firm for legal, economic, or administrative reasons— these employees and their performance can be as much a part of the business as the regular staffers and jobs that are the core subject matter of the HRIS.

Many will say: Our reason for leasing employees or hiring contracted help is to *avoid* record keeping, administrative work, government reporting, and the use of management systems to do these things. Well and good, up to a point. That point can be reached surprisingly early, however, when government regulators insist on them attending safety training or when high turnover rates among leased engineers cripples a vital project; when dissatisfaction with compensation policies creates morale problems in the secretarial pool; when half of your systems analysts are reaching full social security benefits age at the same time; or when it turns out that contracted employees are largely incapable of adapting to your newly introduced technology.

To the extent that these outside or nonregular human resources are part of the business, these and other kinds of information are important matters of human resource management. It may seem to cost less to hire retired pensioners part-time, to lease employees, to contract for specialized consultants to work on projects, or to find other ways of keeping the regular workforce from expanding, but monitoring employment costs are only one reason for having effective control over these people, and they are not always the overriding one. These contingent workers also need to be included in or at least connected to the HRIS for work scheduling purposes, so that supervisors can prepare weekly and monthly assignments, and so that the HRIS can help supervisors properly account for the pay and benefits issues that arise.

The quality, continuity, performance, and future reliability of business partners' human resources are also matters that should be within the domain of human resource management if these business partners are critical to business success. Do your authorized agents have the technical expertise needed to install your equipment properly, so your warrantee program's costs won't skyrocket? Is your only supplier of vital parts about to have a strike over wages? Is the lack of a management succession plan at a major partner jeopardizing that company's future? What skills and talents are required by business partners, and how is their future availability being planned for and assured?

Depending on the nature of the business and its customers, human resource management information about customers may also be within the proper purview of the extended HRIS. Especially when customers are represented by business organizations whose continued viability as a valued customer depends on their own human resources, certain key information about people and jobs in these customer organizations may be worth tracking and analyzing.

For example, a client database in a consulting organization or service-providing firm can provide much more than billing information and the names of client contacts and decision makers. Depending on the nature of the services provided, the system also include such information as the client's organizational configuration, marketing programs, use of technology, competitive posture, and workforce characteristics that will affect the future of the client relationship.

More specifically, when outside organizations are regular, year-to-year clients who are served by account executives or designated consultants, client information can help "match" clients with the human resources assigned to serve them. Client needs and requirements—distinguishing characteristics such as corporate culture factors, management style, and the values of the client organization—are in effect "position requirements" for the account executives or others who serve these clients. In deciding which account executives to assign to a specific client or what kinds of developmental activities will best prepare a consultant for a specific client assignment, these client requirements can serve the same function in a HRIS as the position requirements of a succession planning or management development system. For organizations that provide specialized services to clients in a range of industries and locations — such as accounting firms, systems consultants, advertising agencies, financial institutions, and others — client requirements (or position requirements for those assigned to serve clients) can be highly customer-specific, and need to be linked to the service provider's human resource planning and development programs. (In accounting, there is an added reason for linking client databases to succession planning, in particular: Securities and Exchange Commission regulations say that the same auditor cannot sign a company's annual report more than seven years in a row, so accounting firms must rotate individual senior auditors among clients.)

For all of these external constituencies — irregular and contract employees, business partners, suppliers, and customers — the types of data that should be collected, maintained, and linked to organizational human resource programs in an extended HRIS will depend on organizational business strategies and objectives, the HRIS planning issues addressed in Chapter 4. How much information is needed, who should collect and update this information, how it will be used internally to support decisions or shape policies and programs, and other questions can be answered only in the context of specific organizational needs and objectives. The key question to ask in all cases, however, and the one that will determine how much of an initial investment and continuing budget should be allocated to the acquisition and maintenance of extraorganizational human resource data, is: "How much is this (outside workforce, supplier, customer, etc.) a part of the business?"

Also, it is worth keeping in mind that the kinds of information about nonemployees and outside organizations suggested here for inclusion in a HRIS are often collected and maintained by other corporate systems. The marketing organization often has extensive customer information; accounting has data on business partners and client billing information; engineering may have information about suppliers; and so on. As discussed in Chapter 7, totally integrated systems developed with a view to minimizing redundant data collection and maintenance can be a cost-efficient starting point for expanding the HRIS. In many cases, the new data needed to build HRIS files on external people and jobs may represent minimal additions to data that can be fed to the HRIS through automatic interfaces with other corporate systems.

Involving Employees Through Interactive Benefits Systems, Career Development Systems, Systems to Communicate Policies and Procedures, Surveys, Idea Sharing, and Other Means

For some human resource managers, the most intriguing new HRIS technology permits extending the reach of HRIS information and processes to the employee population generally, through interactive terminals, kiosks, electronic bulletin boards, telephone links with systems, or other networks. In some organizations and for certain types of HRIS data and HR functions, direct access to the HRIS can provide benefits that go well beyond employee morale or the promotion of the company's image as a "caring" employer.

Benefits Communications Systems

For example, systems used to communicate benefits information to all employees can have significant bottom-line effects on the costs of benefits and their administration. Especially when flexible or "cafeteria-style" benefits plans are made available to employees – offering choices and in some cases tax advantages among a range of insurance, savings, day care, and other benefits from vacation time to personal time off – direct access by employees can optimize the economies the company anticipated when installing flexible benefits, and help control administrative costs.

In a kiosk-based or similarly constructed computer terminal benefits communications system (just one type of technology that is used today to make all employees part of the HRIS user community), employees can use a touch-sensitive screen and easily used keyboard to find out both general information about benefits and – restricted by the use of their personal ID and PIN codes – individual information about their own plans. More, employees can be permitted to make changes in their plans, enrolling in new benefits, adding or changing dependents, changing the amount of monthly savings deducted from paychecks, or making a cash withdrawal or loan or withdrawing from a plan altogether. In some systems these decisions are supported by a simple "what-if" analysis that shows the employee available choices, pension projections, how much would be saved after five years at a certain rate of deduction, and so on.

The cost savings to the company come in two areas. First, the corporate justification for installing any type of flexible or employee-choice benefits plan is to provide choice and is, at least in part, based on expected cost savings. Employees not only do not receive benefits they do not want or need—such as medical coverage that duplicates a spouse's coverage under another employer—they get what they do want, even if they must participate in the cost. Therefore, employees treat the insurance plan as something in which they have a personal stake. Even more important from a benefits cost perspective, flexible plans can sometimes be shaped to control employees' use of more expensive benefits, and to encourage participation in those that have equal value to employees but cost less to provide. Health-care benefits costs might also be reduced through moving to a managed-care network or preferred provider (PPO) arrangement away from a pure indemnity plan. Or employees might be encouraged to enroll in a deferred-income savings plan that reduces both employee and employer taxes. In order for the company to present cost-saving options to employees, however, and to encourage their use when that is company policy, employees need to understand their options and be able to exercise them according to their own best interests. Hence the importance of direct, comprehensive access to HRIS data on benefits.

Second, direct access to benefits plans and employee ability to self-enroll or change benefits reduces staffing requirements in the benefits department, eliminates paperwork, and otherwise improves the administration of benefits. A new employee who wants to know when she is eligible to enroll in a certain plan can find this out without going to the benefits department; a change in dependents covered by health insurance can be made without paperwork; retirement benefits at different ages can be projected; and so on.

Career Planning and Management Staffing Systems

Another set of human resource functions where extending the reach of the HRIS to employees generally can have important advantages lies in career planning and staffing systems. At the lowest level, these are represented by electronic bulletin boards that list basic job posting information; at their most elaborate, by management staffing systems in use today which include on-line position descriptions, job advertisements when openings arise, résumés of all covered employees, knowledge-based assessment modules, and systematic procedures that link quali-fied candidates and open positions worldwide, providing managers with backgrounds and résumés of employees and/or applicants with relative "degrees of fit" as to how the candidates meet the position require-ments.

The distinguishing characteristic about career planning and staffing systems that are accessible to employees generally is that they permit the direct involvement of employees in their own career development or movement in the organization. A career development system located at a kiosk, in a "career room," or accessed through desktop computers, can provide a wealth of information in job briefs or, at the next level, de-tailed job descriptions; about steps in career paths leading to certain po-sitions; about training and development activities that may be required; and give companywide information about trends in force movement, surpluses and shortages, and other career-relevant information. In some systems, the employee can select a training class or other develop-ment activity from a schedule, or create an entirely new career plan, subject to authorization—which can also be handled electronically.

Increased systems capacity also permits the on-line storage and re-trieval of resume information on thousands of employees, in systems that combine two-way processes for identifying qualified job applicants and for employees to apply for posted job openings. With systematic limitations reflecting company policies—such as the need for supervi-sory approval or edits that stipulate time-in-grade, specified levels of performance, certain skills proficiency, or geographic limitations—such systems can provide the technology needed to fully utilize the best avail-able human resources in the organization when job openings occur, wherever they are located. These systems can also be very helpful when targeting selected groups for retraining, or redeployment due to layoffs or the impact of technology. The résumés of these affected can be given priority for placement, if that is company policy.

Increasingly, global and diversified organizations are coming to the realization that the skills and talents of managers and professionals at all locations and in all business units are vital organizational resources, and need to be identified and strategically deployed to optimize their value in achieving organizational goals. More important in the context of ex-tending the reach of HRIS to employees, these same organizations re-alize that a key principle of effective career management is that it in-volves the employees being managed: Most career development is essentially self-development, and requires individual motivation, com-mitment, and clear linkages between individual effort and career re-sults.

Communicating Policies and Procedures

The obvious advantages of electronic policy and procedure communication over written manuals—printing and distribution costs, ease of use, the cost of changes—is supplemented by at least one other major benefit in diverse, multilocational organizations. Computerized systems permit automatic communication that addresses an essential paradox in many such organizations: the need for companywide uniformity and consistency of some policies and procedures; and the need for audience-specific variations in others.

For example, each location may have individually discrete pay policies for hourly employees. Regional pay levels may influence hourly rates, different labor contracts may be in effect in different locations, paid holidays may vary, and so on. Yet companywide policies with respect to nondiscrimination, privacy, and the like, as well as legislation such as the Fair Labor Standards Act (FLSA) and other federal legislation affecting nonexempt employees, apply to all U.S. employees, requiring overtime pay and record keeping. And the accounting department needs financial data in consistent formats and timing cycles, possibly from locations throughout the world. Computerized systems are made for this kind of "consistency with diversity," using tables and other mechanisms to create written or on-line documentation that is as variable as it needs to be, yet uniform in other characteristics.

Organizations are increasingly using the power of technology to offer quicker access to company policies in an on-line mode. Entering the systems, managers (and sometimes employees) can examine the company policy with respect to treatment for time off, vacations, holiday pay, or infractions to discipline. Further, merit pay guidelines, performance appraisal instruction, access to training programs, or instructions on how to transfer or hire an individual can be provided on-line. These and more are examples of policy and procedures which should be made available to line managers to make their jobs easier.

Employee Surveys and Suggestions

The extension of systems access to all employees also can permit instantaneous, virtually automated employee attitude surveys and the "electronic suggestion box," a means of letting employees worldwide make their views and ideas known to management in a timely, cost-efficient manner.

When employee attitudes are important to the organization, the timeliness, accuracy, and the identification of different attitudes and perceptions among different types or categories of employees are important characteristics of surveys. On-line or phone systems linked to HRIS data can provide these characteristics for several aspects of surveys, especially timely input on current issues. They eliminate time-consuming administration of paper-and-pencil surveys, and automatically summarize data and trends—including key changes in attitudes that may deserve prompt management intervention. Perhaps most important, they can incorporate programming that retains the anonymity of respondents while identifying responses by categories. Linked to HRIS data, an automated attitude survey can produce summaries of responses by such groupings as management level, job function, location, or demographic characteristics—all automatically, without manual analysis.

For as long as anyone can remember, bosses have been telling their employees, "My door is always open" if they have problems related to work, suggestions, or want to make their views known to top management. The sentiment is admirable, and founded on sound employee relations practices as well as the perception that employees may at times have worthwhile contributions—both positive and negative—to make. In larger geographically disperse multiestablishment organizations, however, employee access to the ears of top management is simply not feasible, unless an extended system acts as an "electronic suggestion box" linking all employees to the top.

Going Beyond Today's Human Resources Domain for Corporate-Wide Training and Performance Support, Nonaccounting Payroll Functions, and the Management of Office Technology

In some organizations planning an expanded, more comprehensive HRIS, the concept of extending the reach of human resource systems includes cross-departmental extension into areas that have not traditionally been part of human resources. Since the late 1980s there has been a trend toward the integration of payroll department functions in human resources, supported by interfaced or integrated HR/payroll systems. Other areas that have been or could be covered by a HRIS include corporatewide training, performance support, marketing, operational planning, and office technology.

It should be stressed that human resource systems expansion into nontraditional HR areas has been and will continue to be driven by one factor: the importance of human resources to organizational success in achieving overall objectives. We are not talking here about "empire building" on the part of the HR manager or HRIS director, or an unjustified arrogation of other departments' responsibilities for the sake of one big system, managed by HR. Rather, the extension of human resource system data and processes that lies in the future for some organizations will come because human resources and their management are at the heart of business success, and the management skills of HR professionals—even more than the technology of one integrated system—are critical to the success of these traditionally non-HR functions.

In each of the examples discussed briefly below, the driving force or central reason for extending the reach of HRIS to cover the application is human resource department expertise. The systems efficiencies of integrated or mechanically interfaced systems, discussed in Chapter 7, provide further benefits when previously separate management systems are linked. But the emphasis here is on business-based outcomes, the achievement of overriding business objectives rather than the creation of a technically and procedurally efficient system.

Training and Performance Support

Human resource department assistance in the administration and management of corporatewide training is astonishingly rare in America today, considering the critical link between training in increasingly demanding work environments and the quality of work. Typically, the only link between companywide training conducted by a training department, operations, manufacturing, or line organizations and the HRIS is the provision of course schedules and completion data to a career development system. Human resource management is usually involved in training after the fact, and data about training are usually entered into the HRIS as just so many data fields on an employee profile or skills inventory. The only training many HR departments create, deliver, manage, and assess is generic training such as stress or time management, or direct training for HR positions, including HRIS user training.

In an extended HRIS, incorporating job analysis data, productivity data, skills and competencies information, performance ratings, applicant qualifications, test results, and potentially dozens of other types of information relevant to training, the information needed to support effective training management is already available. Moreover, human resource managers are usually already in the business of relating training to performance, as professionals in career development and work analysis. The further benefits that HR managers could bring to companywide training development, delivery, and management include:

- Tying job requirements to training and sequencing training to meet critical business needs for new product development, delivery, and support. This could include competency-based training and assessment.

- Analysis of HRIS demographic data for the training population, to develop audience-specific curricula and training formats that are most effective for different groups.

- Analysis of vendor-supplied training courses.

- Analysis of the relationships between training and performance ratings, turnover, compensation, and other variables, to establish cost/benefit data on specific types of training.

- Delivery, through the HRIS, of computer-based training and performance support tools, such as on-line reference guides for customer service representatives.

- Analysis of learning modules and employee history to prescreen requests for training, to help reduce the use of training.

- Development of new recruitment practices, preemployment tests, and other employment process tools based on analysis of training data and the requirements of positions.

In a sense, the effectiveness of training an increasingly heterogeneous workforce where available skills do not match the requirements of increasingly demanding jobs is the most critical human resource issue of our time. In this environment, effective training is conditioned by a number of human resource management issues, not just the content of a course or the acquisition of a certain level of skills proficiency. Motivation, employee involvement in career development, job design, and other issues are involved in effective training—and the HRIS may be the best available repository of data on these issues.

Payroll Processing

Little needs to be said about the integration of payroll operations with the HRIS and benefits unit in HR, a trend evident on all sides. This is a trend driven by past and impending government regulation, the complexity of benefits in many organizations, and management pressures for the efficiencies gained when payroll and HR systems are interfaced or integrated, such as reduced data entry and maintenance.

When payroll operations (not necessarily including accounting functions) are moved to HR, the benefits and compensation expertise of the human resource department assures that benefits plans remain qualified under government regulations, assures the accuracy of payroll deductions for HR-managed plans such as deferred-income plans, and provides a "one-stop" source to answer employees' questions about pay and benefits, either in person or through interactive kiosk-type HRIS technology.

Technology Transfer and Work Restructuring

The missing ingredients in the implementation and ongoing use of office technology in many organizations today is productivity analysis in the first place, and productivity improvement support on an ongoing basis. The introduction of computerized systems of all kinds — electronic mail, co-resident performance support tools, computer-based training and testing, voice-activated systems, and the range of telecommunications technologies — is often not accompanied by the desired gains in performance or productivity, and the reasons for this, in many cases, are essentially human resource issues.

The integration of people and technology is a complex, multifaceted function, with somewhat different critical issues in each case. The selection and recruitment of the right people, ergonomic or "human factors" engineering, job analysis, training and retraining, organizational diagnosis, and productivity analysis and improvement, are all part of today's HR vernacular.

What we have found, however, is that even before such issues as the selection of people or human factors enters the picture, the larger question of what work gets transferred to the new technology must be addressed. A cardinal sin of the companies that installed human resource systems in the 1970s and 1980s was that they fitted the system to the existing work — often by substituting a screen for a note pad — rather than examining the work itself for possible improvement. In the newer systems environment, we believe that extension of the HRIS into the work — by changing it, eliminating steps, rerouting it, altering it to provide a better process — is essential. If we don't, we will not have gained an awful lot.

Chapter 5 sets forth a program for utilizing reengineering principles to help achieve such improvement.

3
First Steps

Principles of HRIS Planning and Development

In this chapter the basic principles of HRIS project planning and development are briefly outlined and explained. They range from rules that are simply good sense in any enterprise, such as the precept that you can't do just one thing, to principles that address the reasons that HRIS projects fail, such as an implementation plan that postpones the hardest part or fails to design for decoupling.

At the risk of a certain amount of redundancy, the principles have been grouped into sets: Some apply during initial project planning; some are overall organizational effectiveness principles; some relate to HRIS project management; and so on. While this scheme is not perfect, it is hoped it will provide a context for understanding each principle (many of which are discussed further in other chapters) and support the reader's "browsing rights."

Finally, these principles should be viewed in the spirit in which they are presented, not as a complete compendium of all the information management, project management, or job restructuring principles nor as inviolable rules, but as ideas gleaned from scores of HRIS projects, large and small, and as guidelines for creating the kind of modern, business-based, strategically valuable HRIS which will help shape a more effective HR function.

The reader should also refer to my earlier work (see page 11) for more on the basic HRIS principles, such as an integrated database or establishment of an HRIC, since they are not discussed in detail here.

1. Initial HRIS Project Planning and Scheduling Principles

1.1 Prepare a Statement of Objectives and Scope

The field of HRIS is notorious for "runaway" projects, projects that extend for months or years beyond their original time frame and end up costing many times their planned budget (if they are finished at all). Quite often, the reasons for such disasters have little to do with the quality or dedication of the people working on the project, the technology, or management's commitment to HRIS. More typically, it's "the nature of the beast," the type of data and processes being automated, and the lack of experience of the HRIS project team. Human resource data and functions are far more variegated, diverse, and potentially voluminous than the subjects of most other computerized systems, and project planning that does not take this into account can doom the project to constant revision, expansion, and in-progress changes.

Thus, the first requirement for successful HRIS project management is a clear definition of project objectives: the scope of the project and what it is expected to accomplish. This should be a written statement of objectives guided by the critical success factors discussed in Chapter 6 and include a schedule showing when each objective will be accomplished. This document will thus serve as both a focusing beacon and a means of dealing with potentially disastrous add-ons during the course of the project. If top management decides to change the agreed-upon scope of the project—and business changes or other factors may require changes after the project is underway— it is the project manager's responsibility to return to the original statement of objectives, redefine the project's scope to include the changes, revise the schedule accordingly, and get a new commitment from all concerned to the revised statement of objectives. Doing this is not just a way of protecting yourself as project manager: It will underscore Principle 3.7, that you can't change just one thing, and it may also serve to convince top management that there may be better ways of achieving their objectives than tampering with a job that has already been defined, planned, and scheduled.

1.2 Use the "Dry Sponge" Approach to Needs Analysis

The first phase of any successful HRIS project, once the overall scope of the project has been established and approved, is a detailed analysis of user needs. Needs analysis, typically an interview-intensive process that asks all existing and potential users of the HRIS what they need from the system, should result in a prioritized set of systems requirements that will be met in the finished HRIS or new application.

The key to an effective HRIS needs analysis is to treat it as a project in itself. Even though the overall scope of the full project may have already been defined, and top management may have already decided to install a certain vendor's packaged system (which is not a good idea before the needs analysis, by the way), the project team responsible for needs analysis should approach this task as "dry sponges," ready to soak up all the information they can absorb and analyze. There is no such thing as too many needs; no matter how extensive HRIS user needs or wants may be, sound HRIS project management requires that *all* should be known and fully understood in advance but that they will need to be prioritized. In needs analysis you are not creating the system, just trying to identify needs, and to understand them well enough to establish which ones are true requirements, which are most important, and when various needs must be met by the new HRIS or application. The analysis that answers questions of priority may or may not be driven by the users, but there's no escaping the need to work intimately with users to identify and understand their requirements.

1.3 Tackle the Hardest Part First, with Your Best People, Without Forgetting "Carrying Capacity"

Our next principle consists of three inseparable parts, because the whole project may come unglued if the project manager forgets any one of the three. In beginning work on a HRIS project, it's almost always a good idea to:

- Begin immediately on the hardest part, if possible, avoiding the temptation to postpone difficult or troublesome work until later.

- Put your best person or persons on the most difficult tasks.

- Never overload anyone or anything, whether it's your hardware or your best people working on your hardest jobs.

By starting with the part or parts of a major project that appear to be the most difficult, project managers avoid one of the more common pitfalls of HRIS development: a situation where you are still on schedule, but are suddenly faced with an impossible deadline for final completion. Worse, the hardest part may be hardest because you don't fully understand how it's going to be accomplished, you don't know its implications, or you have not been able to identify the resources, plan, and schedule you will need to complete it. When that's the case, postponing this work can lead to revisions to previous work, changes to changes, failure to select the right technology to handle the system, and the total collapse of the original schedule. Working on the hardest portions does not mean, though, that this part has to be the first to be implemented or completed.

By putting the most competent people on the toughest jobs, the project manager is simply allocating resources correctly. But the third part of this compound principle should be borne in mind: Anyone or anything can be overloaded, and "carrying capacity" should never be overlooked.

A tendency in any work performed by teams is that certain individuals end up doing more than their fair share or at least their originally apportioned share of the work. Some people simply work faster, have more knowledge or experience, or otherwise demonstrate heroic behavior. There is a natural tendency to let Mary do it if Mary is almost always effective. And Mary may be the type of person who simply overloads herself, taking on others' chores in the interests of the project.

But especially when Mary has already been assigned the "hardest part" of a project, this type of individual heroism needs to be kept in check and monitored. Good project team management and communications, as discussed in the third set of principles, will help prevent such overload.

1.4 The Triage Principle: Start with the Most Critical Cases

Always start with the critical areas. This is *not* to say, "If it ain't broke, don't fix it." Rather, "Don't fix it now," in the initial phases of the project, if it is working well enough and does not need to be dealt with immediately.

Entering a large, complex HRIS project—with numerous business and HR needs, management priorities, and a limited supply of resources—can be daunting for all concerned. Not everything can be accomplished all at once, and not everything should be attempted or even begun at the same time. The triage concept employed by medical professionals at the scene of a disaster or a battle is operative: The critical cases should be treated first; those who can survive for a while without attention can wait a bit.

For example, the EEO/AAP system may be outmoded and scheduled for replacement, but if it is turning out monthly EEO reports and other required reports and data, the company is in no immediate danger of legal action for noncompliance. Similarly, the pension calculation system may need to be fully integrated with the new pension module next year, but for now it's adequate and can be interfaced with the new system.

What makes an area critical, and deserving of immediate attention, is not always related to how well it's working, of course. Management priorities, as discussed in Chapter 4, may require that the project team start at once in certain areas. Also, Principle 1.3 needs to be kept in mind: It's usually a good idea to start with the hard part. And in other cases, a necessary sequence may emerge in project planning and scheduling: You have to complete A before B, or B will have to be redone after you've fixed A.

In many cases, however, the parts of a project that involve systems, procedures, or other HRIS-related components that are working satisfactorily at the present time can be put off until critical parts have been addressed. When you can't do it all at once, you do what you must to assure that the organization survives.

1.5   Plan for Adequate Project Staffing over the Life of the Project

Project work of all kinds requires adequate resources to successfully achieve objectives on time. This has been a particular pitfall of many HRIS projects, and the resources that many HRIS development projects seem to run out of are often human resources. What is needed is adequate project staffing over the life of the HRIS project to do the work, and to do it well. Continuity is also important. Unfortunately, project team members may be reassigned to other, "more important" work in the organization, some become turnover statistics, others are assigned temporarily with no provision for replacements, and some simply lose interest in projects that are not well managed and that drag on beyond team members' expectations.

Even in the smallest HRIS projects, it is essential that a critical mass of human resources be available at all times to successfully achieve objectives. At times, HRIS projects are analogous to warfare: The enemy is work that needs to be accomplished, and without the forces needed to continue to pursue this enemy vigorously and effectively, the project team may stagnate and fail at critical points in the campaign.

HRIS project planning and scheduling requires the allocation of different levels of human resources over time. Certain phases require more people than others, and different skills and talents may be needed at different points. More than this, however, project planning requires adequate consideration of the realities of what happens to the best-laid plans.

2. Organization Effectiveness Principles

2.1 Use Technology to Improve the Way People Work

To be as effective as it should be, technology must improve the way people work. As discussed elsewhere in Chapter 5, this principle underlies many of the early failures of HRIS, and is at the heart of the reengineering approach needed to develop a truly effective, strategically viable human resource system for the modern, global organization since it is coupled with the review and examination of the process *before* automation.

Computerized systems that simply automate existing processes, without changing procedures or other aspects of the work to take full advantage of mechanization, achieve only a fraction of the benefits potentially available with systems. This is particularly true of human resource systems, which support a diverse array of company-specific functions, policies, user communities, and reasons for being. Unlike relatively simple, production-oriented systems with linear work flows and standard output—such as inventory control systems or payroll systems—a HRIS is intended to automate scores of dissimilar activities, and provide management with information for a range of purposes and potential users. To gain the full advantages of HRIS technology, each of these uses of the HRIS needs to be reexamined before being automated, to see how the technology can improve the work itself, not just make it faster or more prolific.

For example, the personnel actions required when an employee is leaving the company may now be performed in several different offices, supported by several different manual or automated systems. A payroll clerk processes payroll data and creates the final check; benefits specialists close out active employee records and create a COBRA file; the EEO specialist might need to make changes; and so on. Instead of simply automating all of these functions in place, a reengineering approach might lead to a single termination screen, activated by the supervisor (using technology earlier in the process) who in turn handles the necessary processes and assures that all of these and other activities are completed.

2.2 Localize HR Policy Making, Programs, and Decision Making

Organizational effectiveness for the human resource function in modern organizations will increasingly require the ability to transfer some analysis, planning, and procedure formulation aspects of HR programs "down the line." Whether this trend is called decentralization, empowerment, smaller-is-better, local autonomy, or some other management catch phase, a growing number of major organizations—especially complex, global organizations with a heterogeneous mix of business objectives, jobs, and people—need a new approach to HR management that is flexible and situational rather than didactic and monolithic. This is happening even when management maintains a standard, core set of values and policies.

Different business units, different localities, different functions, and other localized distinctions present human resource management situations and needs that cannot be readily addressed by inflexible, centralized policies and programs. The same recruitment practices that attract chemical engineers in the United States don't work for data processing people in Japan; benefits valued by married Southern Californians are not necessarily valued by married employees in Maine; the requirements of marketing positions vary by products and markets; jobs in the plastics division are different from those in the pharmaceutical division; and so on. For human resource management policies and programs to be effective, these localized distinctions need to be taken into account, keeping in mind the central core component. This requires a local ability to plan, develop, and administer local HR programs and policies, usually with an organizationwide core set of HR plans as well.

The implications of this principle include, in many cases, the ability to lower approval levels in the organization, so that new programs or other departures from standard operating procedures are not caught up in bureaucratic dicision-making processes. In general, the fewer inflexible HR policies a local manager has to follow, the more likely the manager is to be innovative, responsive to local needs, and effective in addressing local business requirements and HR needs. Management can also achieve standard practices for the core functions, those that simply must be uniform.

2.3 Centralize Specialization

One of the most compelling reasons for centralizing any function is to take advantage of specialization, and to maximize the application of unusual skills or talents of those who perform the function. Whenever possible, it's a good idea to "leverage" these specialized technical and professional skills, making the specialists parts of the organization.

The most obvious reason for this is simple economics: Why have an EEO lawyer or pension actuary at every business location, duplicating one another's work or not fully utilized? Centralization of such functions can also add the synergies made possible by a "professional" group at staff headquarters, complete with reference works, specialized support staff, and the availability of co-professionals who share knowledge and experience.

A related issue with particular application to HR specialization is the need for security in many human resources functions—from executive compensation to medical record keeping. Not only are the skills of personnel performing these and other sensitive functions specialized, the work they do should usually not be distributed to many sites or available on desktop PCs throughout the organization. Although there are ways to make data secure in decentralized systems, the proliferation of users simply adds to the chances of breaches in security.

Other factors came into play as well when dealing with centralized functions. Grouping these select people together forms a nucleus of individuals who can support each other, train new employees easily, and discuss new or different methods of handling the work.

In addition, it should go without saying that the centralization of these specialties does not need to be physicially all in one place, given today's communications technology. The lawyers could be in Boston and the actuaries in Philadelphia, if necessary.

2.4 Focus Upward: Efficiency Is Not Enough

For human resource management to continue its upward climb as an increasingly vital business function, its focus must remain on strategic, business objectives that improve profitability or competitiveness, not just cut costs through administrative efficiency. The value of the work being done by the HR professional should never stop at mere efficiency. Sooner or later, someone will say, "Yes, it's very efficient; but do we need it at all?"

For example, the most efficiently run benefits department in your industry may have reduced its benefits administration costs by 20 percent through automation and organizational restructuring. But are the benefits offered attracting and retaining needed employees? Are they understood and valued? Are they cost-effective in terms of overall compensation? How should they differ from place to place, function to function, or among employees with different needs? The savings realized by administrative efficiency make sense only *after* these questions and others have been answered affirmatively.

The modern HRIS, when well designed and implemented, permits this upward focus on HR management and helps shape it to be more effective in its support of the line businesses. Human resource managers are thereby freed from administrative record keeping, by technology that obviates the need to command and control every issue, and deal with the ever-present paperwork.

2.5 Create a Common Administration Instead of Organizational Mimicry

When an organization has a number of different locations with local administrative functions, each a microcosmic "clone" of the headquarters administrative structure, restructuring to create common administration may be in order. Common administration is made possible by computerized systems such as a HRIS, and its advantages in terms of organizational effectiveness can be monumental.

Quite often, organizations with a number of major locations—such as plant sites, regional offices, large stores, or distribution centers—create administrative organizations at each location that mimic headquarters administration. Each satellite has its own financial organization, and human resource functions from employment and training through benefits administration and career planning are handled by a local organization that is a scaled-down version of the headquarters organization. The data and transactions that result from local administration may be passed on to headquarters, but day-to-day administration remains at the local level, and requires a staff of managers and professionals in an organization that mimics the main location's administrative staff. These local administrative groups are often roadblocks to achieving higher-valued HR work. And this can be highly inefficient in addition to being downwardly focused.

Further, it may be totally unnecessary for users of today's technology. The same on-line systems and telecommunications technology that permit local access and processing in an HRIS permit centralized or common administration. For HR functions and other administrative jobs where this is appropriate, common administration eliminates redundant functions, provides improved consistency and accuracy, and permits HR to reach the analysis and consulting level of operation.

It should be remembered that common administration does *not* centralize the functional use of a HRIS. It is the development and administration of an application, not the application itself, that is centralized. For example, an on-line computer-based training (CBT) library may be available to PC users at numerous locations, but it is created and updated at the training center, where the development team sits, records are kept about who takes what courses, test scores are monitored, and other administrative matters are handled.

2.6 Push Work up the Value Side; Cut into Routine, Repetitive Tasks

Throughout this book, the reader will come across one reference after another to the idea that technology must change the way people work. One key aspect of this maxim with particular relevance to human resource systems design and operation is that a HRIS must find ways to eliminate or reduce routine, repetitive, time-consuming tasks such as record keeping, and "push work up the value-added side," freeing managers and HR professionals to spend more time on more important work.

This principle, which is also supported by others, is critical to HRIS success because the ultimate value of these systems is not in their ability to spew out huge volumes of reports or massive calculations, but rather in their value as access systems, providing decision support information, analysis, and the data needed by managers and professionals seeking better ways to manage human resources. This seems paradoxical: If a HRIS is *not* primarily a system for automating boring, repetitive tasks and eliminating time-consuming manual work, how can it be expected to free up managers by doing these tasks?

The paradox is readily resolved: As it applies to HRIS, the automation of work that is the underlying reason for computer-based technology means the automation of work that should be automated, not necessarily all the work that *can* be automated, which is usually the goal of production-oriented systems. And in a HRIS, with its immense range of functional uses and applications, work that should be automated is invariably the repetitive, boring, routine tasks that do not require human analysis. The human aspects should be reserved for intervention and decisions that are beyond the capabilities of HRIS systems (even those with a knowledge base).

"Beyond the capabilities" also means beyond the desirability of automation, of course. No one wants a succession planning system to pick the next CEO or divisional head automatically.

As discussed further at Chapter 5, the HRIS and the processes that surround it should always focus on ways of shrinking the base of the triangle in typical work structure. That base is usually made up of detail work: the collection of data from numerous sources, manipulation of detailed reports, record-keeping chores, repetitive calculations, and so on. A HRIS should shrink the time and cost devoted to these chores, not only freeing HR professionals for more important (valuable) work but also bringing a level efficiency to jobs that is unapproachable without this technology.

3. HRIS Project Management Principles

3.1 Communicate, Early and Often, with Top Management

Communication with top management, early, often, and in terms managers can understand and appreciate, is vital to the success of any HRIS project. The senior managers whose approval is needed to budget the initial and continuing costs of HRIS development should not be taken for granted once their approval has been obtained: As a rule, each budget cycle will require new approvals, and HRIS costs do not disappear once the system is up and running.

The old approach of "tell them what you're going to do; tell them what you're doing; and tell them when you've done it" applies here, and it applies to all phases of a multistage project. (As discussed under Principle 3.4, it is usually a good idea to break long projects up into shorter ones, a principle that makes it easier to communicate news about complex, long-term projects). At each step of the way, top management should know in general terms what it is you're doing and why—what will be the business-based end results. And whenever a milestone or achievement has been realized, top management should be the first to hear the good news.

How far into the hierarchy should you reach with this type of communication? Starting with the top, you may wish to include all executives, department heads, and functional managers who will be using the system, line managers, and other business unit leaders. When developing the kind of modern, widely used HRIS recommended by this book, the senior managers whose support you should have and whose understanding of the reasons for your work is essential may be at many levels in the organization. Even if they were not part of the approval process last year, they may be part of it next.

3.2 Encourage Project Team Communications

Perhaps the most important of the team-building skills that are so valuable in modern business organizations, and which are vital to the success of a HRIS project, is the ability to communicate. The differences between one person working alone in a laboratory on a project and a group of people working on the same project can be disastrous without effective communications. It's a problem the "lonely genius" never has to deal with (everything's in her head), but one that can escalate geometrically as the number of individuals on a project rises.

Effective communications takes nothing for granted. The project leader cannot assume that a team member who understood his role last month is still performing the role; or that two people who should be working together are doing so; or that the systems professionals are still talking to the HR user representatives. Regular meetings of appropriate groups, written communications that spell out responsibilities and communicate progress, and constant monitoring of what people think they are doing—listening is half of good communications—are necessary.

Other team-building and project management skills depend to some extent on the particular management style of the project leader. Some managers encourage, some threaten, some lead by example, and some wise managers do all of these things to different people or at different times. Whatever the management style, project management generally and HRIS project management in particular call for virtually constant attention to communications. At times, especially on HRIS projects that involve a heterogeneous mix of skills, professional disciplines, and levels of full-time participation, effective communications can be the difference between success and failure. No matter how qualified and dedicated people are as individuals, the project can fail if they do not share the same overall goals, understand their roles in relation to others, respect and benefit from the work and knowledge of others on the team, and sense the importance of their own contributions to the team.

3.3   Maintain User Communications Bonds

The second main constituency with whom communications must remain vigorous throughout a project's implementation cycle is the user community. Too often, users are the initial focus of HRIS planners and developers in the needs analysis phase of implementation, then become the forgotten men and women until it is time for user tests and conversion. By then, their needs may have changed, they may have a different set of priorities, and they may even be different people than they were when you first interviewed their predecessors. Ignored long enough, forgotten users will go on their own or stage a "palace revolt" and cause a change in HRIS management.

Users are the ultimate reason for having an HRIS, it should be remembered. If the system does not bring efficiencies to benefits administration, make the EEO manager's job easier, solve payroll's check-processing problems, or provide a line manager with the staffing models she needs, no amount of technological sophistication or paperwork elimination will justify the HRIS.

In a well-managed needs analysis, the project team typically builds strong bonds with users, many of them line managers. Interviews, work analysis, repeat interviews "to first determine their needs and their satisfaction levels today, to initial design to see if we got it right," and the presentation of the costs and benefits of various systems alternatives become part of functional users' daily lives. These bonds can be maintained as the project team moves into other phases. Users can and should be involved with the reengineering steps, prototypes, design, specifications, and testing, such as being asked to try out a function or a screen. Procedures that may need to be changed because of a new system should always be reviewed with users. In short, the "ties that bind" the project team to users in the needs analysis phase should not be allowed to go slack. It's *their* system, after all, and they should never be allowed to think otherwise. Even if users are not involved directly in implementation work being performed this week, it's a good idea to schedule some time just to "walk around and see how they're doing," if time does not permit more formal meetings or individual visits.

3.4 "Shorten" Long-Term Projects to Provide Goals

Systems work is usually complicated work, with many factors to consider in a complex project plan. When a project is both complicated and long-term – involving dozens of functions, hundreds of procedures, and years of work – the overall project is difficult for any one person to grasp. Therefore it becomes increasingly difficult to think of as a "project" at all, much less one with clearly understood goals. In these long projects people come to work as they would come to work on any job, "punch in" and "punch out," do what they're told to do, and every so often are surprised to learn that a "milestone" has been reached, or that a new phase is about to begin.

Effective project team work is usually imbued with the sense of urgency that comes from delivering important work on time. And the job satisfaction of team members is closely linked to the achievement of goals. At any one time, those working on the project should be able to "see" what it is they are trying to accomplish, why it's needed, the end result, and understand that the time they have to achieve the end result is not indefinite. Perhaps coming to an "open house" would help.

This means that project management, when faced with a long, necessarily complex project, should find ways of making interim goals part of everyone's working life, a reason to come to work and a motivating force from day to day. One way to do this is to "shorten" projects into less overwhelming, more easily understood segments or phases.

What has worked is to plan and deliver projects in phases that never extend beyond four to six months, even 90 days if feasible. For example, the needs analysis work could be a project by itself, as could be a pilot of a new technology, the building of a new DB2 database, and so on.

In addition, the communication effort needed to gain and retain management support for the project, and the continuing participation and interest of others affected by the project (such as users, line managers, and sometimes the entire employee population), is made much easier by short-term depictions of work and its objectives. It's easier for people generally to see and appreciate progress in short time frames.

3.5 Use Charge-Backs: People Only Value What They Pay for

Throughout most of the history of the personnel function, including most of the years since it has been known as human resources and supported by HR systems, companies have had relatively little knowledge about what they spend on overall HR management, or the value they receive for what they spend. There are HR budgets. But to arrive at total HR costs—what training, staffing or other programs really cost—is very elusive. Compared to manufacturing, financial, or marketing (where millions may be spent on corporate image campaigns that are difficult to cost-justify), personnel management generally has not been able to fully quantify its services, been made to identify specific values added to the organization, or otherwise been asked to justify itself with bottom-line results. Usually, it's been part of corporate overhead, and even today's multifunctional HR departments rarely sort out their products and services by value-added or cost measurements.

For HR management to reach the position it should hold in modern organizations, this has to change. There has to be a mechanism that more closely identifies HR costs and services. The cold truth is that people only value what they pay for, and as long as they're not paying for HR products and services, the personnel function will not be fully appreciated. Line managers become critical of HR work and are quick to circumvent the function when they perceive it as non-value-added, or they ask that their pro-rate be altered since they view HR as nonproductive.

Of course, a charge-back process that asks HR "customers" in the organization to pay for HR services requires the delivery of products or services which in fact *do* have measurable value. This implies a need for the HRIS project not only to help keep such costs, but in turn to be a service which has a defined value and a method of delivering the value to the customers. What is required is a cost/benefit analysis such as is described in Chapter 12.

Most important, however, it should be kept in mind that not only traditional HR systems products and services need to be given a value and "charged" to internal customers. It's not just the automated procedures or data people are paying for — it's the applications and functions supported by systems. Automation for its own sake is rarely valuable. By identifying the value added by the function — whether it is benefits cost control, regulatory reporting, payroll processing, or management development — the value added by systems that support these functions is identified. This is an important principle to keep in mind when deciding what to do first in a complex HRIS project, a decision that should be based in part on the potential for immediate payback, fast results that show on the bottom line.

3.6 Generate Some Return During Installation If You Can: Pay as You Go

Pay-as-you-go together with Principles 3.4 and 3.5, is the third leg needed to support a good start to long, possibly costly HRIS projects. Tangible, early payoffs and continuing pay-as-you-go benefits are as important in large-scale HRIS projects as they are in any new venture, both to retain the support of "investors" and to help create and build confidence among the "cast," the project team, users, and other participants in HRIS development.

Project planning that breaks up long-term projects into segments with more immediate, understandable objectives, as recommended in Principle 3.4, and an approach that puts a value on all HRIS products and services (Principle 3.5) and then "sells" these results back to those in the organization who receive them, make a pay-as-you-go project that much easier to achieve.

For example, if the overall HRIS project involves a multinational corporation's development of a comprehensive executive development system, the first phase of the project might focus on the identification and management of international transfers among expatriates as third-country nationals, including relocation costs. Employee transfers, involving relocation costs, especially at the managerial level, have become extremely expensive at many large organizations. They are a major human resource expense item in multinational firms with ex-patriate managers. A contributing factor in these transfers is that top management does not have the decision-support information needed to create more cost-effective policies and programs that could better allocate resources at the managerial level, thereby reducing relocation costs. Who is being transferred and relocated, and where? At what cost? Most important, why? If relocation is largely the result of a job rotation component in the management development program, for example, perhaps localized training and development and staffing programs will be more cost-effective.

By focusing on this problem early and examining the new technology and procedures needed to collect, monitor, and analyze managerial staffing and associated relocation data, the project development team can deliver a quick payoff, a visible, appreciated return on investment (ROI) — and one that can potentially be charged back to the organization responsible for controlling management movement and relocation. The same principle should be applied to subsequent parts of major projects: Whenever possible, look for ways to show some ROI as you go along, both to keep top management's support and to keep the enthusiasm of project participants at a high level.

This principle needs to be weighed against the need to satisfy the overall project objectives and critical success factors among others, but all things being equal, try to put the HRIS on a pay-as-you-go basis.

3.7 You Can't Do Just One Thing.

This principle is one of those "rules" of life that is nowhere more obvious than in the kind of work involved in HRIS development or improvement. What it means, essentially, is that it is very difficult to isolate tasks from their interrelated parts: Doing one thing, whether it's installing a new part in a machine or creating new data fields in employee profiles, has implications and effects that require you to do other things.

In life, we're often asked to do one thing that at first appears relatively simple, and only later do we find out what we've let ourselves in for because of related tasks and implications. Say, for instance, you are asked by your professional association to send out the next meeting announcement, using labels that will arrive at your home on a Saturday, two days before the announcement needs to be mailed. Fine, you say. This is "one thing" you can do to help your professional society.

But then you discover that the meeting announcement has to be rewritten because a speaker has canceled; your home-town post office closes earlier than you thought and you need stamps; envelopes are not available on the weekend; and you've got a critical management meeting at the office at 9:00 a.m. Monday.

This may appear to be an example of some corollary of Murphy's law: anything that can go wrong, will go wrong. In fact, in life and in HRIS work, things don't need to go wrong to cause problems, extra work, or potential project failure. They simply need to be there as unexamined consequences, related tasks, or tangential issues that should have been considered and planned for in advance.

By remembering that you can't do just one thing—whether it involves the reorganization of a department or the addition of a new data element to the EEO system—managers can plan for the implications and contingencies that surround all activities that create change. In reorganizing a department, job responsibilities are redefined and shifted to other people, lines of authority are changed, and so on. In systems work, a code change or a new procedure can have similarly far-reaching implications. I have yet to come across a significant act in systems work or organizational change that was "an island unto itself."

3.8 Teach as You Go: Create Backups for All Positions

The ideal HRIS project team is both multidisciplinary as a group and individually multidisciplinary: Each member of the team understands or at least is capable of learning both the technical side and the functional side, or what the system is going to be used for in the organization. The individuals selected for the project team should be chosen with this in mind, and the project plan and schedule should take into account the need for a certain amount of on-the-job training, especially for those without previous exposure to the other area.

Taking this concept one step further, effective HRIS project management should also assure that individual team members can do more than just one job or type of work. Technical people should be able to write systems documentation as well as write code for the system; the user representative from the benefits department should be able to help with salary administration applications; and so on. Each position at any given time on the project team, in fact, should have a backup person available, a team member ready to step in and keep the work moving whatever happens. This approach also has a positive effect on customer satisfaction, since it will reduce the number of "I don't know" responses by members of the HRIS team.

Job rotation, on-the-job training, project team communications, and the use of small "teams within the team" to perform tasks all help to expand the basic multidisciplinariability of a HRIS project team. Further, the ability to understand and appreciate what it takes to perform other team members' jobs is likely to enhance the "team spirit" essential to effective teams. Nothing promotes an understanding of the other person's problems and priorities better than a walk in the other person's shoes.

4. Fundamental HRIS Design Principles

4.1 Build Today's System for Tomorrow's Technology

Modern human resource systems should be built with an eye to full utilization of today's—and perhaps tomorrow's—technology. When appropriate, systems design may even consider mixing some or all of the technologies that go beyond databases, knowledge-based applications, imagining, pen-based, LANs, and standard computer terminals, as voice-activated systems, video, and telephone access systems, to name a few.

Applications of telecommunications technology, for example, are one way of extending the reach of HRIS to sites and people who do not normally have access to on-line computer terminals. Anywhere there's a phone—at a construction site, in a store, in a car, or at home—an employee can find out anything from what's covered by her insurance plan to what hours he is expected to work under next week's flextime schedule.

Linking the HRIS to technology that permits teleconferencing can permit the display of participants' images and related information on computer terminals as they discuss a work problem or attend a training session. As a further step, live photos may be appropriate in the staffing area, permitting HR and/or line management interviewers to see job candidates, and vice versa, as they respond to questions.

Already, voice-activated systems exist that permit a manager to ask the computer for messages, ask for a new report, summon the day's labor distribution, or put through a call to the Paris office without touching the phone. Other systems, and some still emerging, permit voice input and document creation.

Multimedia computers that incorporate sound, video, and live pictures may also be appropriate in the HRIS being planned today for the personnel office of the future. Imagine conducting performance appraisals for managers worldwide—or performance appraisal training for their supervisors—with the help of live pictures, videos that demonstrate or explain key points, voice-over instructions, and the ability to move back and forth into the performance appraisal system.

Today's technology must be utilized, of course, in building today's systems; but the HRIS team should keep an open mind regarding tomorrow's possibilities.

4.2 Build in Flexibility; Design for Decoupling

How often has an HR manager been told that "the system is down" because some relatively small part of the HRIS—say, the edit program— has a bug in it? Or that reprogramming of the benefits system is holding up the weekly payroll run? Or that a loan provision to the savings and investment plan may have to be delayed until next year, so it won't interfere with the new flex plan or the year-end tax reporting module?

Quite often, these kinds of problems can be avoided by systems designers who build flexibility into a HRIS and related systems through various forms of "decoupling," an approach to systems design that can take a number of different forms. For example, the use of tables can separate vast amounts of data from the database itself, where it can be worked on or changed separately. Independent, self-contained code sets can be designed for specialized functions. Systems can be designed in technically linked but separable modules, so that you can replace vendor A's payroll system with vendor B's without an inordinate amount of reprogramming.

Other forms of decoupling HRIS operations may involve planning for alternate procedures as well as design flexibility. For example, are systems and procedures capable of letting the payroll department process checks for 20 locations without waiting for the 21st location to report?

Many systems are so complex in their design and operation that there is little tolerance for mistakes or for making routine updates. Systems have been so reworked over the years—often with little or no documentation—that even small changes take enormous amounts of time to make. And the IS shop and user community all breathe a sign of relief when the changes are finally made. Unrolling the HRIS "spaghetti code" has become an art form in many companies.

What is needed is to build what are commonly called subroutines, and similar modules, where the IS programmer can isolate the particular part of the program being worked. Also, avoid building unusually long sequences of preset calculations, screen chains, or similar functions which may need to pulled out of service while they are enhanced.

4.3 Include Outside Data as Well as Internal Information

In order to do their jobs properly, human resource managers (and virtually all others involved in critical management functions) need data from outside the organization as well as internal information. This has always been true to some extent for some organizations, but the modern HRIS serving organizations in today's more competitive environment will usually require much more and much better external data than may have been necessary in the past.

As discussed in Chapter 1, the early impetus for human resource systems came largely from equal employment regulations requiring, in some cases, affirmative action plans. Such plans required comparisons of internal workforce demographics—percentages of women, blacks, and other protected classes—with those "available" in relevant labor markets. Then and now, external labor market data has been relatively easy to incorporate into a HRIS, in the form of Census Bureau data.

Salary survey information, educational statistics, cost of living and relocation information, medical statistics based on epidemiology, global and local economic data, and much industry-specific information is also available from outside sources today, and much of this data is essential to strategic planning, HR planning, and a full range of HR management functions. What should be covered in the medical insurance plans being considered for a new flexible benefits plan? What is the availability of data processing specialists in a proposed new office overseas, and what will they cost? How many Ph.D. chemists will be graduating and from what schools?

Health Care experience data on costs and plan utilization is needed to monitor medical costs as is managed care data.

Increasingly, the HRIS that fully supports modern human resource management must also incorporate competitive data, a somewhat more difficult task. Industry-specific salary survey data—showing what others in your industry are paying people in similar jobs—is one form of competitive data. But what are your chief competitors *getting* for their wage and salary dollars? What are their productivity rates, turnover rates, and what costs and benefits are they getting out of their recruitment programs, benefits plans, and other human resource policies and programs?

And in the expanded HRIS recommended by this book, what other business information about competitors can and should be collected about competitors? Marketing and sales information, suppliers' prices, production costs, and a score of other types of data may be relevant in some cases, and available to managers to compare with internal data.

4.4 Create "Public" Data for Multiple Users

It is in the nature of a HRIS database that some data is "public," i.e., available to all authorized users, and some is not public, but is used by one user or for a specialized application. Public data includes such information as a person's name, social security number, job title, or employment history; nonpublic data might include individual performance appraisal ratings, test results, or medical information.

The early identification of which data elements are public and which are not has implications that go beyond privacy issues, though privacy is certainly a consideration. Most important, a multifunctional HRIS that can cover a dozen or more different HR functions and may—if extended beyond HR—be used throughout the organization, should have as much public information as possible. Each data element that is needed by more than one user and that can be standardized—such as a job code, department number, training course, or social security number—can then be used by all functions and organizations that need that data element, such as telephone operators, mailrooms etc. It is entered and edited once, updated (when necessary) just once, and maintained as needed in the HRIS database—available to meet functional needs.

The advantages of public data elements extend beyond simple efficiency, though efficiency that eliminates redundant work or maintaining separate databases is always a HRIS goal. Almost equally important, especially over time, is the consistency that public data brings to information systems. If "John J. Jones" is a person's name in the HRIS, he's not Jack Jones in the pension system, J.J. Jones to EEO, and J. Jerry Jones to payroll. And the variations possible in spelling a person's name are nothing compared to the variations possible in showing job titles, skills inventory data, benefit plan enrollments, or other data that can usually be made public and used by a number of different functions.

This principle might need some enforcement by the HRIS team, since it implies adherence to a standard. The users, if they are to share the data with others, are by definition using public data. Standardization means that they are not free to stray from the screens, code sets, and other data conventions established.

4.5   A System "Built for History" Pays off in Many Ways

One thing a HRIS can and should be built for is history. At any given time, it should be possible for the user to move back in time to any date or period, and have a complete record and chronology of events and data regarding that time. The historical information can be in active HRIS files or stored on secondary files or archives, but all history should be available in some machine-readable form for later analysis.

Some HRIS history is used regularly in a number of different applications. Individual work history, for example, provides data used in skills inventories, career development, pension planning, and other functions. Other historical records are required by government regulation, or may be required by the company to defend itself in potential litigation based on employment law. The payroll law's Fair Labor Standards Act requires retention of wage and hour data for two years; and laws on equal employment, pay, age discrimination, health and safety, and other employment conditions, if applicable, call for similar record retention. Further, the company may have to prove that actions in past years did not violate employment law, or make it vulnerable to an employee's suit. Health and safety regulations call for data to be kept for up to 30 years following termination, retirement, or death.

HRIS historical data also permit the reconstruction of parts of the business and events that may have changed greatly over time, but which the company wants to look at again for one business reason or another. What happened, for example, to relocation costs, pensions, unemployment benefits, when we closed the Akron plant five years ago? How did we manage staffing of the office we opened in Toledo, and the expansion of our Ohio marketing department? Although circumstances change over time, much can be learned from the company's past experience in many areas covered by human resource data. And, of course, those who do not learn from the past are doomed to repeat its mistakes.

4.6   Design the HRIS for Regulatory Compliance

It should go without saying that a HRIS should be designed for compliance with employment law and regulations. From the equal employment laws, benefits laws, safety laws, and others as well as, federal, state, and local payroll laws require most employers to file regular reports on employees with government agencies and to have other employee data available for efficient extraction.

Just as the equal employment legislation of the 1960s and early 1970s justified the costs of some of the nation's first human resource systems, the systems of the 1990s and beyond will often pay their way by their ability to cost-effectively collect, store, and report data needed for regulatory compliance—and not just in the United States, but in countries throughout the world, some of which have far more restrictive employment laws than America.

Compliance-oriented human resource systems not only collect and store data for currently required legislation—such as the data that may be needed for record-keeping aspects of EEO, ERISA, EPA, ADEA, OSHA, ADA, FLSA, and other regulations, but in addition, should anticipate future regulation, and take into account the burgeoning array of case law developed in litigation based on issues in the employment exchange—such as privacy rights, wrongful termination, negligent hiring, and other issues.

4.7 Build in Training and Documentation

Whenever possible, a HRIS should be built for tomorrow's newcomers as well as today's users. One way to do this is to build training and documentation into the system, in the form of on-line help, performance support, user-friendly inquiry capabilities, and computer-based training.

On-line access to information and instructions that guides users through procedures, explains unfamiliar terms or transactions, and otherwise coaches the user is potentially the most powerful type of on-the-job training available to systems users. The instruction or information is part of the job, integrated with the work itself, and available instantly as the user needs it. When well designed, computer-based training has the further advantage of empowering individual users to move beyond the instruction needed to perform tasks required by his or her current position: Courses can be made available that are prerequisites of promotion, and the empowered user can spend the lunch hour or other times during the day or after work in career development sessions with the system.

User friendliness does not need to be "relative" as it always was when systems capacities were limited and computer languages, database architectures, and retrieval tools were less sophisticated. Today, it is genuinely possible to make computer use as simple as a video game or a bank's automated teller machine. By adding English-language instruction and information either within programs or on linked programs that can be entered and exited at the touch of a screen or keyboard; with a "windows" environment, split screens, and high-definition graphics; the technical aspect of the systems are very easy to learn and use. What is needed as well is to explain the application and/or process to the user, and to guide the user through the staffing activities, pension calculation process, and the like.

4.8 Extend Data to Employees, the Largest User Community

Whenever possible, the design of a modern HRIS should find ways of extending the reach of the system, as discussed in Chapter 2, and the largest potential user community that should be reached by the HRIS is the employee population as a whole. The modern HRIS can be designed to provide access to all or most employees—providing information about benefits, HR policies, career planning, work procedures, and other matters—and it can provide ways to enter and change HRIS information, an ability that can vastly improve the effectiveness and efficiency of some HRIS applications. For example, when an employee can use a desktop computer or centrally located kiosk to enter the fact that his wife had a baby, the technology can take over and make all relevant changes to benefits, payroll deductions, and other files.

The HRIS should allow a wide range of on-line interaction. The employee should be able to make a change in benefits, respond to an employee attitude survey, check the accuracy of personal data, send a résumé to a department with a job opening, buy company stock with payroll deductions, or sign up for the company picnic—all without help from human specialists who may or may not be in the same building, or even the same country.

Controls on this type of all-employee use of the HRIS can be systematic. Employee ID numbers, passwords, and PIN numbers can assure that only the employee's own records are shown; the résumé may go first to the employee's supervisor for approval; a change in personal data may need verification before the database is changed; and so on.

Systems designed for more than mere employee "access"—which permit employees to create data or make changes—can take advantage of the fact that for much HRIS data, the best source is the employees themselves. Whenever possible, the elimination of people or systems that come between these sources and the HRIS should be a high priority in systems design.

4.9 Build in Measurements, Both of HR Costs and Organizational Health

Whenever possible, HRIS design should find ways to correct one of the longest-standing criticisms of the human resource function in the organization: "We don't know what it costs." Because people are not steel ingots or other raw material with unvarying characteristics, predictable potential, and known value after the application of known costs, the basic subject matter of human resource management has never been readily amenable to strict cost accounting methods. The variables involved in managing people — individuals with different talents, motivations, energy levels, needs, intelligence, skills, and so on — appear to defy the usual production-oriented "value-added" approach. The traditional measurement approach was: "We *can't* really say that a benefits plan that costs X amount per employee adds X amount to each employee's value to the organization, or that a given training program added a certain value to each employee who took it."

At the same time, however, much of what occurs in the management of human resources *can* be measured in terms of operating costs, and a HRIS that is fully extended to the line managers and employee population — presents unparalleled opportunities for tracking and reporting these costs. In many ways, a HRIS can help human resources become as cost-driven as other functions in the organization, without necessarily attempting to put an exact price on each individual in the employee population. For example:

- When do we have the most effective workforce? At what mix of skills and levels?

- Are the true costs of hiring people being measured and tracked — by location, function, source, or other variable — and related in some way to outcomes, such as performance appraisal ratings or absenteeism rates?

- What does turnover really cost, in terms of lost productivity, replacement costs, or other "lost investment" factors?

- Do we know all the costs of training and development, and can we relate these to measurable outcomes?

- What does my HR function cost?

Each of these and many other questions regarding human resource management costs involves a number of factors that can and should be considered in HRIS design.

In addition, beyond the costs of HR programs and policies, a number of measurements relating to the overall health of the organization might be incorporated in HRIS design. These include productivity measurements, the efficiency of decision making, responsiveness to market demands or opportunities, and other factors specific to the organization's corporate mission and objectives. Wherever possible, HRIS designers should be on the watch for measurement data relevant to organizational effectiveness—data that an automated system can readily supply to management so they can assimilate and analyze it—as part of the normal HR operating procedures.

4.10   Include Policies and Procedures in the HRIS, Not Just Data

In the early days of HRIS, mainframe systems that carried as many as 100 different data elements were considered behemoths. Today, microcomputer-based systems that can be acquired for several thousand dollars can handle many times that number, and can include or be linked to provide instant access to whole libraries of text, performance-support data, and knowledge-based systems that guide users through the HR professional procedures. This explosion in the capacity of systems should be fully exploited in HRIS design, so that the system contains not just the conventional data about employees and jobs, but many underlying HR policies and procedures. These other parts of the HRIS help people perform their jobs, inform HR professionals throughout the enterprise about relevant policies, and in some cases inform the employee population generally. A few examples of such applications:

- Supervisors can inquire regarding overtime payments the day after a holiday.

- What are the rules for enrolling an employee in a training program and the procedures for signing up?

- Plant managers in all locations can ask the HRIS for vacation policy information, such as what options are available if the plant will be short-handed this month.

- A benefits specialist asked to perform an unusual or complex task—such as an executive's exercise of her stock option—can move into a program that provides step-by-step expert instruction, eliminating the need to refer to a written manual or ask a colleague for help.

- Employees throughout the organization can use terminals or centrally located kiosks to read company policies about benefits, business ethics, career opportunities, or other matters of interest.

- Electronic mail systems can be used to provide instant communication without duplicative paperwork, such as when the HR vice president wants to send the same memo to 30 business unit heads.

Now that the functionality of the HRIS has been extended beyond the traditional database and its carrying capacity is no longer an obstacle to the inclusion of vast amounts of text and other information that in the past was part of paperwork, the issues to be addressed in HRIS design are not so much whether to include policies and procedures, but how to include such information in easily accessed formats.

5. HRIS Operating Principles

5.1 Collect Data Early and Edit Locally

For the sake of data quality and plain efficiency, it's usually a good idea to design HRIS systems and procedures that permit the early collection of data and its editing in the field, at the source of its origination. By "early," in this context, we mean as close as possible in time to the event that creates the data and at the location where it was created.

Prompt data collection and local editing assures that information gets into the HRIS database more quickly, without the data preparation and mailing, duplicate handling, or back-and-forth procedures usually associated with traditional systems. It also avoids the bottlenecks that occur when large amounts of data need to be keyed in all at once—say, at corporate headquarters where input is collected on paper on forms from many sources.

Systems that permit local data entry and editing mean that when an event such as a new hire or a performance appraisal occurs, the event's consequences on the HRIS database are immediately reflected, without delay and therefore available to all users instantaneously. Not only is the newly hired employee entered in all relevant files and paid on time, but also, data entry has not been allowed to pile up, either at a central source or at satellite locations in the field, only to be rehandled later.

In many cases, local editing also helps improve data quality. The source documents used to create data are on hand locally; persons familiar with the event and its data characteristics originate and check the data; and many potential errors that could slip past both systems edits and the review of data-entry people at another location are prevented. This also promotes user "buy-in" in terms of ownership of the data. The HRIC management does not *own* the data: The user line management or the employee does. For example, the identification of Jan Smith as "M" for male passes systems edits, and is not necessarily caught by people in the HRIS management department who have never seen Jan, a female. Or, as discussed in Chapter 11, better technical edits are possible relating data to other data that might only be available locally.

The costs generally are lower in this type of system as well, since there are fewer edit failures and rework, fewer people handling the data, and the same amount of time (or less) spent by the data originator who is inputting the data—now on-line rather than onto a paper form.

5.2 Design for Security and Controls but Remember that the System Can't Do It All

The HRIS and its database are corporate assets, of continuing value to the business of the organization. This is the justification for many HRIS design features, procedures, and policies that assure the security of the system and its data. But HRIS security is not merely a matter of protecting the past investment in the system. Measures that prevent outside intruders from entering the system, or that assure that data and programs are not "lost" in the event of disaster, are only part of database security. These measures are relatively easy to install and implement, through the use of user ID codes, passwords, and proper backup and recovery procedures. A more critical issue in HRIS security, which grows out of the fact that an HRIS is essentially an "access" system dedicated to providing information and automated processes to numerous users throughout the organization, is "who sees what," and its corollary, "who changes what."

Each data element, from social security number through salary, needs to be assessed in terms of its required security level. And the investment must be scaled to the potential loss: Not all data can be protected to the maximum level at all times. In the early days of HRIS, user codes based on a function such as salary administration permitted users to read or change whole categories of information — whatever they seemed to "need to know." Today, data element security and control measures can assure that some users in the salary administration department see only certain salary ranges, or codes that relate to tables and not to individuals; others can see but not edit selected salaries or salary grades; and others have the authority to make specific changes to selective organizations or locations.

Security and control of data then extends not only to who can gain access to the various system components, but who can alter the data as well. And in a fully extended system, complete hierarchical tables of who works for whom may be needed in order that supervisors see only the records of those who report directly to them.

Effective database security assures that the quality of data is not harmed, inadvertently or deliberately, by users. Data quality involves not only accuracy, but currency, availability, and usefulness to managers, as well as other technical limitations on who uses the system. It also involves policies and procedures that protect the HRIS from both human error and natural disasters. Controls such as needed audit trails and transaction logs are to be provided for as well, so that records of usage are maintained. HRIS administrators always need to "know their users," one way or another.

For example, what happens when a user leaves the company or goes on vacation? Does the office temp get the user code and password? Where are backup tapes or disks stored, in the same building or at another location? What happens to hardcopy reports that include access codes? Are remote modems being controlled and monitored? In short, do all users throughout the organization know to and follow security procedures?

5.3 Ensure the Privacy of Personal Information

Privacy is often confused with security in an HRIS, but it is an entirely different issue that needs to be perceived from a different vantage point and addressed through a privacy policy that goes beyond database security measures. Security says that the HRIS and its data are corporate assets and need to be protected; privacy says that some data is also personal and belongs to individual employees; some should not be collected at all; and if it is collected, it should not be misused or carelessly disseminated by the organization.

Laws in this country and in Europe have put some limits on the uses of computerized information about individuals, but privacy principles that apply to an HRIS—the ultimate "people inventory," capable of carrying a person's entire professional and personal career—should be driven by more than mere legal requirements. There are fairness and ethical considerations involved. In the extended HRIS envisioned by this book, individual employees throughout the organization are potential users of the system, and their confidence in the HRIS as a safe repository of sensitive personal data that will be handled responsibly is essential to continuing operations.

Privacy policy should usually cover these principles, first spelled out in the United States in the Privacy Protection Act of 1974, covering federal employees:

- Collect and store only business-relevant data.
- Provide employees with the opportunity to see and correct inaccurate data.
- Prevent unauthorized disclosure.
- Do not allow data collected for one purpose to be used for another.

In addition, all of the above should be clearly spelled out in an HRIS privacy policy and communicated to employees, with appropriate sanctions to assure compliance.

What information is "personal" and deserves to be covered by privacy policy? Anything that relates to an individual, from social security number through medical history, is private, which means that the lion's share of HRIS information needs privacy protection. Operating measures and management practices that help assure both database security and privacy are discussed in Chapters 9 and 11.

5.4 Disaster Recovery Investment Should Match Downtime Costs

The HRIS envisioned by this book, a vital part of the business side of the organization, needs to be fully recoverable in cases of "disaster," a word that takes in a broad range of events and conditions that can prevent continuing use of the system. All new HRIS data and changes should be backed up on separate files or data sets at the end of each day, and together with everything else needed to run the HRIS—programs, documentation, forms, equipment, and even user manuals—should be kept at a location not likely to be affected by the same disaster that might disable the HRIS. Usually, this means another building, if not another city.

Disaster recovery has always been considered a worthwhile investment in other types of systems. When a bank loses deposit records in an earthquake, or Defense Department programs are infected by a virus, or a strike prevents telephone company operators from getting at their computers, the consequences are potentially enormous—threatening enough to justify the costs of adequate security measures.

A HRIS that has become a vital part of the business of the organization, providing essential data and automated processing that has bottom-line effects on everything from payrolls to savings plans and pension funds must also be recoverable in cases of disaster. The cost/benefits analysis that is discussed in Chapter 12 forms the basis for answering the question, "How much should we invest in assuring (1) that we don't have to rebuild all or part of the HRIS from scratch; and (2) that HRIS operations will be continuous, despite a temporary inability to use the system?"

Additional analysis may be necessary to estimate the potential costs of temporary disabilities, such as a bomb threat or a strike that prevents HRIS use for a day or two. What will be the costs of the overtime needed to bring the payroll system back into its normal cycle? What additional resources will be required to process other daily functions such as benefit claims or employment and staffing? And so on. The costs of reconstructing the entire HRIS or rebuilding certain programs and files—huge as it may be—may be only a fraction of the total costs incurred when the system is not available for use over a period of time.

PART 2

Bringing the Vision to Life

Principles and Practices
of the Development Cycle

4

Business Analysis and the Identification of Needs

In developing new business strategies for HRIS development and management in the years ahead, the maxim that no two human resource systems are exactly alike will have more validity than ever before. Unlike production systems such as accounts payable, each human resource system has always been unique, because each population is different, different types of work require different types of organization, user communities differ, and employment policies and HR programs have never been uniform and grow more diverse each year. If one considers as well the growing globalization of human resources, and the idea of a "standard" or ideal, HRIS becomes even more unrealistic.

Packaged HRIS software and standard systems architectures have brought a certain superficial similarity to systems, but the similarities are largely technical and only "screen-deep." A HRIS is not defined by how it looks and feels to users, or by technical features. Rather, a HRIS is defined by what it does, and these functional differences—why the HRIS will exist—are the focus of the discovery process outlined in this chapter.

Business Analysis

Different businesses have different needs. For example, for an organization that is moving into overseas operations which will involve different cultures, business environments, and ways of operating, analysis for job redesign will have particular importance. Consider, for example, the differences between management positions in a regional sales office in the United States and in office with the same functions in Europe, the Pacific Basin, or a more socialist country in Africa. In one office a regional manager's job requirements may include intimate knowledge of local political and governmental issues. In another the manager's most important task may be to motivate the sales force. In yet another locale, training in the use of available office technology may be the sales manager's first priority.

Job analysis, whether for a position in production, sales, management, clerical services, or whatever, must examine the total requirements for the position within the context of the organizational unit in which it functions—not just a textbook definition of tasks and responsibilities. A management style or mode of behavior that succeeds very well in motivating the engineering department in Silicon Valley may be totally inappropriate in Taiwan, and job analysis must reflect such differences.

The continuing expansion of the HR management function in the years ahead is likely to include more job analysis and more participation in redesign than was common in the past. As discussed in Chapter 1, the integration of people and technology is no longer merely possible by relying only on industrial engineering, time-motion studies, and job design that treats human workers as interchangeable parts. The skills of human resource professionals in analyzing both work activities and the needs of workers, and in identifying appropriate technologies for improving the productivity and performance of employees, will be increasingly critical in the years ahead.

For example, analysis of customer service or telemarketing positions that involve telephone response to a potentially complex range of inquiries and requests must focus on both the nature of the work and the skills, capabilities, and attitudes of the representatives answering phones—people the organization has decided to pay a certain amount in salary and benefits, not an unlimited amount. Overall, the issues might include:

- Whether telecommunications technology should replace all or most service representatives, and what would be the cost/benefit impacts of automation
- Whether one highly trained representative can do the work of two or

three whose training is merely adequate, and what the training costs would be

■ What kinds of performance-support technology—such as on-line reference guides, artificial intelligence systems, or telecommunications tools—would improve this function, what it would cost, and what skills would be needed

All of these and similar issues involve human resources. On paper, the technology available to support a customer service representative answering phones may look like the greatest thing since the invention of the switchboard. But what are the actual requirements of the position, today and in the years ahead? What skills will be needed to use the technology, and how will they be learned? What kinds of human resources will be required, and what kinds are available?

Should these positions be limited to phone-answering responsibilities, or is there other work that service representatives can be doing—perhaps on a word processing system co-resident in the computer—between calls?

How can the HRIS analyst determine such needs and the relationship between the needs and the supporting technologies? The answer lies in the involvement of both line management and the HR planning function. This is especially important in a decentralized, highly dispersed organization.

Senior management and strategic plans will identify the overriding issues. For example, improved customer service in an increasingly decentralized company, with diverse products, made more demanding by a global economy, will require particular HRIS support responsibilities.

Applications of human resource systems that help unify widely dispersed locations or provide corporatewide information for local management decisions are examples of how an increasingly decentralized environment can be supported by HR technology. In these applications, one or more specific human resource functions or programs are run on a decentralized, usually microcomputer-based subsystem of the HRIS, with its own function-specific database, data collection procedures, reports, and a set of users defined by the function. Information can then be gathered from these local systems for corporate use.

For example, an organization with facilities at a number of locations and a need for consistent, universally managed hiring practices may decide to install a micro-based applicant-tracking system that links all hiring locations. Such a system would provide functional help, keeping résumés on qualified candidates and government-required data on the demographic characteristics of job applicants, assuring that companywide standards and policies are being met at all locations, and bringing other consistencies to the employment process while leaving actual employment processes and hiring decisions in the hands of local managers.

Another activity that is frequently decentralized in large organizations with scattered business units is succession planning. When managers throughout a far-flung organization are potential successors to key positions, a system that provides consistent, corporate-wide procedures and policies, for succession planning can be more promptly responsive to organizational change. At each location, top managers use the same screens or data-entry forms to update their individual profiles; succession planning managers meet with managers in front of a computer terminal that provides instant information about developmental activities, openings, and other succession data; business unit managers at all locations can quickly identify available or qualified candidates anywhere in the organization; and senior HR management and planning officials have access to up-to-date, corporatewide information on such factors as management development needs, performance appraisals, the future availability of successors to key positions, blockages preventing timely promotions, and other issues relevant to succession planning.

These two examples—applicant-tracking systems and succession planning systems—represent two types of business needs which have developed different structures in terms of their usual linkage to the overall HRIS. Applicant-tracking data is typically carried in its own database, because subjects are not yet employees; if and when they are hired, their files might be automatically transferred to the HRIS. A succession planning system can and should be linked to the HRIS technically, so that basic personnel data on successors and positions can be downloaded and used to update the subsystem—say, with newly eligible successors or new position requirements. The succession planning system remains a separate system, with its own unique data elements such as potential assessments and its own security restrictions to limit access to appropriate managers, but systematic links with the HRIS and other systems such as career development or training systems can improve data collection efficiency and help integrate both HR systems and HR policies.

A third type of business need which is driven by the organization of a company can also be found in decentralized operations. These instances where separate subsystems have links to the HRIS might be called the "business necessity" model, since they are driven by the need for distinctively separate systems and processing at different locations or in different functions. For example, an organization may require different payroll systems at a number of different locations, because of different workforce characteristics, union rules that apply locally, regulatory issues, or the nature of operations. While one of the overall trends in HRIS is the functional and systematic integration of payroll processing with HR departments and HR systems (see Chapter 14), global organizations with different regulatory requirements affecting pay and benefits are likely to decentralize payroll, whether integrated with HR or not. Still, each separate payroll system should be able to produce data for uploading to top management.

Sources for Identifying Needs

Business needs, usually dictated by the pressures and strategic direction of the company, are best discovered by reviewing existing business planning documents (one year or five-year plans). These can serve as background data for a meeting between the HRIS designer and senior management where the use of technology to support business initiatives can be explored. Such meetings can be used to discover or verify the major issues and needs—from worker productivity to COBRA record keeping—which the HRIS team must address. It should be noted here that there are many other sources of needs, such as legal and the HR plan requirements, which will form the foundation for HRIS requirements. Chapter 5 will also show how a redesigned work process will also generate HRIS requirements. However, the most beneficial sources for *future* management needs is interviews with line and management personnel.

Senior Line Management

With as clear a perception of overall organizational goals and plans as can be formulated from existing information and top management, the HRIS planner or project team must next test the validity of these objectives with the senior line managers responsible for the day-to-day and long-term running of the business, and determine the key specific issues that must be addressed by new human resource management technology. These interviews or analyses must cover all divisions, departments, major locations, and otherwise defined operating units. The view of the HRIS as a global system incorporating data and processes that support the total organization may remain a long-term vision—one that may not be fully accomplished for many years—but the planning scope at this stage needs to encompass the broadest possible overview of "permanent" HR systems development for the years ahead. If the organization indeed has a foreseeable future as an international conglomerate pro-

ducing diversified products in 20 countries, the HRIS being planned today should not be made obsolete by this expansion—no matter how far
away the future lies. As discussed in Chapter 1 and 2, the technical limits to HRIS development are largely a matter of history: The "next" systems can be flexible and adaptable enough to last longer than the CEO's
youngest son.

Senior line managers are the men and women responsible for achieving the immediate objectives of the organization, objectives framed by
such criteria as production levels, market expansion and penetration,
sales, cost control, and profitability. But as senior managers, they are
also responsible for managing for the future, and the implementation
of programs and policies that will achieve organizational goals beyond
quarterly profits or annual growth statistics. The difference between
corporate strategic planners and line managers as prognosticators of
the future, quite often, is the difference between a focus on broad environmental issues and the labor cost of production, sales trends, or the
impact of a new competitor on pricing strategy.

For example, futurists armed with demographic data including birth
rates can safely predict the number of native-born 18-year-olds who will
be available to begin working 10 years from now, and can make some
estimates of the qualifications of the future labor pool by reviewing immigration trends, educational data, and future needs of the organization that may change because of technology. The senior line manager
responsible for using 18-year-olds with specific entry-level qualifications
to accomplish known work has a much less generalized view of the future, one that incorporates specific numbers, skills levels, and the costs
of alternatives to hiring 18-year-olds.

Senior HR Management

Armed with the business goals of the organization as a whole, the
project team or HRIS planner should now turn to the human resource
department, where the first focus of inquiry is senior human resource
executives. The subject of interviews at this stage may be a single person, the vice president or director of human resources, but more often
the perspectives needed will come from a group that includes top HR
executives in a number of business units, as well as several senior corporate managers heading compensation, HR planning, and other major
components of human resource management.

The objectives of these interviews are to identify existing human resource programs and policies throughout the organization, assess their
alignment with corporate needs and objectives, and, most important,

find out what senior human resource managers see as the most important issues they need to deal with today and in the years ahead. At this level, the examination of existing HR programs and policies should focus on the general outlines and purposes of the components of HR management in the organization, and the management rationale for the way things are done today. For example, what are the scope and objectives of management development in the organization, and how is it integrated among business units? How dissimilar are benefits plans in the overall organization, and why? What synergies exist or should exist between different human resource programs, such as training and career development? How consistent are human resource policies throughout the organization, in all business units, and what are the reasons for variations or anomalies?

The key issues in senior management interviews all relate to the future: What's needed to address the issues we face as an organization, as soon as possible and over the next 5 to 10 years. Because the one constant in life is change, and because change in the human resource management environment is no exception, the human resource manager who believes that "business as usual" and the maintenance of existing programs and policies will suffice in the years ahead is not only rare, but is likely to become extinct. Senior human resource managers, however, may not see the same future or the same future human resource needs as senior operating managers. The HRIS planner may be confronted with a set of conflicting, or at least dichotomous, perceptions of the most critical issues faced by the organization in the years ahead. For example, senior corporate management may agree that the highest priority is the need to open up new markets for company products while controlling human resources costs, using human resource strategies that focus on training, retraining, and redeployment of existing personnel. Human resource executives, focusing more on workforce demographic changes than on the business goals of new markets and cost control, may see the demographic diversity of the available labor force as the most important issue facing human resource management.

For the HRIS planner, these different perceptions of the organization's greatest need imply distinctly different "first priorities" in a human resource system. Training and redeployment call for data and systems to support job analysis, competency testing, training, and restructuring to improve the organization's ability to leverage existing resources and broaden market penetration. The demographic issues commend themselves to data and a system that supports programs and policies designed to attract and retain a changing workforce, perhaps including child care, flexible benefits plans, flextime, or job sharing.

The project team or individual in charge of HRIS planning is in a unique position to act as an agent of change, helping to identify and resolve different perceptions of critical issues and the organization's response. By bringing such differences to the surface for discussion, inviting all participants to review one another's assumptions and priorities, and facilitating the broadest possible review of issues, the HRIS planner can often help assure that senior human resource management and senior line management follow the same game plan for the future.

This does *not* mean, necessarily, that one or the other of two or more different perceptions of critical issues must be found "right" and the other wrong. More often, differences of opinion unearthed among different corporate constituencies or at different levels of the organization are the result of different functional perspectives, not disagreement on the substantive facts or the appropriate business response. In the case cited, for example, the apparently dichotomous objectives can be addressed in a training and redeployment effort that is conditioned by changing demographics, such as increased emphasis on basic skills and education to qualify more lower-level employees for promotion and company-specific training, or job redesign that features the option of flexible hours.

Also, it should be stressed that while the process of interviewing the groups discussed here is sequential, starting with top management to help focus on the most important business issues and needs facing the organization, it is also an iterative process. After any set of interviews or after the entire spectrum of sources has been interviewed, the HRIS planning team should review all findings with all participants. Refinement of goals, corroboration, and an eventual consensus of views on critical success factors come at the end of the iterative process.

HR Professional Staff

Below the level of top human resource managers are a potentially vast array of human resource professionals, specialists in HR functions from recruitment to pension administration, with varying needs for data, automated procedures, and management information. In large, complex organizations with fully developed human resource programs, a dozen or more distinctly different functions, each with its own needs for data and automated processes, will need to be examined and evaluated. The professionals or functional representatives to be interviewed may include, for example, managers of the employment process, EEO, compensation, several types of benefits (insurance, pensions, savings, etc.), training, management development, succession planning, HR planning, and other discretely different functions. Moreover, needs should be assessed in each business unit or location where requirements may be different: Benefits data needed for German employees is considerably different than that needed for U.S. workers.

These interviews and the analysis of functional requirements typically offer a rich source of cost/benefits data that can be used to support the case for an investment in human resource systems technology. Each function has clearly defined requirements, such as the need for data and reports to meet the requirements of government regulatory agencies or procedures needed to administer an insurance plan, that are currently being handled in some way or another, manually or through an existing automated system. In some cases, direct, tangible benefits — such as staff savings, reductions in outside costs, or time savings — can be identified by comparing current procedures and output with the results of a planned system. In many organizations where an HRIS has been in existence for a number of years, for example, a number of different application systems have been "added on" to the overall HRIS, usually in the form of microcomputer-based subsystems that may or may not be downloaded with basic data from the HRIS. Are these systems fully integrated with other systems? Are their data definitions consistent across functions? Are they linked to the HRIS efficiently, providing updates when needed and in the most cost-efficient manner? Quite often, the subsystems used to manage the EEO/AAP program, the applicant tracking process, and succession planning — or any of a half-dozen other applications — represent a piecemeal evolution of human resource systems in the organization. Each was a "good idea at the time," and was designed and implemented according to unique functional requirements. But they may not be fully integrated to achieve optimal efficiency as parts of an overall HRIS.

Evaluation of the specific functional requirements of different user constituencies in human resources more closely resembles the traditional HRIS needs analysis than other parts of the objectives-setting process. When conducted as part of an overall analysis that begins with the identification of top management's strategies and human resource management priorities, the specific needs of staff professionals responsible for various functions can be put into context, weighed against other options, and used to produce more relevant, meaningful recommendations. For example, the training manager may be convinced that a major systems investment must be made in a subsystem that will track, monitor, and manage classroom training in computers now being conducted at 20 locations throughout the country. Senior management may know that this training is soon to be replaced by computer-based training that will be centrally managed.

Systems Management

Interviews with the technical people in the organization, representing any existing HRIS and its subsystems, MIS (Management Information Systems) or IS, payroll systems, and possibly telecommunications managers or others responsible for separate technologies that will possibly be integrated with the new HRIS, are essential to determining the current technical environment and future possibilities.

The first and primary objective of these interviews is to determine if there is an overall information system strategy in the organization, what it is, and how human resource systems fit into the overall framework. Further, the project team conducting these interviews and analysis should focus on current information flows, database structures, degrees of systems integration, information access, and the timeliness and accuracy of data and reports.

In creating the kind of expanded, business-based HRIS envisioned at the outset of this book, a view of the role of HRIS in the total technological environment of the organization is essential. In some cases, as discussed earlier, the HRIS of tomorrow will be *the* information and management system in the company, the main repository of decision-support information on the products, services, costs, and other factors responsible for business success. More often, of course, the HRIS will continue to be one of a number of separately designed functional systems; but the need for its integration and compatibility with the overall technological environment and other systems will be more important than ever.

Questions to be considered include: Does the overall systems strategy in the organization call for a standard system architecture? What kinds of equipment are part of the plan? What corporate databases are currently maintained, and what will be their design in the future? What investment strategies are in place or planned, and what kinds of budgetary or financial mechanisms are in effect or in the works? How will decentralization be supported by systems, or other needs brought on by reorganization?

Technologies that are not strictly information systems should not be overlooked in this part of the analysis. Voice and data communications, electronic mail, new methods of data collection, teleconferencing, computer-based training and performance-support tools, and a host of other impending technologies should be considered for their impact on the HRIS.

This phase of the HRIS planning effort, like the interviews with the human resources professional staff, is typically a major source of highly tangible cost/benefit data. The costs of existing manual or systems procedures needed to support human resource functions can be clearly identified, and planners can estimate the savings or other benefits that can be realized with the new system.

First-Level Line Managers and Employees

First- and second-level line managers have often been the missing ingredient in HRIS planning and development. Their nonparticipation in the planning stages of human resource systems is a typical trademark of "old" human resource systems — systems that merely automate HR functions and keep personnel data needed by human resource managers, and that have little or no relevance beyond personnel.

In many large, complex organizations, the most effective methodology for gaining the insights of line managers and other employees is through focus group meetings. These groups permit the interplay of ideas and suggestions, and the identification of common threads that can be addressed in the systems strategy. For example, line managers representing a number of different departments — shipping, production, office administration, and outside sales — typically have a correspondingly varied set of needs and objectives for data and automated processes. Taken separately, these systems requirements could constitute a virtually endless list of "needs," from the automation of job requisitions to companywide productivity data on the use of comparable word processing software. In a focus group, led by a skilled planner armed with overall business and systems objectives in the HRIS-to-be, issues and needs representing common types of data, ways of accessing information, reports, or other features of HRIS technology can be identified.

Another group of "users of the future" who should not be overlooked are employees at large. If the planned system is one that will be used by all or most employees — say, for benefits communications, job posting, career development information, to answer payroll questions, or simply as an electronic bulletin board — focus groups or surveys discussing the planned application will assure its full utilization. What skills levels will be needed to use the system? What technology is appropriate: phone communications, desktop computers, interactive kiosks, data centers? For a given application, such as benefits communications, what kinds of data and user capabilities will have the greatest impact on employees?

When all interviews, fact finding, and analysis have been completed, the project team planning the HRIS should have a fairly well-defined set of business and human resource issues that can be used to identify the critical success factors for a new system. Critical success factors are the systems goals which, if attained, will most effectively achieve business objectives, such as improved profitability, market expansion, or operational efficiencies.

The identification of critical success factors for a HRIS is not a simple process, given the range and complexity of issues that represent business goals, HR goals, and technological objectives in modern organizations. It is not as easy as taking the CEO's 25-word mission statement and converting it into a system to support that mission; or as simple as translating the five leading HR issues into a HRIS architecture that addresses all five issues.

Figure 4-1 identifies the major influences on the analysis leading to systems success factor development, but it should be stressed that the analysis and review stage is potentially the most time-consuming, detailed stage of the planning process. Critical success factors do not emerge from any magic formula for weighing business, HR, and technological issues and objectives, but require extensive analysis of the rationales behind issues, cost/benefit analysis, and repeated reviews with key managers to assure that issues have been clearly identified and understood.

For example, interviews with senior human resource management may have identified "benefits communication" as a leading objective. The company's newly installed flexible benefits program is perhaps not widely understood or fully utilized by employees, and the HR vice president envisions the installation of centrally located kiosks at all locations across the country, and later worldwide, where employees can use interactive computer systems to learn more about benefits, adjust or select new plans, and get answers to specific questions.

The rationale behind this systems objective may be sound, from the HR management perspective. Given the complexity of most flexible benefits plans, and potential cost savings and employee morale benefits of such systems, communications are a critical issue. But is the flexible benefits plan part of the company's future? Are the costs of interactive kiosk technology justified? What other technologies—such as local area networks, telecommunications, or video—might be more appropriate? In short, is this a critical success factor that should shape the architecture of the new system, or is it an issue to be addressed once other factors have identified systems architecture and its use?

A methodology for identifying critical success factors and the application of cost/benefit analysis to HRIS development issues are discussed in greater detail in Chapter 6.

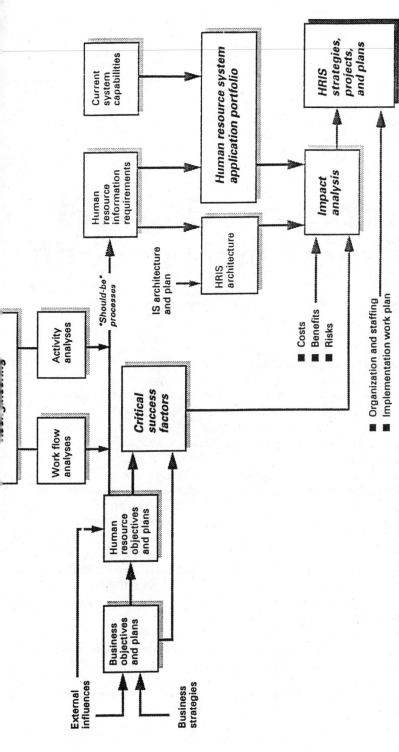

Figure 4-1. Human resources systems planning methodology.

101

5
Reengineering and Work-Flow Analysis

Changing the Work before Automating

One of the central principles of this book is that technology can and should change the way people work—it is hoped, for the better. This is particularly critical in human resources management, which has been slow to arrive at information management systems and continues to face obstacles to full automation, starting with the indisputable fact that the basic subject matter of HR—people—are infinitely variable and constantly changing.

But a human resource information system is more than a database of information about people. It is, or should be, a technology that automates an expanding range of processes and procedures needed to manage human resources effectively—from payroll processing and benefits administration to work analysis and strategic planning. More, HRIS technology can be used to change the quality and effectiveness of work throughout the organization, if the systems and the decision-support information they can provide are extended beyond the HR department to corporate management, line management, parallel staff functions, and individual employees.

The first step to fully exploiting HRIS technology has already been taken in many organizations, because the traditional approach to information systems development has not worked well in the human resource department. This traditional approach is to look at existing tasks, procedures, activities, and data requirements as "given," needs that are accepted as requirements, and simply to automate these functions. Thus the traditional approach to systems development, which has worked well for many non-HR systems such as accounting and inventory management, goes to work on a function as it exists. It breaks the function down into inputs, processes, and outputs; traces the information flow; identifies needed data elements; and then automates at the end, depending on the need for human intervention and the technological environment. And very often, systems designers have avoided the most difficult parts of the function, or made a case for a trade-off between 90 percent mechanization and a more costly system. But the basic approach to systems development has usually been the same: Automate the function and its surrounding processes and procedures; don't question the validity or effectiveness of the function itself.

Some examples of what this has meant in HRIS development help illustrate why this is not the best way to develop systems that automate HR functions:

- Systems developers are told that a salary increase requires six approvals, and develop an unnecessarily cumbersome approval process to handle this process.

- Software is developed or acquired to "interface" the common data elements of the separate payroll and HR systems, so that each of these dozen or so items of information needs to be entered or changed only once. But the basic systems (and their staffs) still represent wasteful redundancy.

- Throughout the organization, at dozens of locations in the United States and abroad, employment managers and their staffs write and send letters to unsuccessful job applicants.

Such examples could go on and on, given the complexity and diversity of human resource management functions, and the processes and procedures that support them. Underlying this diversity is the simple fact that human resource management is not the same as accounting or inventory control—both relatively rigid disciplines with universally applicable standards and optimal procedures. In no other area of organizational management is it more true that policies, procedures, and objectives are company-specific. Quite often the "right way" of handling a HR function at Ajax Company would be a disaster at Acme Company—because of differences in workforce characteristics, customer service goals, skills requirements, or the many other variables that influence optimal HR management in different organizations.

In this chapter we will look first at some of the reasons why early HR systems—and many being developed today—have not dealt successfully with the principle that systems should change the way people work. Then we will examine the critical process steps in work-flow analysis, a "reengineering" approach that will help assure the full exploitation of HRIS technology.

Background: Early Mistakes and the Need for Work-Flow Analysis

As discussed in Chapter 3, the environment in which early HRIS developed created some myths and misapprehensions that persist to this day, and that have prevented the massive reengineering effort needed to change the nature of work through technology. This environment typically included some or all of these factors:

- *Little or no personnel automation.* Manual record keeping, paper forms, and file cabinets full of personnel files were the rule. Any automation at all was welcomed by the personnel department, whose first exposure to the wonders of mechanized information was often the ability to get headcount data from an automated payroll system.

- *Information systems (IS) influence.* Most systems people—then as now—are so in love with the technology that they believe computerization is an end in itself. Anything that can be converted to computer language or automated by a system can be improved and made "efficient," never mind the business reasons for the data, process, or procedure. The view was that the HR function was no different from order processing, inventory control, accounts payable, billing, or other functions that IS had improved.

- *Insistent pressures to automate.* Demands for information and mechanized procedures have always been insistent in HRIS development, from the early need to identify protected classes under EEO to benefits administration systems that permit more flexible benefits plans without becoming administrative nightmares. Top management, information systems, and human resource people all agreed: The purpose of an HRIS is to collect, store, and retrieve data—never mind the underlying processes that drive data creation, transactions, or management application of the technology.

To the extent that such views prevailed in an organization, it was widely believed—and still is in some quarters—that computerization alone would improve personnel department productivity enormously. Forms would be eliminated, clerical jobs slashed, file cabinets trucked away and replaced by desktop computers, and for the first time, any manager in the company would be able to summon any information about HR at the touch of a few keys. When none of these things happened, or happened only partly with the infusion of new corporate resources and increasingly expensive HRIS management organizations, the stage was set for the explosion of "packaged systems" in the late 1970s and 1980s, when companies began letting software vendors tell them what a HRIS should do. By this time, HR managers had moved even further away from what should have been their original mission. Once the organization started listening to a software vendor about what data to include in the system, how data should be defined, what reports are needed, and so on, the study of work itself was forgotten. And no matter how thorough the original needs analysis, requirements definitions, and vendor evaluation process, the focus was still likely to be on the way things *have been* done, not on the way they *should* or *could* be done.

To be sure, automation of existing data and procedures has provided significant benefits to HR management. Data that was not previously available in *any* form, such as up-to-date headcount and staffing information from multiple locations, is now available for analysis. Reports of all kinds, from benefits statements for employees to salary planning reports for compensation specialists, are now available. More recently, technical advances and labor-saving devices such as Computer Assisted Systems Engineering (CASE) and other software tools have also allowed systems to be developed or customized more rapidly, and systems using relational database technology, graphical user interfaces, and other user-friendly features have made it easier for nontechnical users to take advantage of today's systems.

Too often, however, the original questions have been neither asked nor answered. Is this process or procedure necessary? How can the process be improved, not just automated? In short, how can and should the work itself be improved by technology? The goal should be to raise the quality and improve the direction of HR services, not merely provide data faster, more uniformly, less expensively, or more efficiently. This is the central issue of HRIS development if the final system is to be genuinely effective in serving business and HR objectives.

Definition of Work-Flow Analysis

Work-flow analysis is generally defined as the analysis of work on a sequential basis, over time and as it passes from person to person or place to place, at the greatest possible level of detail. As this concept is applied in HRIS development, it involves the examination of all HR tasks, procedures, and processes *before* the needs analysis that defines user requirements for a new system (though work-flow analysis can be applied at any time to improve existing systems or add new applications).

Also, the term *work-flow analysis* as used here employs a range of industrial engineering, job restructuring, organizational effectiveness, and chronological flow techniques. The goal is not only to make work more efficient, but to make sure the right work is being done and in a more effective manner. Thus, work-flow analysis in this context will identify opportunities to eliminate some tasks and processes, simplify others, and so on. The overriding objective is to create an optimal or "should be" state for all tasks, *before* they are automated or presented to HRIS developers for mechanization. This means that organizational policies and business objectives that drive the work play a key role, and will condition decisions made in each of the following stages, from the initial definition of the scope of the analysis through the development and implementation of optimal process models to be automated in the HRIS.

Selecting Processes to Be Analyzed

Depending on definitions, there can be hundreds of different functions or processes in HR and payroll work, each made up of numerous tasks and steps. In order to be effective in reengineering work, the work-flow analysis team needs to examine each specific task in a process and where it fits into the overall process, in order to identify areas for improvement or change. The scope of such a project can be so wide that the task is never completed. The team should understand that "process" as used here is not precisely the same as one HR function. Rather it is a series of linked steps, generally triggered by an event — e.g., a hire or a termination — and which may cross organization boundaries.

In selecting which processes should be analyzed — first at the macro or overall level and later at the detailed task level — several considerations should apply:

- *First, identify the possibilities.* The team should create a list that can be shown to top management, IS, and users to help select high-priority processes. Depending on the organization, this list might include a dozen general categories, such as benefits administration, training, and payroll, or might list hundreds of different processes within these categories, such as payroll check processing, accounting data entry, posting to general ledger, tax reporting, FLSA record keeping, and other processes associated with payroll work.

■ *Apply critical success factor methodology.* As will be discussed in Chapter 6, the early identification of critical success factors—the things that must be done in human resources for the company to be successful—is essential to any project. The critical success factors should also, where possible, include cost/benefit analysis of how improvement in a process will benefit the organization.

■ *Identify management, information systems, and user priorities.* Depending on the organization and the current state of the HR department, different "constituencies" in HRIS development may have different priorities regarding processing to be improved. Top management may be looking at benefits cost control, and may want to start with various managed-care or reoriented benefits administration processes; the systems organization may realize that unless better ways are found to get a person on the payroll system, all subsequent activities in payroll and HR will suffer; a user organization such as the EEO department may point out that the company is facing major noncompliance action because of its inadequate EEO tracking system. Top management will eventually make the decision, but it is up to the project team to present all sides and make recommendations.

■ *Select the processes to be analyzed.* The final step before proceeding to actual analysis is to select the processes to be analyzed and then perform some initial analysis to be sure everyone understands the scope of what the team is expected to accomplish. Remember Principle 3.7, that you can't do just one thing? This initial set of processes selected for review should reveal whether or not the analysis of the payroll functions associated with benefits deductions will require revamping the procedures used to assure tax law compliance, savings plan administration, COBRA tracking, and any other processes that are inextricably linked to the payroll functions.

There are two ways to develop a list of functions for possible work flow analysis, both of which may be appropriate. At first, to determine which general area of "macro" process is most important in the organization, a listing such as the one on the left side of Table 5-1 helps set priorities. Then, a more detailed list of functions, as on the right side of the table, helps define the scope of the work-flow analysis project.

The selection of HR department processes to be analyzed in work-flow analysis does not mean that other human resource and payroll processes will not be analyzed at a future time; rather, the approach recognizes the immensity of the job involved in analyzing all processes in large, multifunctional HR departments, and the fact that most of these activities have never been subjected to the rigors of work-flow analysis from a systems development point of view.

In the long run, the "extended" HRIS envisioned by this book and

Table 5-1. Listing the Possibilities

Examples of a macro list: HR functions and processes	Examples of a detailed list: payroll function
Payroll—termination	Check processing
Pension management—retirement	Prepare/pay payroll taxes
Benefits administration—flexible enrollment	Regulatory compliance
EEO/AAP—EEO goals	Posting to general ledger
Career management—development plan	Quarterly compilations, e.g., FICA, SUI, FUI
Management development—annual review	Account reconciliation and balancing
Compensation—salary change	Bank reconciliations
Training—course registration	COBRA tracking/compliance
Performance appraisal—salary review	Savings/deferred-income plans
Succession planning—backup process	New hire processing
Employment process—new hire	Expatriate processing
Work analysis—crew scheduling	Bonuses/merit pay
Employee communications—SPD distribution	FLSA record keeping
Labor relations—grievance	Reports for financial planning
HR planning—annual forecast	Response to check inquiries
Health and safety—accident	Year-end accounting
Relocation—household move	

discussed in the early chapters can be used to analyze not only HR processes, but work of all kinds throughout the organization. Using cost data and other resource allocation information resident in a HRIS, the same methodology that identifies optimal processes for hiring a new employee can be used to identify the best way to handle customers' hotline inquiries, decide on a new office site, or plan a marketing campaign.

Flowcharting Current Processes

Once a process has been selected for analysis, the work-flow approach charts the sequential series of tasks (some of which actually happen concurrently) from a "trigger" event that starts the process to the completion of the process. In this step, everything that is being done now—whether or not it makes sense—is identified and described. The triggering or initiating event could be receipt of a new hire form in the payroll department, the arrival of a job applicant at the employment office, or the preparation of a job requisition by a manager with an open position, as shown in the example in Figure 5-1.

Clearly, the level of detail required—what each person or function does as a piece of paper is processed or an event unfolds in the organization—suggests one reason why early HRIS developers abandoned this approach. It was, and remains, much easier to focus on data than on work: Automate the data, and let users figure out the best way to initiate, validate, retrieve, and use the data. In fact, the mechanization of data is rarely useful in itself. It is the work that must be improved by technology, and work that is not first analyzed in this way cannot be fully grasped or understood. The data needed to perform the process or task will follow.

In developing task-level work-flow charts such as these, it is important that a common descriptive methodology be applied. Both to simplify a complex process and to assure that uniform standards are applied by analysts in later stages, common definitions of words and the use of symbols that always mean the same thing can help. For example, the words "calculate" and "determine" may mean the same thing in some applications, but not in others. To a user—say, a benefits administrator entering a benefit level—"calculate" may mean an arithmetic process; "determine" may mean the level of benefit or premium which is to be looked up in a table.

In addition, a symbolic shorthand can be developed to identify tasks or procedures that recur throughout the process, such as filing, entering data, copying, or approving. Care should be taken, of course, not to "force-fit" symbols or standardized words. Distinctions in different tasks need to be reflected; for example, if one person looks up information in

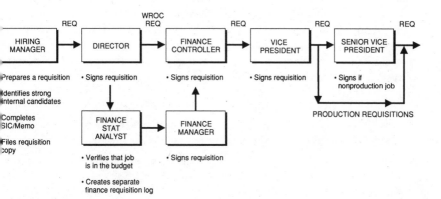

Figure 5-1. Work-flow analysis of existing process. Prepare a requisition (current approach).

a table and another looks up the same information electronically, both should not be described in the same language or symbols.

The method used to create work-flow charts such as this is a combination of interviewing and observation. When documentation is available that spells out tasks in sufficient detail, this is a Godsend. More often, however, what people in white-collar jobs actually do—and why they do it—has never been spelled out at the level of detail sought by work-flow analysis.

In identifying the "why" of tasks and procedures, a word of caution is in order. The team members responsible for identifying the current process should avoid giving the impression that they are judging the tasks in any way. The objective of this stage is to learn what is happening now, not whether what's happening is a good idea. Open communications with people who perform the tasks is necessary—especially when confronted with tasks and procedures that are "in someone's head," and that have never been fully documented or reviewed.

On the other hand, if an interviewee offers comments or ideas on how to improve a task or a series of tasks, these should be noted for possible use in the next step, when tasks will be analyzed for improvement.

Analyzing Processes for Improvement

For people who believe in the overriding mission of work-flow analysis—to improve the work—this is where the fun begins. Once current processes have been charted, team members work with managers and others in the human resource department to determine which tasks can be eliminated, which should be improved, and how the overall process can be made both more efficient and more effective.

Using the work-flow documents as walk-through documents, the team should question every task within the overall context of the purpose of the process. For example, in the simplified chart of the new hire process shown in Figure 5-2, the existing process for hiring a new employee is examined using questions such as these:

- Why is this process being done at all? Can we eliminate it entirely?

- Why is the initial entry of the new hire being done in payroll and not in the human resource department?

- Is it necessary that reference checks be confirmed before all new hires are entered, or is this procedure essential only for certain employees holding positions of trust?

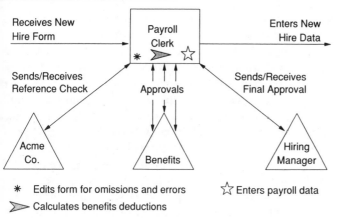

* Edits form for omissions and errors   ☆ Enters payroll data
▷ Calculates benefits deductions

Figure 5-2. Existing new hire data-entry task.

- Should the needed reference checks be completed at an earlier stage, perhaps by the interviewer completing the initial new hire form?

- Can an employee enter some data directly? Why take staff time to enter what the hiree put down on paper?

- What information could be scanned in electronically, from paper forms completed by the new employee?

- Why return the new hire form to the hiring manager before data entry? If final approval is necessary, why not send it electronically?

These and similar questions may have simple, logical, or otherwise compelling answers. Then again, some may never have been asked before, or they may have been asked and answered without focusing on the real reasons for the new hire process and its associated tasks.

In the distant past, for example, someone may have been hired as a security guard without a check on his military record, which would have revealed that he had a "Section Eight" discharge, emotionally unfit to carry a weapon. After a negligent-hiring lawsuit, a new company policy came down from the top: Nobody would be hired for any job unless cleared by the Acme Security Company. Worse, it was decided that the most certain way to enforce this new policy was at the point of new hire data entry in the payroll system: Nobody would go on the payroll without reference verification including a security check. Now, paperwork verifications to and from Acme represent the "critical path" in entering a new hire, an essential task that takes longer than all others put together, and whose duration is beyond the hiring company's control, and which is performed too late in the process to suit the users.

One of the most important attitudes that should pervade work-flow analysis at this stage — and one of the most difficult to establish in many cases — is a visionary perspective of how work *should* be performed. At the start of this process, in sessions that are as much "brainstorming" meetings as anything else, it is vital that the managers and users being interviewed by team members be as open as possible, consider all possibilities, and be willing to suggest the fullest possible range of improvements, no matter how "blue sky" or impractical the changes may first appear. Later on in work-flow analysis, each suggestion will be examined for its potential impact on workers, jobs, customers, and other factors, and both long-term and interim models can be developed with varying levels of automation or work improvement. At this point, however, the team should seek to elicit the most creative new ideas, and approaches that challenge the status quo.

The difficulty of establishing this approach among managers and others who have become accustomed to performing work in certain ways can be eased somewhat if project team members stress that a long-range or "futuristic" model for the process is an essential part of the exercise, but will not necessarily lead to job changes this year, or even in the forseeable future. A discussion of new and emerging technology — the possibilities created by voice response, scanning, imaging, multimedia computers, pocket-sized terminals, and so on — might usefully precede brainstorming sessions. By stressing that anything is possible in the long run, team members may uncover some break-through ideas that can be put to use today, either fully realized or as a step toward the ultimate goal of a "should be" process.

Although each process and its associated tasks represent unique opportunities for improvement, the following general questions are usually applicable in all cases.

General Guidelines for Work Analysis
- Is this process necessary? Why?
- Can it be done by someone else?
- Are all tasks in the process essential?
- Which tasks can be eliminated?
- What can be automated?
- What's the optimal or "should be" solution, long range?
- What can be done now as an interim solution?

The answers to these questions are of course conditioned by organizational priorities, business needs, and the objectives of the function being analyzed. Some processes and tasks, for example, perhaps should be "farmed out"; a third-party administrator may be the best way to handle benefits administration in a particular case. And even if this option is not currently available, it might make sense to begin preparing for the possibility.

Sometimes, process and task improvements will practically "jump out" at you. For example, a process that includes the need for three or four approvals when an employee changes her name or address is obviously bureaucratic and unnecessary. At other times, work-flow analysis will show that changes are being forwarded to people or functions that neither approve nor need to know the changes, just because "that's the way we've always done this."

While the outright elimination of tasks or procedures is always a first consideration, most work analyzed in this phase is more susceptible to restructuring or redesigning than total elimination. In this context, restructuring means job redesign, such as the combining of work done in two places or distribution of tasks that can be done more effectively at another level.

Throughout this stage of work-flow analysis, automation should remain in the forefront of the team's thinking. As a general rule, work that cannot be eliminated can and should be automated, now or in the long-range or visionary process.

For example, restructuring some tasks may require the introduction of technology that does not yet exist. Work that should be performed in one place—at one terminal instead of at three located in different offices and linked to three different systems—can be consolidated only by introducing new interfacing software that permits access to all three systems. The work-flow analysis team should not rule out such options at this point. In a later phase, when developing the optimal model for the process under analysis, the team will apply cost/benefits analysis and other perspectives that will help establish the feasibility of work improvement changes.

Developing an Optimal Model

There are at least two schools of thought about whether development of an initial model should precede or follow the identification of business requirements and policy issues implied by the model. Some say that approval "from the top"—a budget commitment that will permit the introduction of technology-based work improvement—should happen as early in the process as possible, and that senior management needs to "buy in" before specific changes are recommended.

Our view is that top management is already on board, to the extent that they are willing to heed the team's recommendations, or at least listen to a clearly stated case. At this stage, the case is developed, so management can see what's being proposed, what it will cost, and what its benefits will be. The political maxim that "you can't beat somebody with nobody" is relevant here: To the extent possible, business requirements and policy issue evaluation should proceed from an explicit, clearly enunciated vision of what the optimal process will be—not some vague idea of "efficiency" or procedural "streamlining."

Figure 5-3 shows an optimal restructuring of the tasks outlined in Figure 5-1. This is the final outcome of work done at this stage of workflow analysis, and is supported by detailed cost/benefit information, documentation spelling out the reasons for change, and other relevant considerations.

The level of detail and the extent of cost/benefit analysis at this stage will depend on organizational needs and other issues brought out by management as outlined in Chapter 4. Also, note that certain processes are more susceptible to cost/benefit analysis than others: It's usually easier to measure the direct benefits of a process that produces tangible results such as paychecks than it is to measure the indirect benefits of a good succession planning system, for example.

As a rule, however, development of optimal process models requires consideration of factors such as the cost of labor, computer systems support, supplies, facilities overhead, maintenance fees, and similar expenses of the current process. These costs can then be compared to the costs of the optimal model, whether the improved process calls for transferring the work to another unit, a third party, restructuring, automation, or some combination of solutions.

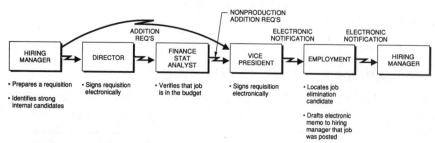

Figure 5-3. Optimal work-flow chart. Prepare a requisition (optimal approach).

When cost/benefit analysis is conducted at the task level, critical information needed to develop optimal models is available to the project team. The purpose of detailed work-flow analysis, it should be remembered, is to subject all aspects of work to the harsh scrutiny of team members seeking a "should be" approach that produces results more effectively and efficiently than any other approach. This may mean that certain tasks should be left alone, others consolidated, others contracted to a third party and some eliminated. Without knowing what individual tasks cost and what they contribute, the team is only partially equipped to devise solutions that may involve a "mix" of answers, rather than wholesale automation of an existing, unimproved process.

This type of task-level unit-cost analysis can be facilitated by work sampling techniques that measure such factors as the time taken to complete specific tasks, the number of transactions, the number of incoming and outgoing phone calls, forms used, documentation required, etc.

Regardless of the cost/benefit methodology used and the level of detail sought, the team needs some time-related data showing what actually happens in the process at the task level, so that comparisons can be made when estimating time and work in the optimal model.

In addition to developing an optimal process model, the team may also be well advised to create alternatives that might serve as interim improvements, or changes that do not require immediate investment in technology or other costly solutions. For example, Figure 5-4 shows a company's current process for making a change in an employee's payroll deductions—say, because of the birth of a new dependent. Figures 5-5 and 5-6 show two alternative processes for effecting the changes. In alternative 1 (Figure 5-5), the employee prints out a paper form and sends this to payroll for processing; alternative 2 is a paperless solution, which saves the company even more in resources. Cost justification of an HRIS project based on similar savings is discussed in Chapter 12. The rationale for making changes should indicate the benefits and implications, as this rationale for alternative 1 shows:

Recommended Changes

- Allow employees to model their tax withholding amounts interactively, and to update their final decision directly in the system.
- Payroll (of Human Resources) monitors and files hard copies of forms for legal purposes.

Benefits

- Reduces inquiries/requests to payroll department.
- Improves timeliness and accuracy, since employee is fully accountable.

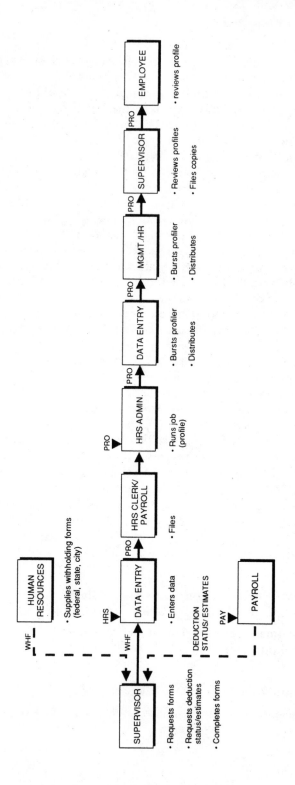

Figure 5-4. Change tax withholding (current approach).

WHF = Withholding Forms   PRO = Profile

HRS = Human Resources System   PAY = Payroll System

116

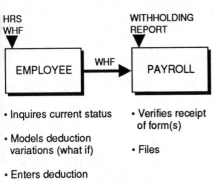

HRS WHF	WITHHOLDING REPORT
EMPLOYEE	PAYROLL

WHF

• Inquires current status

• Models deduction variations (what if)

• Enters deduction

• Prints form and signs

• Verifies receipt of form(s)

• Files

WHF = Withholding Forms
HRS = Human Resources System

Figure 5-5. Change tax withholding (alternative 1).

HRS
WHF

EMPLOYEE

• Inquires current status

• Models deduction variations (what if)

• Enters deduction/approves

Figure 5-6. Change tax withholding (alternative 2).

■ Improves employee relations/service levels with inquiry and modeling capabilities.

Implications

■ Assumes a printed version of tax forms (rather than actual forms) is legally acceptable.

■ Assumes work stations and printers can be made readily available to most employees.

■ Assumes good employee-level security (e.g., PIN).

■ Assumes system is very "user friendly."

- Assumes that interface with payroll system is very "tight": Requires timely date from payroll (current deductions, tax tables, etc.) Requires timely data feed to payroll for updated deductions.

Business Requirements and Policy Issues

The next stage has two components: The first is an extension of the work done in developing the optimal model, which presents implications of the new model, both technologically and for the organization; the second involves a review of the procedural issues that drive the process, and offers opportunities for top management to reassess and possibly improve policies that may have been taken for granted in the past.

The business requirements part of this analysis should produce not only a list of the implications of change, like the one shown in Figure 5-5, but should also address the human implications of the new model. What will be the impact of restructuring on positions, autonomy, working relationships, reporting lines, and so on? Will the net result eliminate jobs? Will some positions be downgraded? There are many potentially disruptive results of work redesign, and issues such as transfers, relocations, union agreements, reductions in force, new training requirements, and other human issues need to be recognized by the project team.

This stage also provides opportunities to reexamine the policies that created existing processes and procedures. When the benefits administration procedures were first initiated, different requirements than today's may have dictated operations. Relocation costs may suggest a new policy for moving mid-level managers around the company. The insurance plan rules of your current carrier may be more cumbersome and costly than necessary. By examining all policy requirements from the fresh perspective of effectiveness and efficiency—or asking management to look again at policies—the project team may be able to identify opportunities for cost and time savings that will justify the overall project, with or without new automation.

Identification of these policy issues may appear to the team and the user community as potential "show stoppers." Questions involving plan design, perceived legal questions, or audit rulings will often seem too large for the team to handle. Some companies have established "policy clearing teams" to handle such problems as they arise, so that they can be dealt with in an expeditious manner and not slow down the streamlining process unduly.

Selecting and Testing a Model

At this point, management and users must decide on a course of action. There are always three options: leave the process as it is; implement the optimal model; or implement one of the alternative, less ambitious options. If the process is to be changed at all, however, it is usually essential that a prototype of the newly reengineered process by tested first by users and managers, to assure that all of the project team's assumptions are borne out and that no important obstacle to change has been overlooked.

The selection of an "optimal" model, it should be stressed, is based on standards of both effectiveness and efficiency, and involves consideration of a broad range of technical, operational, economic, human, and policy issues. The eventual model of "should be" process is developed through the application of a number of disciplines and perspectives. It may, therefore, be closer to being "ideal" from one perspective than another. For example, a technically perfect solution that optimizes the efficiency of scanning technology for data entry may be part of the optimal model, but the level of accuracy needed because of government regulation or corporate policy may make this solution less than optimal. In short, there may be trade-offs that turn out to be unacceptable. This is one of the things you learn only by testing the new data-entry process.

The field test should replicate the new process, as nearly as possible. Depending on the process, this may involve creation of new screens, forms, reports, and job descriptions, use of new technology and an 800 number, and many related procedures. By having those who will use and manage the new process test the prototype, the project team will be better able to define the technical support needed, edits and controls, and all other implications of change. Additional policy questions may emerge, such as whether it is a good idea to allow a whole new category of users access to sensitive data on salary administration.

Testing a new process has two important objectives. First, and most important, it gives the project team a chance to correct mistakes or make necessary adjustments. As discussed earlier, many processes in modern organizations are highly complex, with numerous tasks that are not always fully understood, even by the people performing the tasks. The trial provides designers with the opportunity to see a "drawing board" optimal model come to life, so that it can be fine-tuned at least, and totally restructured if necessary. Usually, in a rigorously conducted work-flow analysis project, changes in this testing phase will amount to revision of screens, formats, and a few procedures—alterations that do not change the basic improvement of work reflected in the optimal model.

The second benefit of testing is that it provides users with early exposure to the new way of handling work. Getting people to change the way they perform work is always difficult. But when they are asked to participate in a "test" of a new process, rather than being presented with the final, unchangeable version, the implementation of change is usually more manageable. User participation in testing, as discussed in Chapter 10, treats users as partners in the process of change, rather than as "victims" or mere objects of redesign.

It is also necessary to ensure that the benefits that were sought are actually achieved, so measurement of the work before and after the trial is vital.

Implementation

By now, with the results of testing in hand and any alterations decided upon, the real impacts of changes in the process being subjected to automation should be known. The required technology, new forms and procedures, new job descriptions, and documentation for the new flow of work have been developed and refined, and all that remains is to put the new process to work in the organization. Depending on the scope of the work-flow project, this can be a major undertaking in technological change. But the human aspects of this change should never be underestimated, and may require management skills of the highest order.

The basic reason why work-flow analysis and reengineering can provide the long-awaited quantum leap forward in the efficiency and effectiveness of human resource management is that it can change everything about the way work is done. New work flows, new procedures, new policies, and other changes created by the optimal model will not only change the work itself, they will also change working relationships, the content of jobs, spans of control, management autonomy, skills requirements, and other aspects of working. Some jobs may be eliminated, others enriched, some farmed out to third parties, and many replaced by more efficient technology. All of these changes need to be planned for and managed in advance, through effective employee communications, training and retraining, outplacement, or whatever other human resource programs have been decided upon to match organizational objectives with the need for a qualified, motivated, effective workforce.

Measuring Results

Finally, the work-flow analysis project should have developed a set of benchmarks of organizational effectiveness that can be applied after implementation. The measurements and standards used in cost/benefit analysis should be applied to see if they actually occurred in operation. Costs of operations, timeliness, accuracy, responsiveness to requests—all of these and other factors should be reportable as data. As discussed at the beginning of this chapter, a work-flow analysis project rarely begins with all the processes in the organization that *can* be automated. The funding and commitment needed to move on to the next process or set of processes is far easier to obtain when concrete proof of past success is available.

And although we have frequently referred to the human difficulties of projects of this type, stressing the importance of user involvement and the avoidance of negative reactions, care must be taken to avoid the *Hawthorne effect* in assessing the success or failure of a project. This effect grows out of a study that showed all participants in a work-improvement project—in this case conducted at the Hawthorne Western Electric plant—reported positive improvement at the end of the project, just because the company took the time to ask their views and act on employee suggestions. Eventually, if not all at once, technology will improve the quality of working lives—or so we in this business believe. But the goal of work-flow analysis and the restructuring of jobs is not to make life easier for employees or to make them feel better about the company. Rather, it is the first step in using technology to change the way people work, improving both effectiveness and efficiency.

6
Identifying Critical Success Factors

Measuring Success

After completing a typical HRIS needs analysis, the project team responsible for developing technology that will improve work usually has a list of needs and requirements that runs into the hundreds. Some of these needs are driven by business requirements, some by regulations, some are technical, and all users or potential users have their own sets of needs, which may run into the hundreds for each function. Some needs are obviously more important than others, some belong in subsets or categories, and some of the categories—possibly including systems, procedures, staffing, and other functional needs—are more urgent than others.

In visionary HRIS development projects that may require a major investment in new technology, more is needed to support and drive a major change effort than a laundry list of unmet needs. Above the detailed cost/benefit analysis or the specifics that grow out of task-related work-flow analysis, there needs to be a set of clear, measurable objectives—agreed upon by organizational leadership and all who will use the HRIS—as guideposts to the allocation of priorities, time, and other resources. In other words, a "short list" that subsumes and categorizes the hundreds of different activities associated with needs emerging from the needs analysis is required.

One approach to meeting this requirement is to develop *critical suc-*

cess factors (CSFs), major issues and areas that can be defined as the primary reasons for HRIS development or improvement. These are the things that must be done right, or issues that must be addressed and resolved, if the HRIS is to be successful. Their characteristics, described below, include their "size," limited number, clarity, and strategic implications. And wherever possible, a critical success factor should be measurable as to results, so that the project team can work toward specific goals and report measurable progress or success.

A CSF is not a strategy. A strategy is a means of achieving the goals driven out by critical success factors. A clearly stated CSF identifies an overriding reason for the application of new technology and procedures, reasons which—whenever possible—imply measurable goals and objectives.

Relationship of CSFs to Cost/Benefit Analysis

There are a number of ways of arriving at the most valid, powerful set of six to eight critical success factors driving HRIS development, but the general approach that usually works best is to "start at the top," getting at the agenda of senior executives responsible for guiding the organization. This can usually be accomplished by examining all available strategic planning documents, board minutes, and other documentation emanating from senior management, followed by direct interviews with key managers at the highest and most influential levels.

Valid CSFs reflect the intent and plans of senior management, their business needs and priorities, the goals and mission of human resource management in the organization, and what they expect or want from HRIS technology. In some organization, CSFs have already been articulated and written down, the result of planning sessions or management consensus taking. More often, HRIS developers are not so lucky—hence, the interviews. In the context of developing CSFs to guide HRIS development plans, several points about interviewing methodology are worth considering.

Senior executives should first understand that the purpose of the interview is to obtain relevant input regarding the use of technology to better utilize human resources. Once the interviewer has established that as a goal, it is fairly easy to transfer the agenda to one of determining what senior managers feel are the most important aspects of the HR function, the use of technology in that regard, and how best to use this technology to help achieve business goals.

Probing for the most important services that HR can provide, and the best way to use technology, is a very effective method of obtaining the critical success factors. While other methods, such as survey documents and consensus meetings, are helpful, one-on-one interviews with the top 20 or 30 people in a company are usually a cheaper and more direct method of obtaining the same information.

Interviewing also has the advantage of allowing two-way communications to develop, using the discussion between the interviewer and the interviewee to help clarify points managers may raise—such as the relationship of an HRIS to a payroll system—or other organizational matters. In some cases, interviewers can help overcome initial resistance to technological change simply by explaining the technology.

The interviewer should try to elicit the two or three major areas where HR and related technology can help the business achieve its objectives. Also, what barriers to the business managers see in the next three to five years, and how an HRIS can help remove them, should be probed in the discussion.

Asking the same questions of a widely representative number of managers will build a fairly good base from which to develop a trial set of CSFs. The interviewing team can then judge their relevance by examining the strategic fit of these CSFs with stated business goals, and their relevance to the project at hand.

The team also needs to decide which executives have the clearest vision of the future. In other words, priority alignment and "whom to believe" are next for the team. For instance, most senior executives may feel that acquiring new markets and increasing business share might be the most important business goal. This may well be supported by other interviews, as well as the relevant business planning documents. If, however, one senior exec feels that a nontraditional goal might be more important—such as to sell out one business to the competition, enter a different business line, or divest a business unit—this should not be ignored. This view may not have been supported by other interviews or found in a business document, so it becomes an "outlier." Bring it up in later interviews, or go back to a few executives and double-check this view.

Determining Critical Success Factors

For critical success factors to be meaningful, forceful drivers of the kind of change we envision in human resource systems, they should be tested against the criteria listed in this section. These characteristics and issues to be avoided help the project team shape CSFs from the wealth of information gathered in the needs analysis and subsequent interviews with senior management.

Select Large, Businesswide, Enduring Issues

As a "short list" of critical business drivers, critical success factors should obviously be large-scale subjects that genuinely affect the success or failure of the organization, not minor problems or issues that will take care of themselves with the passage of time. Technical problems that can be resolved with a known systems fix, new legislation that requires relatively minor changes or the addition of a few reports to regulatory agencies, a temporary skills shortage that can be resolved through intensified training, an issue affecting one or two business units or locations out of a dozen or more operating units—these issues usually do not deserve to be listed among the critical success factors. One of the most difficult perspectives in this regard is the type of analysis that identifies permanent or inevitable issues from among transitory or "possible" issues. Before the Section 89 amendments in the Tax Reform Act of 1986 were repealed, for example, the onerous new data and reporting requirements of this legislation certainly looked like a critical success factor to many HRIS developers.

Limit the Number: Usually Six to Eight

There is a no "magic number" of critical success factors, but usually there should be not fewer than five, nor more than 10—six to eight is recommended. The reason for limiting the number is to underscore their special meaning as *critical* factors, of major import to the organization. In addition, when CSFs are translated into HRIS objectives, a longer list of goals presents the traditional HRIS development trap of trying to do too much, all at once. At least five or six critical success factors are usually necessary to cover the various business, technical, and human resource management issues driving a major project or new investment.

Provide Organizational Balance

In planning for a major HRIS development or improvement project, all business units, functions, departments, and other entities should be considered. To assure this, the full list of critical success factors should not be disproportionately weighted toward one area, so that, for example, five of eight factors involve compensation. Balance for the sake of symmetry is not necessary, or course, but no major issue, function, or province of the organization should be totally ignored in CSF development.

When all or most critical success factors emerge from within one function or part of the organization, the companywide support needed to translate CSFs into driving goals for a major technology effort may not materialize. Even more important, the extended HRIS recommended in this book usually transcends the boundaries of one issue or department. On the other hand, if one of the six or eight factors is powerful and compelling enough to gain management's support for the entire project, the team will have found its driving CSF.

Seek Discrete, Measurable, Nonoverlapping Goals

To ensure their clarity, measurability, and precision as objectives, critical success factors should be discrete, standalone statements of goals rather than broad, overlapping goals or compounds of several issues. When a CSF is vague or diffuse, few people in the organization will understand exactly what it means, and it will be difficult to measure how well the existing or proposed HRIS meets its objectives.

For example, "improving the accuracy of the database" is potentially a vague and overlapping objective. A better CSF would be "to improve the accuracy of compensation data from 92 percent to 99 percent," or from today's 8 percent error rate to 1 percent. In itself, this goal may or may not deserve to join the six or seven other critical success factors that will shape the HRIS of the future, but it should stand or fall on its own merits as a discrete objective, and not be generalized, compounded with other goals, or otherwise obfuscated.

Similarly, a CSF that says "to increase the accuracy of compensation data to 99 percent and permit new variable compensation programs" does not meet the requirements of a discrete, measurable CSF. In fact, very few statements that include conjunctions such as "and" or "in addition to" are specific enough to drive action and provide measurable results. If each of the two objectives in a CSF is indeed a critical success factor, they should probably be separate CSFs.

Be Inclusive: Don't Ignore What You Don't Like

It should go without saying that the list of critical success factors should be complete, covering all of the major issues raised by a large share of senior executives. At times, there may be a tendency on the project team to avoid tough issues, or to impose conceptual biases on what top management says should be the critical success factors driving the company's success.

For example, if manager after manager focuses on an issue such as "cost savings" or "productivity," these should show up in the list of CSFs. They may need to be refined or more sharply focused—usually through repeat interviews—but the project team should not unilaterally decide they don't belong. The entire process of CSF identification can be defeated by HRIS developers who distort or ignore the outcome of management interviews.

Select Issues That Will Last

Avoiding short-term, transitory issues or linking critical success factors to concerns or technology that will soon become history is, in part, a matter of selecting large, "strategic" issues, as discussed above. Short-term recessionary pressures, start-up pains with new production facilities, and near-term financial objectives that will always be present have little or nothing to do with future financial strength and are examples of issues that a strategic view will help put into perspective. If the start-up is one of the most important issues of the next five years, it belongs. On the other hand, most companies have new product introductions every year. The team has to take a macro view.

Therefore, the project team developing critical success factors must assure that the issues and related factors implied in each CSF—including technology—are in fact time-insensitive, and will not become obsolete within the foreseeable future. This can be a difficult thing to do without a crystal ball, but it should be part of the review and analysis of all CSFs developed after interviews with top management. It clearly has to be done before setting out a plan for HRIS development that includes applications and the technology platform, since the models will have to endure over the next five to 10 years.

The obverse of this is that some of today's most troublesome issues can at times be dealt with through immediate, readily applied technology, thereby quickly removing the CSF from the short list of critical issues. For example, a data-collection problem in a management staffing system might be easily resolved by integrating on-line résumés with staffing requisitions that are already on-line. If the objectives implied by a CSF can be quickly and easily met, the CSF probably does not deserve the stature of a major issue driving new systems development or other large-scale change. In short, avoid transitory issues, whether they'll disappear on their own or because they can be easily fixed. Neither type properly reflect what may be a major change effort.

**Consider Your Competitive Position
in Your Industry**

As a rule, each industry is driven by somewhat different business requirements, and critical success factors should be considered in light of their "fit" with the organization's industry environment and competitive position. For example, a retail business might be driven by the need for low margins, customer service quality, turnover control, and real estate costs. A high-tech company may depend on professional qualifications and technical training. And so on. When critical success factors are genuinely business-based, they invariably incorporate industry-specific goals and objectives, or imply such goals.

Incorporate Key Services

One of the key missions of any major HRIS project should be the improvement of services now being provided, both in payroll and in human resources. Even when senior management has not gone out of its way to identify problems or needs in these areas—say, because they take it for granted that the current payroll system is serving the company as well as could be expected—the project team should consider whether changes in the way things are done today will improve the work even before automation. As discussed earlier, the one-on-one interviewing technique provides the two-way communications format needed to raise these issues with senior management, if necessary. Streamlined work flows, improved decision making, technical efficiencies, and improvements in data quality are some of the objectives that can be incorporated in critical success factors relating to existing services or systems.

Figure 6-1 lists some sample critical success factors.

Matching with HRIS Objectives

Once an initial set of critical success factors has been developed, they need to be analyzed, reviewed by senior management, and related to

Generic
- Attracting and retaining employees
- Increasing employee–management communication
- Meeting legislative/regulatory requirements
- Streamlining HR policies, procedures, forms

Specific
- Attracting and retaining entry-level employees
- Strengthening effectiveness of first-line supervisors
- Increasing managerial "bench strength"
- Providing more variable compensation and benefits programs
- Streamlining the HR/Payroll work flow and information retrieval
- Creating a three-way employee–management–HR communications channel
- Increasing the ability to manage an extended workforce
- Minimizing the risk and expense related to legal compliance

Figure 6-1. Sample critical success factors: generic and specific HR functions.

their specific implications for HRIS development. The initial analysis stage will apply all of the criteria discussed above—are these major issues, are they clearly stated, etc.—but review will require additional input from senior management. One way to facilitate this review is to form a steering committee or advisory group of senior managers to judge the CSFs. Another approach that can save time is to return to the most visionary and influential managers interviewed, both to assure the validity of the critical success factors selected and to help assure the support needed to achieve the objectives they imply.

Several methodologies for helping analyze the validity of critical success factors and their implications for the change effort are shown in Figures 6-2 through 6-5. Figure 6-2 is an impact matrix, displaying critical success factors and their impact on business goals. The development of a matrix like this helps align CSFs with specific goals, and can help sharpen vague or inadequately defined factors. Another version of this concept is to list the work processes that might be reengineered to see the potential benefits, as shown in Figure 6.3.

Another approach, illustrated in Figure 6-4, is to assess the adequacy of the current system against the critical success factors. This can produce a "gap analysis" showing weaknesses or omissions in the current

Company Strategy/Business Goals

Critical Success Factors

Critical Success Factors	Bringing New Generating Capacity On-Line	Upgrading the Quality of Operations	Moving to a More Customer-Oriented Focus	Managing the Environmental Concerns	Managing Organizational Change
Increasing Management Effectiveness	XXXX		XXX	XX	XXXX
Upgrading the Quality of Operations	XX	XXXX	XX	XXX	X
Increasing Employee Utilization/Performance	X				XX
Obtaining and Training Competent Supply of Workers			XXXX		
Creating Three-Way Employee Management Communications Channel		XX		X	XXX
Achieving Higher Degree of HR Systems Integration		XXX			
Streamlining/Supporting HR Program Portfolio			X		
Meeting Growing Legislative/Regulatory Environment Needs	XXX	X		XXXX	

X = *Weight of potential impact*

Figure 6-2. Are we aligned with company strategy?

Critical Success Factors

Critical Success Factors	External Hires	Employment Status Change	Terminations	Time and Attendance Reporting	Absence from Work	Workers' Compensation	Pension Plan Administration	Health and Dental Plan Administration	Insurance Plan Administration	Payroll Accounting	Job Evaluation	Performance Appraisal	Compensation
Increasing Management Effectiveness	X		X								X	X	
Upgrading the Quality of Operations	X		X	X	X				X				
Increasing Employee Utilization/Performance		X	X	X							X	X	
Obtaining and Training Competent Supply of Workers	X	X								X	X	X	
Achieving Higher Degree of HR Systems Integration		X							X		X	X	
Streamlining/Supporting HR Program Portfolio							X	X	X	X	X	X	
Meeting Growing Legislative/Regulatory Environment Needs						X	X	X	X	X		X	

X = Potential positive impact of re-engineering

■ Major impact   ▨ Minor impact   ☐ No impact

Figure 6-3. Which operations are we trying to improve?

Pay/HRIS Processes

Critical Success Factors

Critical Success Factors	External Hires	Employment Status Change	Terminations	Time and Attendance Reporting	Absence from Work	Workers' Compensation	Pension Plan Administration	Health and Dental Plan Administration	Insurance Plan Administration	Payroll Accounting	Job Evaluation	Performance Appraisal	Compensation
Increasing Management Effectiveness			X									X	X
Upgrading the Quality of Operations			X	X					X				
Increasing Employee Utilization/Performance		X	X	X	X							X	X
Obtaining and Training Competent Supply of Workers	X										X	X	X
Achieving Higher Degree of HR Systems Integration	X	X							X	X			
Streamlining/Supporting HR Program Portfolio						X	X	X		X	X	X	X
Meeting Growing Legislative/Regulatory Environment Needs					X	X	X	X	X	X	X		X
CSF Count	2	2	3	2	2	2	2	2	3	3	3	4	5
System Quality (Excellent, Good, Fair, Poor, Nonexistent)	N	F	P	G	F	F	P	P	G	F	F	G	F

X = Areas in which our current systems are adequate

◼ Major impact   ▨ Minor impact   ☐ No impact

Figure 6-4. How do our current systems stack up?

system, identifying what needs to be built in the future to meet needs and assure success.

An opposite approach is shown in Figure 6-5. Here, the "system of the future" with all applications or modules is presented, showing how this system would address critical success factors. In effect, this approach asks management, "Are we building the right system?"

Whatever method is used to help analyze CSFs and show their relationship to the HRIS, a final step in this review/analysis stage is to identify CSF priorities and the systems solutions they mandate. Even though the CSFs have already been distilled and sharpened from perhaps hundreds of issues and needs, some of the few will still be more important than others, and these should drive the initial development phases of a new HRIS.

As discussed in Chapter 3, HRIS developers should tackle top-priority issues first, work toward quick results, and avoid becoming bogged down in multifaceted projects that attempt to do too much at once. Further, if the vast majority of senior managers have indicated that one CSF—say, the extension of data access to all line managers in the organization—is of paramount importance, the project team can ill afford to postpone this part of the project while spending resources on less critical needs.

In summary, critical success factors should be initially derived from senior management, reviewed and shaped by the project team, users, and a steering committee or other representatives of top management, and further distilled and "prioritized" to establish the driving forces behind the change effort.

Potential HRIS Applications

Potential HRIS Applications (columns, left to right):
- Employee Setup/Change Processing
- Time Reporting/Employee Scheduling
- Internal Vacancy Records
- External Applicant Records
- Job Evaluation Administration
- Salary/Performance Administration
- Group Benefit Plan Administration
- Pension Plan Administration
- Grievance/Disciplinary Actions
- Collective Agreement Management
- Human Resources Policy and Planning
- Organization Planning
- Employee Development
- Employee Training
- Exposure Management
- Safety Management
- Affirmative Action Management
- Pay Equity Management
- Company-Employee Communications
- Company-Line Communications

Critical Success Factors (rows):
- Increasing Management Effectiveness
- Upgrading the Quality of Operations
- Increasing Employee Utilization/Performance
- Obtaining and Training Competent Supply of Workers
- Creating 3-Way Employee-Management Communications Channel
- Achieving Higher Degree of HR Systems Integration
- Streamlining/Supporting HR Program Portfolio
- Meeting Growing Legislative/Regulatory Environment

Legend:
- ■ Major impact
- ▨ Minor impact
- □ No impact

7
User-Driven Models of HRIS Architecture

Changing technology, shifting organizational structure, and the escalating needs of human resource users have led to the rapid obsolescence of many HR systems in recent years. Increasingly, systems designers are being asked (or have decided on their own) to rethink their approach to HRIS architecture, the overall framework into which are structured mechanisms and procedures for input, data transmission facilities, storage devices, processing units, access points, and other elements.

It is also true, however, that some systems have survived admirably over the past 25 years, adapting to changing times, new needs, and new technologies. Why were some systems more resilient than others? It may have been that their client organizations changed less rapidly than others; it may have been the availability of technical resources to modify or update existing systems; but sometimes, I believe, it was a matter of choosing the right overall system architecture—a holistic framework, if you will—to meet current and future business needs.

One reason why a holistic, overall approach to HRIS architecture has been slow to arrive in this field has been the typical development process of HR systems in large organizations. This process usually followed a pattern such as this:

1. Initial development of a system, whether designed internally or acquired as a software package and customized, that meets some but

usually not all of the organization's needs for HR data and automated processes.

2. The emergence of these unmet needs; as business requirements change, and as new benefits, compensation arrangements, and employment regulations arrive, users in an expanding array of HR functions want more data and more automated processes. Further the initial system users become more knowledgeable and demand more sophisticated processes.

3. The development or acquisition of new systems or subsystems, each more or less linked to the original system but not fully integrated. Payroll, for example, has traditionally been interfaced with the HRIS rather than integrated.

The result of this pattern, of course, was system fragmentation. New applications were sometimes created by users, sometimes by MIS, sometimes by software vendors, sometimes by outside HRIS consultants. Each new application was thus likely to have different standards, different relationships to other systems, and other characteristics unique to the application.

But this pattern is not necessarily something to be deplored or viewed with alarm, for several reasons. First, it has always been a fundamental principle of effective HRIS development that you can't do everything at once. The complexities of multifunctional human resource departments—even the complexities of a pension administration system alone, in a large organization—mean that initial systems development projects usually require a phased approach that achieves some objectives immediately, some in six months, and some in a strategic future.

Second, it should be noted that the "problems" of this pattern are driven by user needs. What's wrong with that? The fact that users often went outside the MIS or HRIS organization to fulfill their unmet needs, together with the microprocessor revolution that brought the price of HRIS technology within reach of most budgets, may have had unfortunate consequences. But the reasons users did this usually arose from the mismatch between their real needs and available resources: They had no choice.

As discussed in other parts of this book, today's systems architects do have a choice. New technology that permits the more rapid development of software applications, retrieval tools that effectively translate data from different systems, increasingly powerful hardware and software, new integration tools that can combine data sets, and a range of architectural options are available. And at the same time, the status of human resource management as a business function has risen rapidly in recent years, so that HR managers are now in a better position to obtain the technical and other resources they need to do their jobs.

To make the right choices, however, HRIS builders in any given organization need to perform the kind of business analysis recommended in Chapter 4, make the work-improvement effort that is the subject of Chapter 5, and identify company-specific critical success factors such as those outlined in Chapter 6. This business and work-flow analysis will help provide answers to the issues raised in this chapter.

It should also be stressed, once again, that today's technology—nor even tomorrow's—is *not* going to solve all of our problems, nor present us with a perfect system architecture for all organizations. The overriding reason why no two HR systems are exactly alike is that the *users* of these systems as well as the *organizations* themselves are different. They perform different functions in these different companies, have different needs for information, enjoy different levels of technical sophistication, and so on.

Thus, the "top 10" influences on HRIS architecture, outlined below, are predominantly user-driven. Bearing in mind that the organization itself is a "user," users exist in a range of organizational structures, have different priorities, and so on, it becomes clear that all of the strongest influences on HRIS architecture are essentially "user-driven," or should be.

The "Top 10" Influences on HRIS Architecture

In deciding on a new or improved HRIS architecture, all or most of the "top 10" influences listed below should be considered. As noted earlier, however, the different needs of different organizations mean that these influences will not all have equal weight in any particular organization. Though the most important influence should always be alignment with overall business objectives, company size, geography, the technological environment, and other factors need to be assessed in terms of specific organizational constraints, opportunities, and strategic goals. Chapter 6, on critical success factors, helps identify these goals.

1. Alignment with Business Strategy

An understanding of the business forces at work in the organization should be the single most important guide in developing systems architecture. These business forces usually imply a need for change, such as the organizational and functional change needed to compete in an international economy, the need to cope with technological change, more effective utilization of a changing workforce, regulatory vulnerability or organizational restructuring brought on by mergers, diversification growth, or divestiture. Change alone, however, should not overshadow or cloud the system architect's view of what's needed in an HRIS. Some designers develop "analysis paralysis" when faced with constant change. They become frustrated trying to cope with business directions and demands that seem to change from week to week. Change always has a starting point, yielding a goal or set of goals, and an optimal timetable, so "alignment with business strategy" requires the fullest possible understanding of the issues discussed in earlier chapters, including and culminating with identification of the critical success factors driving the business.

2. Size of the Organization

Obviously, it is one thing to design a system for a company employing 500 people and quite another to design one covering 100,000 employees. Other factors besides headcount are involved in the "size" of a company and implications for HRIS architecture, including:

- Characteristics of the employee population, which may be highly differentiated as to number of hourly or salaried employees and their skills, and which may be a "mixed bag" of employee types (part-timers, temps, semiretirees, job sharers, etc.), locations, and so on

- Scope of the database, number of different data elements, type of data (text, numbers), and transaction volumes

- Number and types of users, access points, security privileges, and reporting requirements

- Size of the nonemployee database, which may include data about retirees, competitive data, external data such as labor market availability or medical cost information, or organizational information such as unique job descriptions, myriad benefits plans, or management development activities

Thus, while the "size" of the organization in terms of employees is a major factor influencing design, two companies with 10,000 employees each would not necessarily opt for the same system architecture. And there are other issues to consider as well.

3. Customer/User Priorities

One or more of the customer/user's functional priorities may arise from the identification of critical success factors that stand well above all other HRIS goals. In one case this may mean designing a system to handle flexible benefits program administration; in another it may mean focusing on management development; and so on. If the company is facing massive skills shortages, this might well make all other HR "problems" irrelevant. Therefore a design and architecture that supports these needs and functions is clearly critical.

4. Organizational Structure

A fourth major factor influencing HRIS architecture is organizational structure, both today's structure and the structure envisioned by strategic plans. Highly centralized organizations require a different system than decentralized organizations; multidivisional companies in many lines of business will need a different HRIS than monolithic organizations; different organizational structures—e.g., by product, customer region, or service type—should be mirrored in HRIS structure; global systems imply a different architecture than those operating in a single location; and so on.

5. Geography: How Far Must Data Move?

The geographic dispersion of employees, jobs, and users of a system, in one country or throughout the world, also has a strong bearing on system architecture. This issue frequently relates to the availability of existing or planned technology. A telecommunications network may already be in place and paid for, for example, making it a good idea for HRIS designers to take advantage of this to move data. A good example of this is an international telecommunications network that might be installed, or planned, to meet other business needs. If this network is capable of transmitting HR data, then this would influence the design. It should not, though, unduly weight project needs or create a requirement. Very often, the IS community feels a need to "fill up the mainframe" or "utilize the network since it's paid for." While this is in a sense true, these available technologies should influence the design but not drive the project.

For short-distance transportation of data, designers should of course consider local area networks (LANs) as well as the more expensive wide area networks (WANs), which can move data globally.

The concentration of users will dictate a good bit of the design. If the inputters and users are all local, then a local-access, clustered design should be considered. If the inputters are dispersed geographically but the users are centralized, then a more monolithic, central approach might be appropriate.

6. Available Technology or Commitment to Technology

Although most of us who believe in the value of human resource systems would like to live in a world where anything is possible technologically, and where we would design and develop a HR-dedicated system in which form follows function technically, the reality is that in most organizations IS standards (the available technology) has a big influence on HRIS architecture. In some cases, the MIS organization or other business function may have already established corporatewide standards for hardware and software, and this must be taken into account. Or a decision may have been made to move toward new technology—such as knowledge-based systems and local area networks, or client server architecture—and the HRIS needs to fit into this environment. Further the skill set within IS may not yet permit full service support to the newer, more advanced systems. At least, technology no longer imposes the limits on HRIS architecture that once prevailed, as discussed in Chapter 2.

7. Human Resource Management Objectives

Just as the HR system should be aligned with overall corporate objectives and the project-wide critical success factors, and should satisfy the traditional user needs, there are invariably other human resource management objectives—such as the goal of moving toward a more decentralized HR management mode that empowers line managers—that influence HRIS architecture.

Not only do functional HR priorities need to be considered, but the HR cultural environment and management style can affect the ultimate HRIS architecture. For example, is it a HR goal to make business unit HR managers self-sufficient as HRIS users? If so, then a highly user-oriented, accessible design might be appropriate. How about the need to reach HR customers, not only line management but the employee directly? How would that change the system design? Clearly, there is need for an on-line authorization feature which would give the end user the

ıbility to access his or her own data. This need also includes the require-
nent to know who the employee's supervisor is and permit the supervisor to alter or at least recommend such things as salary increases or
ransfers.

The quest for process improvement, data accuracy, and quality will
ınfluence the design as well as we strive to build systems that have better
edits and access, so users will be able to enter data directly, spot poten-
ial errors, and clear them easily.

Another goal might be to make the HRIS an interactive "conversa-
ional" system (rather than one that is totally transaction-driven), in
which case knowledge-based technology, telecommunications, voice
nessaging, and similar technology may be called for. These and other
management objectives must be factored into the design.

3. Cost Considerations

Although the benefits of a well-designed HRIS far outweigh its initial
:ost, as discussed in Chapter 12, no business decision can escape the
ıeed for cost justification — nor should it. Systems architects need to be
ıure that the functional and business benefits of the proposed HRIS ar-
:hitecture cannot be achieve with a less costly system. For example, a
ɔatch-update, sequential processing system — or a smaller PC system —
may well represent the least expensive system to operate. However, it
may not meet users' needs or satisfy business demands. On the other
ıand, the most expensive systems — including telecommunications networks, work stations galore, and imbedded knowledge — might repre-
ient overkill for the organization at this time. Cost considerations, then,
must reflect the potential benefits that can be obtained from the HRIS.
The amount of investment that a company should make in the HRIS
:herefore depends to some degree not only on the needs but on the fi-
ıances. See Chapter 12 for more on this subject.

9. Flexibility for the Future

The future obsolescence of a HRIS is often "built in" by the failure to
design for flexibility. This means using an architectural model that al-
ows for future expansion, that allows changes to be made to parts (and
doesn't require alterations to the whole), and that permits revised data
lows to match changes in user needs and other requirements brought
ɔn by changing business conditions. New regulatory and functional user
demands can easily bring a system to the critical stage if they have not

been anticipated. We all know that the federal government will pass more invasive legislation and that organizational structures will shift several times in the next few years. The systems design principles discussed in Chapter 3, such as designing for future technology or using modules that can be "decoupled" without affecting current operations, can help create a HRIS that responds to such future demands.

10. Technical Support Requirements

The final factor influencing overall HRIS architecture is its technical "supportability." Building a system that will require extensive MIS or HRIS resources, or the continuing application of other technical resources such as maintenance tools, is usually not a good idea. An overly complex system that cannot be enhanced or maintained without costly infusions of technical help—which may or may not be available when it's most needed—can be inviting trouble. The best type of system in this sense would be one that is user self-supportable. By this we mean that the data, edits, access capabilities, and other features can be used directly by the user, with little or no need for support. Because of the changing nature of the HRIS organization, the highest value of work for the staff will be to develop new applications for the user, not spend time training the user population or supporting requests for data. Therefore the systems themselves should be constructed in such a way as to allow the users to carry out these tasks for themselves.

HR Applications and User-Driven Architecture

The basic premise of user-driven architecture is that user applications—the work itself—will shape the overall design and construction of the system. The goal is not to create a technical marvel or a system that automates everything in sight, including automating some functions just because you have the technology to do so. Rather, user-driven architecture starts with the redesigned work processes and the functional requirements of specific HR management applications, and proceeds from there to a technical configuration that improves the work itself through technology—reshaping the HR function.

In planning a new HRIS, however, it should be remembered that these systems cannot be all things to all people, all at once. The potential number of HR management applications in any relatively robust human resource organization can be staggering (see Figure 7-1, for example). Except in unusual situations, at the start of an overall HRIS devel-

pment project, no more than four to six of these applications should
e included in the initial development cluster.

In addition, it should be remembered that most HR users may not have
he systems sophistication needed to absorb as much change as can be deliv-
red by today's technology. Even within a single application, such as internal
taffing, users' ability to understand and work with new systems may lag be-
iind systems development capabilities. As in so many areas of HRIS plan-
iing and development, this means that the initial delivery of automation
hould be based on priorities such as overall business strategy and critical suc-
ess factors, and not necessarily on the available technology.

But despite these caveats about doing too much too soon, the long-range
objectives of all of the applications that will be automated by a HRIS should
e considered in the systems architecture. Only some of the HRIS applica-
ions shown below, with their typical data content and functionality, may be
n the first modules and clusters delivered to HR and management clients,
ut the architecture they imply must adapt to future needs. Other modules
and applications will eventually be added, so a holistic approach to design is
avored. The original set must be implementable, but the system is never re-
illy finished. It evolves over time as new pieces are added, and these pieces
nust all fit. These processes of course will be examined and overhauled before automation begins as discussed in Chapter 5.

Basic HRIS: Employee Setup, Enrollment, Change Processing, and Access
Handling day-to-day employee record-keeping activities, tracking employee
movements and recording relevant historical activities—front end to HRIS,
payroll, and benefit systems

- On-line access for HR supervisors and managers (also to employees—long term)

- Decentralized access and administration by users

- Relational database—fourth-generation, easy-to-alter and easy-to-
  access systems

- Integrated systems with standard definitions across systems/appli-
  cations—common coding of all key items

- Full employee history—status, compensation, work assignment,
  jobs, awards

- Ease of use—by managers; by HR little use of codes; windows/
  presentation mgr; icons, point-and-click, on-line help

- High level of data integrity—input on-line at point of source; edit
  on-line (no batching)

(Continued)

- Extend ad-hoc/generalized retrieval to HR supervisors and managers
- Pending file to permit future data changes
- Extension of functionality to field HR groups and eventually to line managers and employees
- New employee data maintenance (basic data required for new or rehired employee setups)
- Employee demographic data maintenance (name and address, relevant dates/statuses, emergency contact data, immigration reform data, etc.)
- Employee status change data maintenance (status, salary, job, transfer, promotion, termination, etc.)
- Ability to maintain disciplinary actions, accidents, or other supplementary information on a historical basis
- Employee benefit plan eligibility and relevant enrollment data, both current and historical
- Hierarchical code for organization reporting relationships and to print a directory, with internal mail codes, locator data, and supervisor's name and ID
- Employee formal education data maintenance and relevant history maintenance (schools attended, dates, degrees received, major/minor, etc.)
- System table data maintenance and relevant history (status, job, salary, grades, location, reason codes, schools, etc.)
- Streamlined data-collection procedures (enter data once at source, electronic signature concept, etc.) and support for decentralized data entry
- Full front end for all payroll and benefits processing interface to local systems
- Ability to carry temporary, contractor, agency status

Staffing/Recruitment: External and Internal Candidate Management
Support for posting, receipt, evaluation, and selection of candidates for positions by electronically matching résumés internal and external applicants, and related record keeping

- Applicant/résumé data maintenance (name and address, work experience, job applied for, etc.) and relevant tracking data (dates applied, dates interviewed by recruiters, dates interviewed by requesters, etc.)

- Support for the college recruiting effort (school files, costs/expenses, campus visits, interview scheduling, annual statistics, etc.)

- Production of all letters under recruiter control with a suite of standard applicant/résumé reports

- Job descriptions/functions/competency sets maintained for on-line access, with the ability to match applicant/employee against job requirements to produce potential candidate lists

- On-line access to posted openings, with the ability for employees to apply on-line via minimum data entry for openings for which they are qualified (bidding)

- Location/grade-restricted electronic job posting/match program for job openings within a geographic market

- National job posting/match program for high-potential candidates and upper-level exempt population

- Ability to create new hire transactions to update the core module when an applicant is hired, which implies conformance to standard HRIS data definitions and related code values

- Ability to create, maintain, and report on a "prospect," including exceptional applicants, campus referrals, etc.

- Maintain testing/assessment scores, dates, and types

- Ability to monitor Associates programs and track career paths and retention rates of Associates

- Track sources of recruitment (schools, key contacts, etc.)

- Ability to better support career planning through access to job descriptions and organizational data.

(Continued)

Staffing/Recruitment: Requisition Control Management
Handling the creation, maintenance, and reporting of open requisitions and using these to help staffing and headcount control

- Requisitions that contain job requirements and specifications according to the position descriptions/functions/competency sets decided upon
- Requisition data maintenance and relevant history (requisition number and date, requisition identifiers, requesting organization, budgeted/authorized identifiers, etc.)
- Automated linkages with the applicant/résumé module for external candidates
- Automated linkages with the core module for internal candidates and when a new hire record is processed
- Automated linkages with the job description file for authorized/budgeted job descriptions and job requirements
- Staffing/recruiter measurement data maintenance and reporting (turnaround time to respond to applicants, applicants-to-interviews ratio, interviews-to-hires ratio, cost-to-hire statistics, etc.)
- Open requisition reports, requisition aging reports, measurement reports, budget-to-actual reports, etc., to support the recruitment function
- Advertisement/agency data maintenance (ad copy and costs, with source/date, agency identifier, candidate, costs, etc.

Competencies, Skills, and Abilities
Maintaining an up-to-date record of critical skills, abilities, and competencies based on lines of business, products, and services.

- Support for standardized sets of critical competencies on a defined subset of the workforce
- Ability to map competencies to training programs, training plans, and/or workforce redeployment needs
- Maintenance of information regarding key language capabilities
- Support for job descriptions and position requirements using competencies and to analyze job models
- Mapping of performance to competency requirements, and linking to career paths
- Supply of job briefs/open jobs using competencies for on-line candidate/training matchups
- Development of a job skills directory which will carry exempt and nonexempt approved job codes, descriptions, and definitions
- A potential add-on feature could include a linkage to a forecasting system to analyze future skills needs
- Maintenance of records of certificates and licenses (e.g., CPA).

Organization Analysis
Providing management information with which to more effectively create, maintain, analyze, and manage work groups and teams

- Information on potential downsizing/right sizing efforts by location, type of work, organization
- Software support to identify actual work performed by task for potential overlap, redundancy, duplication, and fragmentation
- Productivity analyses by type of work, products, services
- Span of control, layering of management analyses
- Tracking of surplus employees
- Ability to form and track self-managed teams
- Analysis of impact of quality teams and employee involvement
- Cost studies of work performed and identification of potential cost savings
- Agency and contractor records maintenance—feed to a bill payment system
- Carry hours worked by product/service for all categories of employees

(Continued)

*Management Development: Succession Planning Program Management
Support for the executive continuity program, the management of this activity, and the maintenance of relevant succession planning data*

- On-line access to a profile containing the following information on the succession planning population:
  Formal education (including management education/executive courses)
  Prior work experience — goals/targets met
  Salary/performance history
  Incentive/bonus history
  Job/organization history
  Officer title history
  Licenses/certificates
  Training course history
  Languages/competency sets
  Career goals and preferences.

- Ability to maintain additional data on executives, such as individual development plans, job rotation assignments, detailed performance assessments (strengths, areas for improvement, key accomplishments), backstop/potential successor data, etc.

- Ability to produce key position promotability forecasts, and to identify blockages and leadership gaps

- Automatic linkages with an organization charting program for production of organization replacement charts, proposed new organizational units, etc.

- High-potential identification, promotability, readiness ratings.

Compensation: Job Evaluation Program Management
Support for maintaining job descriptions and duties, for evaluating and grading jobs, and for conducting relevant salary surveys

- Job table maintenance and relevant history (date-sensitive table with job number, job title, effective date, EEO data, FLSA data, job function, benchmark jobs identifiers, Hay evaluation data, salary survey indicators, etc.)
- Automatic linkages with the job evaluation process for edit/validation and for extractions/reporting of relevant job table data
- Ability to link job table and employee data automatically to produce salary survey files/reports required by external survey organizations
- Import facility to bring in external salary survey data, conduct analyses, and produce charts or graphs
- Job description file maintenance and relevant history (job number, job descriptions, job functions, job competency set requirements, Hay and non-Hay evaluation data, etc.)
- Automated linkages with the requisition system, the job description file, and the job table for new jobs which need to be evaluated
- Mass change capability to update new pay ranges—locally and at corporate

(Continued)

Compensation: Salary Administration, Variable Pay (Nontraditional Pay Plans), and Performance Management

Support for the administration of the salary administrative plan, the management of the performance appraisal process, and the maintenance of salary and performance histories

- On-line increase approval capability for line managers to generate performance appraisal and increases—full history of evaluations (up to three)

- On-line salary/merit grid for supervisory use—allowable percentages based on current appraisal, salary level, and relation to grade maximums

- Ability to handle variable compensation plans for a wider group of employees—including incentive plans, bonuses, and awards

- Automated link to external salary survey data and competitive/benchmarking data

- Ability to support productivity-based compensation plans such as gain sharing and other nontraditional incentive plans

- Modeling of effects of future merit or other compensation plans

- Production of total compensation profile/display of all pay components (overtime, base, variable/incentive plans, shift differentials, commission), with effective dates

- Support for executive compensation plans (equity deferred and cash)

- Full compensation history capability with effective dates for all compensation payments and eligibility dates for payment (on-line access)

- Ability to track employees with "red circle" rates

- Calculation of annual merit review pools and distribution to the various departments/operating centers

- Production of salary planning panels, displays, or printed worksheets for use by managers

Benefits: Pension Plan Administration and Calculation
Support for the management, administration, and maintenance of pension plan records (Pencalc)

- Ability to maintain consolidated pension plan data on employees, including eligibility, vesting, beneficiaries, deferred vesting
- Ability to extract and provide active/inactive employee records required by the actuary for actuarial plan valuations for all pension and retirement plans
- Ability to perform estimates and final benefit calcuations on-line, with customized pension worksheets for upcoming retirees—when fully implemented, employees will access directly
- Automatic records transfer from the HRIS to a unique entity status when an employee retires, with the ability to maintain records for name and address changes, medical/life insurance coverages, etc.
- Employee access to an interactive telephone system to receive vesting status, pension estimates, etc.
- Integrate financial counseling products with employee records

(Continued)

Benefits: Benefits Administration and the Group Benefits Plan
Support for the management, administration, and maintenance of the group benefits plan

- Automatically enroll in benefit plans at new hire time and supply information to TPAs
- Variable methods of communicating with employee, e.g., use of telephone enrollment, PCs, and kiosks
- Elimination of manual enrollment cards
- Restructuring/reengineering of work flow in the enrollment, change of status, investment areas
- More timely and accurate data for benefit statements
- On-line absence reporting system for managers to report attendance (could include policy assistance)
- Rule-based, data-sensitive benefit plan tables
- Automatic premium billing
- Ability to feed the savings and investment plan and pension systems
- Assistance with nondiscrimination (HCE), 415 limits, etc.
- Ability to provide new information and estimates for benefits planning for future issues in health and welfare and qualified plans
- Production of all reports and registers
- Maintenance of postretirement records for tracking, costing, and medical enrollment
- Full access by employee to ascertain coverages, balances, and enable inquiries and produce a benefit profile
- Ability to support full flexible benefit system including credit-based plan with enrollment, account control, confirmations, and reporting

---

Medical Utilization

Support for medical-care cost-containment efforts by analysis of medical plan enrollment and utilization

- Positive enrollment for direct certification of health-care plan participation
- Production of data to outside supplier for analysis of dependent, employee, and retiree populations
- Ability to supply information regarding benefit plan options selected, e.g., single, family plan, etc., by enrollees
- Supply of eligibility and enrollment information regarding HMO which employee selected, and comparison with indemnity plan enrollment
- Integration of data streams for claim database for analysis with enrollee demographics/characteristics—data supplied to outside supplier for statistical comparison by age, sex, location, etc.
- Assistance in the analysis of performance and costs of specific health services providers—in/out of networks by integrating data from health-care databases
- Helping managing and standardizing data elements/codes throughout the various systems

---

(Continued)

Training: Course Registration/Facilities/Scheduling Administration
Support for training management regarding course development, registration,
and scheduling of courses, and maintenance of relevant training data

- Training authorizer—allocation based on group/locations/need algorithm with apportions seats—three per year, etc.
- Manager access and enrollment on-line to courses, dates, locations
- Employee access to course catalog on-line and classes they are scheduled for/taken
- Tracking of training courses taken and production of profile (upon demand/display)
- Fully on-line
- Ability to link with development module and core module to permit cross-comparisons with developmental plans and current job location, department, and EEO data
- Pretraining work automatically submitted/sent to employee
- Prerequisites noted and new enrollees screened against them
- Relationship between performance/competencies—evaluation of training
- Course content available, and in history (not just course title)
- Date-sensitive internal course description table linked to the HRIS (course code, description, dates offered, enrollment cutoff dates, targeted participants, prerequisite courses, course instruction, course length, etc.)
- Date-sensitive external seminar description table linked to the HRIS (seminar code, description, targeted participants, location, course length, cost, etc.)
- Ability to link participant evaluation data to the internal course and external seminar tables
- On-line registration facility with the ability to maintain employee status (signed up, wait-listed, canceled attended), schedule courses, and notify participants
- Automatic linkages with facilities/classroom records for scheduling classrooms, allocating equipment and analyzing classroom utilization
- Ability to produce internal course directory, mailing labels, confirmation letters, etc.

Government Compliance: EEO/AAP and Other Human Resource Plan Compliance Management
Support for compliance monitoring and reporting for the various HR plans

- Ability to produce the following EEO reports on demand (including affirmative action systems for goal setting/SMSA data):
  Applicant flow report
  Report on females and minorities (EEO-1)
  EEO job groups by company, division, cost center
  Work force analysis report
  Utilization reports

- Ability to produce the following EEO reports each month:
  New hires/rehires
  Transfers
  Promotions
  Salary increases
  Demotions
  Performance Reviews
  Terminations

- Ability to produce U.S. government reports and relevant antidiscrimination lists required for the following:
  Age Discrimination in Employment
  COBRA
  Department of Labor (5500 etc.)
  ERISA
  Tax Reform Act of 1986
  OBRA 1989
  Section 79(d) of the Internal Revenue Code
  Section 105(h)
  Section 125 (flexible benefits)
  Sections 401(a) and 401(k)
  Section 410(b)
  Section 415
  Training offered and received

- Ability to produce the following AAP reports on demand:
  Availability analysis
  Underutilization analysis
  Goals and timetable variance report

- Ability to maintain and produce data for other plans, such as:
  Equal Pay/FLSA
  Handicapped/veteran and status and employment
  Immigration

(Continued)

Communications
Providing employee and supervisory access to selected portions of the database and to company plans via telephone, kiosks, or PCs

- On-line access for local supervisors to the most frequently asked questions and relevant assistance on policy and procedures with respect to time off, staffing, compensation, labor relations, benefit issues

- On-line access for local supervisors to selected contractual and collective bargaining agreements and, potentially, suggestions regarding disciplinary proceedings

- Employee access to selected personal data items for review and change/update

- Employee access to selected open jobs with appropriate bidding rules and procedures

- Employee access and change capability to benefits, savings plan, deductions, and payroll items

- Employee and supervisor access to vacation and attendance records

- Supervisor access to electronic bulletin board for employee input on key items, opinions, or surveys

- Access to training programs, course data, prerequisites

- On-line employee suggestions, complaints

HRIS Architecture Models, Examples, and Key Issues

There are at least four basic types of HRIS architecture models, with virtually endless variations in terms of hardware, software, and other system features. In this section, each of the basic models is briefly discussed, with some further discussion of other issues that apply to model selection.

Fully Centralized Model

A fully centralized model, generally mainframe-based, is typically appropriate for large companies when significant amounts of data or processing need to be accommodated in a highly secure environment, and common data must be shared by numerous users in the organization.

The computing power of a mainframe-based, centralized system is usually superior to that available to users via PC's. And for large-scale networks, a centralized system works as a host system for others. Centralization often emerges as the model of choice simply because there is no "choice." Highly complex systems requiring constant maintenance and technical enhancements are often best served by an architecture that centralizes the HRIS function where it can be performed most cost-effectively. As new applications come along, the centralized HRIS organization can assure that they are fully integrated with other systems and procedural requirements, and deliver the application to users in a timely fashion.

Another key factor is the size of the database. Even though the raw power of networked PCs is growing, if we are dealing with a fairly large database covering 50,000 to 100,000 employees, and have an intensive computing network, then we would probably stay with a centralized concentration of data on a mainframe system.

Full centralization also implies a high degree of commonality of functions across user organizations. This way, economies of scale can be achieved. If all of numerous users are handling employment, pensions, or staffing — under the same guidelines and principles — then there is a strong argument to be made for centralizing those processes in a common service environment.

Another reason to consider centralization as a model is when local users have little or no reason to be dealing with other users at the same level in the system. In a retail environment, for example, the ability or rationale for having users such as store employees dealing with other stores on an ongoing basis is not as important as having them deal with the benefits department or the compensation department. And retail employees in turn may not deal with the HR function as often as employees in an R&D environment, where an engineer or scientist may in fact often be involved with career development, training, and other modules of the system. In addition to the ever-present cost considerations, the applications themselves, the type of organization, and consequent user needs to a large degree dictate the need for centralization. An example of a centralized model is shown in Figure 7-1.

Fully Decentralized Model

In the fully decentralized model, shown in Figure 7-2, there are no centralized functions at all. This is a true distributed processing environment in which there are local applications, local databases, and local users. Access to the entire data set, if needed, would be accomplished by connecting all the databases or by having each submit a standard data

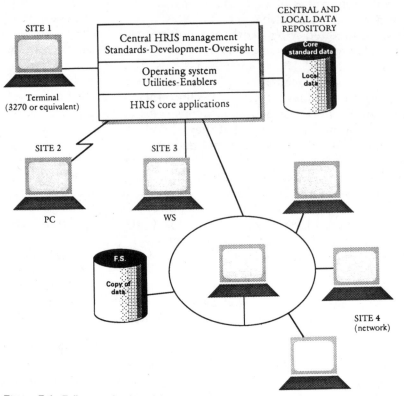

Figure 7-1. Fully centralized model.

set to corporate headquarters. Sharing can take place between units to the extent that some parts of local systems are standard. Standardization does not necessarily dictate centralization. For example, each of these local databases could be using the same data conventions, the same applications on the same technical platform, or on a common platform. The classical centralized functions, such as pensions or payroll, would in this fully decentralized model be accessed at the local level, making them decentralized applications. Autonomy, timeliness of data, and availability are more persuasive arguments for decentralization.

This type of an environment could be found at a local factory, a chemical plant, a regional office of an insurance company, or wherever there are (or could be) different user needs and potentially different HR plans such as pension plans or payroll systems. Each could operate on a different cycle according to the users' requirements. The systems then could be local area networked, or, in a smaller situation, on a stand

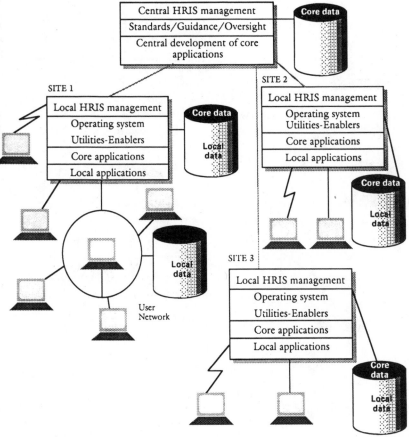

Figure 7-2. Fully decentralized model.

alone PC, if the population were small enough so that work could be handled by one person.

Hybrid Model

In the hybrid model architecture, as shown in Figure 7-3, some functions are decentralized and some are centralized. The determination as to which is which would be made by the users and the issues, based on the similarity of systems and the ability of system developers to write or develop a common application.

For example, it would be fairly normal to have hiring and staffing,

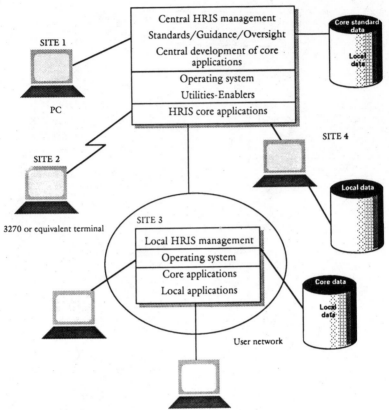

Figure 7-3. Hybrid model.

access to personnel policies, performance evaluations, salary reviews, and wage analysis handled on a local or decentralized basis according to the users' requirements and management's desires. The traditional areas where the data and applications could be centralized would be benefits administration, such as a defined-benefit plan, savings and investment management, relocation, and payroll. Another key determinant of which areas can be localized is the need for information by key decision makers and central staff functions. In this regard, storing the data centrally, and not permitting local databases, might be the better approach, since the data is then available to all the users at all levels. However, the primary determinant should be the application itself, with the screens, panels, computations, and displays that are required by the application driven down to the user level. Access to data can be accomplished in a number of ways, and should not be the single most influential determinant of the architecture, since the data can be accessed under either a centralized or a local configuration. The key items should be the processes and the functionality.

Parallel Model

The fourth type of model is the parallel model, illustrated in Figure 7-4, in which there are duplicate capabilities in both local systems and centralized systems. The application and the data are physically stored in both places, as opposed to the decentralized model where we try to separate the data and the applications. In the parallel structure, we have

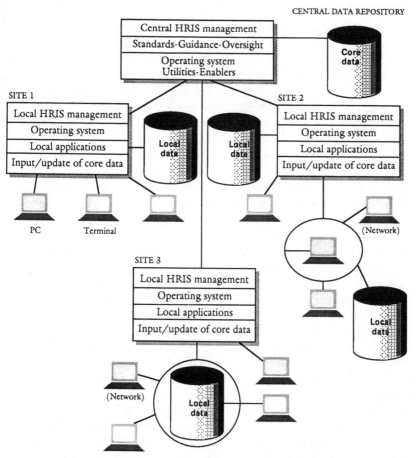

Figure 7-4. Parallel model (shared HRIS management; no core applications; local systems feed central data repository).

the same screens, and the same databases stored in two places. This is a highly redundant model, but one which is used in some organizations.

Additional Models and Issues

Several additional issues need to be examined before one particular type of model is chosen over another, since there are trade-offs based on influences and evolving architectures.

One of these issues involves the possible use of a core module which could be utilized by each of the decentralized systems. The core model could then also be used in a centralized environment to collect the data from each of the subsidiary units. The concept of a core model which could be embedded in local systems evolves because of the efficiencies in development of the applications. The premise is that if the core modules can be developed once and applied in each of the local systems, it would save time and money, and obviate or at least lessen the need for local systems development. The ability of a centralized system to drive down into a local market system, however, is very dependent on user needs and the variations at the local level. Local autonomy therefore might prevent distant system developers from being able to write the application for a decentralized environment.

Another issue is the need to transmit data on a worldwide basis. An international system's need to transmit information over and across transnational borders may preclude an architecture such as a fully centralized model, since data would be moving across the borders of countries with different trade barriers and laws governing personal data rights. Some international systems may need to be decentralized and self-contained, and data moved into the corporate model some other way. Also, language barriers and the applications themselves—with personnel issues covered by different employment laws or tax rules—may preclude a centralized model in a truly global environment. (See Chapter 8.)

Another key issue is standards. The imposition of standards across an organization will, by its very nature, limit to some degree the local designer's ability to formulate an optimal model. For instance, if a given application is available from a commercial PC vendor, the centralized organization might or might not prevent that option because of its own set of standards. The standards might either allow or disallow a particular brand of hardware or software from being used in the organization. By their nature, standards limit the degrees of freedom that a local designer or architect might have.

Other Approaches to Architecture Design

If applications alone do not suggest an optimal design, other activities or methodologies can be employed to help.

The first is the "create-use" model which takes each of the various data entities that might be used in an application and studies its creation and use. This exercise determines who is (or should be) the creator of the data, who is (or should be) the user, and who might be the modifier of the data. In this way one can see whether or not all data originates and is used locally, or whether there are some intermediate points that might have to be accounted for in the model. This is a fairly standard technique used by most systems designers when going through a design or architectural discussion.

Another design methodology and approach that needs to be faced ahead of time is the impact on the organization in terms of how technology changes work. The particular job content and description of users' work must be clear, and the transformation of work caused by a HRIS must be fully understood by the user organization.

One hopes that reengineered jobs (see Chapter 5) were designed and structured in a positive way, to the benefit of both the jobholders and the organization itself. Very often, however, users may not realize the impact of the new work processes on headcounts, budgets, and so on. Thus, a structured walk-through approach of ascertaining "buy in" from the client is vital before the architecture can be fully decided upon. This review should involve users including the administrative workers, the HRIS support group in their role as a consultative organization (as described in Chapter 9), and IS and programmers. All these functions and jobs will change as a result of the new architecture, and users should not be the last to know about these pending work changes. Moreover, of course, the team should have reengineered and changed these work processes sufficiently before deciding on the new architectural framework. If the team hasn't altered the work and moved to a more paperless, managerially extended system through the use of knowledge-based systems and newer technology platforms, then perhaps it has missed the boat.

Integration with other technologies is another exercise that has to be done before or during the design process. What is the potential impact of newer architectures—e.g., voice response moving to voice recognition and then to continuous speech and voice input—on HRIS processing in the future? What impact will these have: scanning and pen-based input systems; imaging and systems with three-dimensional output;

foreign-language translation systems? All the newer technologies will have an impact on architecture, and so designers must take a position with respect to the availability of such software and new technologies, and then decide whether or not they will let these potential new technologies influence the design, and if so, by how much.

Summary

The move toward distributed client-server architecture has been with us for some time. Systems with self-locating data backed by fiber optic networks and fourth/fifth-generation systems will open up many new vistas for the users. However, the design and architecture should be elegant but ultimately simple. Systems must be structurally sound, and as we look back over these upcoming years in another 25 years, many will be asking, "why haven't the basic architectural underpinnings of such systems been more stable?" Why do we continue to build mega applications?

Why do we continue to doubt that the speed with which technology becomes available in the marketplace will always outstrip our ability to use it? These and other questions are perhaps the key ones to be addressed as we enter the next round of systems. Keeping our eyes on the applications, and the true need for information to the correct client in a customer-based environment, is sound way to develop the architecture of a HR systems.

8
The Added Perspective of Multinational Corporations

Increasingly, American-based multinational companies need to manage their human resources from a distance. Few companies among the *Fortune* 500 largest firms have no operations in another country, and the human resources employed there require the application of many of the same HR management functions—and the data and automated processes that support these functions—as are found in the United States.

To begin with, certain data may be required because of oversight, governance, and stewardship obligations, and these may require data reporting from each unit. Also, certain HR functions, such as management development and compensation, span units and may also require data to be supplied to corporate.

This does not mean, however, that HR policies and practices that define these functions are or can be the same in all countries. Compensation plans, for example, are shaped by different economic, legal, and other factors in Europe, the Pacific Basin, and Canada. And yet there needs to be a way for multinational companies to manage compensation worldwide. Whether people are paid in yen or lira, the human resource management principles that apply to effective compensation plans—which attract, retain, motivate, and reward people according to their contributions to organizational objectives—are constant. And so is the need to be able to analyze relationships between pay and productivity, service quality, and other factors; and to compare operations in different countries, business units, and so on. No matter how various and diverse compensation and other human resource functions are, if an organization is to be managed effectively on a global scale, there must be a way to gather, monitor, analyze, and use human resource data from all parts of the organization.

The systems architecture, specific data requirements, and other characteristics of the global HRIS will of course be dictated by some of the same influences that shape domestic human resource systems. Corporate objectives, the HRIS mission, organizational structure, and similar company-specific factors override any "textbook" prescriptions for a global HRIS. One multinational firm may own and staff all of its overseas operating units; another may form financial relationships with foreign firms in joint ventures; and another U.S. organization may itself be a "foreign" operation of a company based abroad. One company may place expatriate Americans in key management positions throughout the world; another may rely on locally recruited managers; and others may seek an optimal mix of local and expatriate managers and professionals—sometimes dictated by social or legal requirements of the countries in which they do business. A company that owns most of its multinational operations outright may find, for example, that the only way to do business in some nations is in partnership with locally owned companies or governments.

Although country-to-country "differences" may appear to present insurmountable obstacles to the development of global HR programs and their automation, most multinational companies find that there are certain human resource management issues—beyond the need for financial accounting and cost control—that are constant throughout the world. For one, it is widely agreed that management skills are universal: A good manager is a good manager, whether the skills are applied in New York or Manila. Professionals working in highly specialized disciplines often have work habits, interests, motivators, and work environment preferences that extend across cultural, language, and societal lines. And to some extent all employees generally have certain characteristics in common: They want to be appreciated; they want to be paid fairly and gain satisfaction from the work itself; and they experience stress and work-related problems when they are mistreated on the job. These similarities, and the company's need for universally consistent products, quality service, or other "global mission" objectives, mean that certain underlying concepts of HR work can be applied universally. The basic purpose of career development, for example, which is to unify the goals and aspirations of individual careers with organizational goals and objectives, holds up well throughout the world. And many human reource management problems are equally universal: Labor costs, for example, are on the rise throughout the world; technical training needs improvement; and the need for effective leadership is felt by organizations in most countries.

Increasingly, then, the growing number of business organizations with global operations are faced with human resource management needs that first require a "sorting out" of what needs to be centrally managed and what needs to be handled on a country-by-country basis. In some areas of HR management, computer-based systems that support functions such as payroll, benefits administration, or health and safety compliance may need to be country-specific. But even in these areas, global data is needed to manage multinational organizations effectively; differences in language, customs, laws, and cultures simply make the job of managing global human resources more complex, not impossible. Certain data elements—gender, marital status, and educational level, for example—may well mean different things in different countries, but this should not preclude the data-collection effort.

A Typical Transition: Global to Local HR and HRIS

In the 1970s and 1980s, many of the companies that were turning into global organizations went through a transitional phase that influenced HR management and the development of international HR systems. At first, these companies developed global strategies to plan and coordinate worldwide marketing, distribution, manufacturing, services, or whatever other types of operations they required. These strategies often resulted in the formation of separate "global" or international organizations within the company, devoted solely to the management of international operations. These centralized staff organizations might include specialists from a range of functions, from finance and marketing to human resources, but the functions and staffers were usually required to follow a "global plan" and account for all nondomestic operations in their plans, programs, and policies.

Quite soon, these companies and others entering the global marketplace realized that their "international" staff organizations were in over their heads. The differences among countries and regions, the need to respond to local changes in markets, resources, and other business factors affecting local operations, and the logistical limits imposed by management from a distance were simply too much for centralized staffs to handle.

The structure that soon evolved in most multinational organizations was one in which management functions were largely localized, with countrywide managers—one in France, one in Malaysia, one in Japan, etc.—perhaps reporting to regional managers. Depending on the nature of the company's operations, management functions that could be localized were moved to the country or region and made autonomous.

This transition was also felt in HR management. At first, headquarters-level organizations handled all "international HR," largely the management of expatriates working abroad. As a growing number of people started working in a growing number of countries—each with its own employment laws, customs, labor market conditions, and so on—the need for on-site human resource staffers became increasingly apparent. Benefits plans offered in Madrid, Munich, and Montreal needed to be totally different, to say nothing of pay scales, recruitment policies, training methodologies, and data privacy policies. And in the HRIS area supporting HR management, differences in available technology are also a factor.

For example, even if all HR programs and policies are the same in the Pacific Rim countries as they are in Europe, computer technology is not the same. Apart from language differences, there are different keyboard conventions, screen displays, and other technological differences. Modifications to systems are possible—using Kanji characters in one place and English in another—but cost efficiency also needs to be considered in planning global systems.

In the remainder of this chapter we will examine some of the key issues that usually need to be addressed in developing a genuinely global human resource system of the type needed to support global HR. These issues include:

- The identification of certain kinds of data on employees—both managers and nonmanagers—that can and often should be part of a global HRIS
- Methods of transmitting data around the world
- Organizational information requirements
- Needs emerging from expatriate administration
- Some current and future trends affecting international HR and its systems support

Corporate Employee Data Needs

Regardless of where employees work, their nationality, or their relationship to the organization, multinational human resource management requires some level of information at the corporate or perhaps regional level. These needs vary according to types of employees and their relationship to the company — expatriates, local staffers, temporary employees, business partners' employees, job skills, and so on. Information requirements may also vary by country, depending on governmental requirements, local skills shortages, economic factors, and other issues affecting human resource management. For most multinational organizations, however, there will be categories of information or data elements that can and should be collected throughout the world and made available to corporate human resource management for analysis, decision making, and management intervention. Figure 8-1 shows a model of some typical international data requirements. These information needs are somewhat more extensive for managers and professionals, as a rule, than they are for nonmanagement personnel. Managers, as

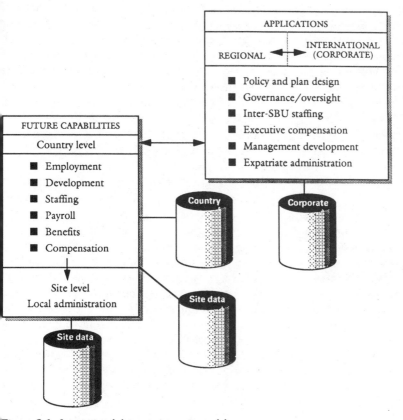

Figure 8-1. International data requirements model.

noted earlier, have more in common from an HR management perspective than nonmanagers. And in theory, at least, they have more to do with the success of the business.

Information About the International Management Population

In a global organization, the need for managers and professionals to achieve business objectives is more critical than ever before. Multinationalism means that operations must be managed in a range of different business environments, using a diverse array of local resources, while at the same time accomplishing or working toward overall organizational objectives that emerge from the corporate mission. A global organization may have 100 different environments for making and marketing a soft drink, for example, but the end result in terms of product quality, profitability, and other characteristics related to the business mission must be the same throughout the world. To assure this consistency of purpose in the global organization, human resource management practices and programs need to be in place that attract, retain, develop, and motivate the best available managers and professionals, the men and women most able to guide the organization's fortunes in locations throughout the world.

Increasingly, enlightened multinational firms are taking the view that all managers are corporate resources, potentially capable of leading operations at the headquarters level. On the practical side, global succession planning systems that incorporate companywide development activities help unify organizational goals and measures of success. For managers, global succession planning helps serve as a constant reminder that they are leaders of an international organization—not just head of operations in Indonesia or North America.

This "globalization" of the management of managerial and professional human resources also requires a wide range of data about the managers, as shown in Figure 8-2. Compensation that attracts and rewards performance is obviously critical, and requires the inclusion of information in both local currency and in a common equivalent. Training data, information about skills and competencies, and other "management development" information is essential to the extent that the company depends on the skills and talents of managers and professionals. Many companies also permit U.S. expatriates and selected other managers to participate in certain compensation and benefit programs, so the HRIS needs information with which to handle the administrative and record-keeping responsibilities.

The privacy considerations that emerge when data about people is transmitted across international borders—discussed at greater length

International Management Data Requirements
Succession planning and development data:

- Historical data on past jobs and positions the employee has held— length of time, countries, titles
- Targeted positions the employee could hold in future
- Potential evaluations or readiness to move
- Developmental plans in order to prepare employee for targeted jobs (including training)
- Geographic limitations
- Language capability and nationality
- Planned backups/replacements
- Next scheduled move—location and data
- Key task forces/rotational moves

Compensation data (amounts and effective dates):

- Base salary in local currency along with equivalent in U.S. dollars or other targeted currency (e.g., DM,¥, or £)
- Date of currency conversion
- Incentives and awards/bonus
- Appraisal rating (or equivalent ranking process)
- Stock or equity position
- Deferred compensation
- Benefits package equivalent
- Total cash/stock/deferred bonus and conversion
- Penetration in salary range

Training and education data:

- Formal Schooling—school name, degree, major, year
- Schooling in progress
- Training courses taken (substantial/company sponsors)
- Training needed (if not tied to development plans)
- Training scheduled
- Other significant training courses

Skills, abilities, and competencies data:

- Strengths in terms of products, knowledge, lines of service, industries
- Competencies and areas of specialties
- Employee's stated interest for next job and career goals
- Team assignment skills
- Technical competencies in fields of potential company interest
- Licenses, certificates

Figure 8-2. International management data requirements.   (*Continued*)

Other

- Citizenship, visas (dates of expiration)
- Relocation or job limitations, if any
- Family situation
- Home ownership
- International experience

Figure 8-2. (*Continued*)

later — are usually not a major issue for management data that is used only within the company, and with the manager's permission. When information is collected and transmitted on the employee population generally, or when it is used beyond the borders of the company, privacy issues are a major concern.

Information About Nonmanagement Employees

Multinational employers also need information about their nonmanagement employees throughout the world, but who needs this data, when, and why are questions that will differ greatly among organizations. There may be little need for corporate headquarters to have a great deal of information about local employees' training and background when most of these employees are foreign nationals, for example; but the same employee information may be needed by a local government agency, local owners, or business partners.

The key is to determine the specific items of information that need to be collected centrally (and locally), and then determine the most reliable and cost-effective way to get this data to where it is needed. For example, if headquarters simply needs the total number of employees on a monthly basis, this number could be phoned in, faxed, or put in the mail for data entry at the central location. If numerous breakouts and additional data elements are required, perhaps it could be sent electronically or on preformatted diskettes, for automatic data entry.

Data requirements for employees generally or for the nonmanagement population are usually more complex than simple headcounts, however. The list in Table 8-1 could be considerably longer, depending on the nature of operations and business objectives. For example, multinational companies engaged in overseas production may need statistics on productivity, resource use, quality measurements, and other manu-

Table 8-1. International Nonmanagement Data Requirements: Statistics

1. Number of total employees at beginning of period and comparison of budgeted headcount to actual number
2. Number of total employees at end of period
3. Number of new hires in the period
4. Number of transfers in from other affiliates
5. Number of transfers out to other affiliates
6. Number of terminations by reason for leaving (turnover)
7. Number of employees and/or FTEs by location
8. Number of employees by department
9. Number of employees by grade level/exempt, nonexempt and hourly
10. Average wages paid in local currency—total
11. Average wages paid in local currency—by grade
12. Number of hours worked (by product if possible)
13. Number of hours of overtime paid
14. Number of promotions/lateral moves
15. Number of training programs delivered/students taught
16. Number of accidents on the job

facturing data, and these statistics may need to be available on a daily or weekly basis to address problems or quality control issues promptly.

The question of whether or not to build local systems with local databases and how and what to transmit to corporate systems is also affected by laws concerning individual privacy rights. Many countries, especially in Europe, have highly restrictive laws regarding the transmission of personal data across international borders without the data subject's approval. The bulk transmission of employee records with personal identifiers as record keys may not be permitted in some cases, requiring different data paths or only local analysis of data, or the removal of the personal identification.

Methods of Supplying Data to Corporate

Legal constraints aside, the two most common approaches to collecting individual data regarding managerial and non-managerial employees from the field and supplying that data for corporate use are the direct entry method and the translation method.

In these models it is suggested that regional users or others requiring data from more than one local entity utilize the corporate database.

Direct Entry Method. The direct entry method illustrated at Figure 8-3 is the method preferred by many multinationals because it requires that the information be collected locally, in the same format and to the same standards as the corporate entity, thereby ensuring that when the data is

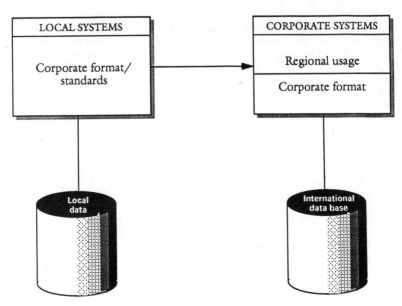

Figure 8-3. Direct entry method (local databases).

received, headquarters does not have to go through a reediting and/or a mapping process in order to use it.

Although it is preferred, it is not all that common to find that the direct entry method will work for all overseas affiliates and all the data elements required. However, such an opportunity might arise when a new application is introduced. In a newly designed application, the systems designers might be able to utilize a common software package, which would automatically provide a standard file for corporate's use whenever it is run by a local affiliate. Alternatively, they might install a standard feature in each local system such as a "dual commit," where data is supplied to two databases (local and corporate) simultaneously when the local system is updated. Either method gets the data to its user in an acceptable format, and accomplishes the direct entry of data.

Another method of direct entry is to use a fully on-line system (Figure 8-4), where the local user and corporate users access the application directly, and the data supplied by the end user updates a single, worldwide database. This assumes there is a telecommunications network, that can be accessed by all users, and that is maintained to a central set of standards.

One weakness of direct entry methods is that most applications have to be standard for all locations and all users. This means that users in Singapore, New Delhi, London, or Buenos Aires must meet both local requirements as well as satisfy corporate's needs, without being trans-

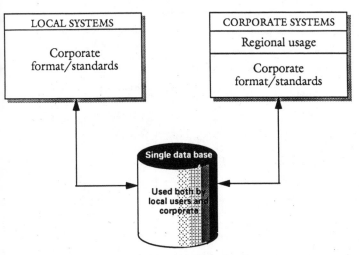

Figure 8-4. Direct entry method (worldwide database).

lated. With these methods there is only one data update format. Whether on-line, via diskette, or EDI, all users are accessing the data created by that single update, and hence the requirement for format standardization. For example, if a new succession planning or compensation plan is being introduced, and with it an application program which requires data on a key set of employees, the direct method would ask that all users supply the needed data via this system, thereby ensuring that the data is uniform among users.

Translation Method. The translation method, as the name implies, is utilized when local databases do not contain the same data in the same format as corporate requires, and must be "translated" before it can be used by corporate or regional users. The translation method utilizes mapping to build its database. The instructions to the local country for the operation of this system would be to generate a prescribed data set of information from your local systems—regardless of the type or content of those local systems—and supply the prescribed data to corporate in a format and to the standards that corporate requires (Figure 8-5). The instructions indicate the conditions under which to supply data; definitions of the elements; edit requirements; and the like. This method of translating to the corporate specification is commonly used due to the variety of hardware and software platforms found around the world. It is also a virtual necessity when differences in languages, data categories, and elements differentiate the various employee populations.

Translation allows more autonomy of local operation, reflects the way

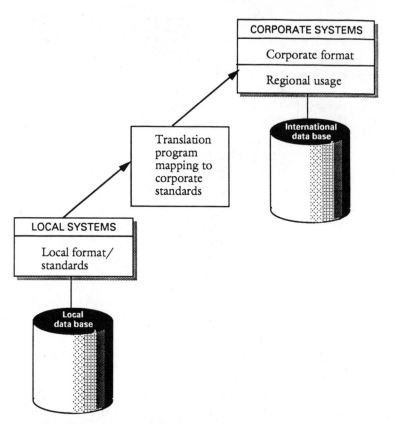

Figure 8-5. Translation method (local mapping).

the primary business is conducted, and therefore is in the spirit of most managerial philosophies. The users, keeping their own local front-line systems in place, extract either employee transactions or copies of employee data elements and save them for later shipment to corporate. Before being sent, data is put into standard language or code set, as prescribed by corporate. For example, local pay grade, if one is kept, would be changed to a corporate standard, the local currency converted to U.S. dollars, and so forth. A major weakness of this method is that data errors cannot easily be detected by corporate. Therefore, there really is no effective way of ensuring full compliance with corporate standards. Unless there is a method of ensuring accuracy (see Chapter 11), there is complete reliance on the local affiliate to generate correct data.

A second translation method involves local countries sending in their data "raw," and putting it through translation by corporate's software (Figure 8-6). If the data cannot be mapped or if there are inconsisten-

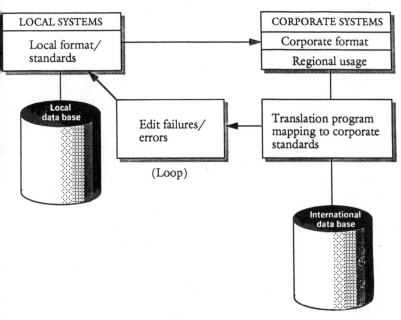

Figure 8-6. Translation method (corporate mapping).

cies, then it is rejected by corporate and the local country is sent errors to clear and for resubmission. Data editing and control standards are more easily put in place with this method, but it is more expensive for corporate to operate, and shifts a good bit of the burden of data administration to the corporate group. Very often an international affiliate will be quite small and therefore have only a PC or a LAN for data processing, and corporate may have little option but to use this method.

Organizational Information Requirements

Employee information from each country needs to be supplemented with information regarding the structure and nature of the organization. In order to perform comparisons regarding operations in various countries, their costs, style of management, productivity measurements, and the like, it is important to have base data over a period of time with which to produce a meaningful set of statistics. And if the multinational has operations in a number of countries which have different social security and insurance schemes, some with runaway inflation and/or highly unstable political climates, key planning issues and data surrounding these critical operations centers should be captured as well.

It is very important to understand the organizational hierarchy in the local countries. In certain cultures the table of organization and protocols may be more rigidly observed than in the United States. Organization charts show a hierarchy which may or may not be strictly observed. Supporting data showing true reporting relationships is therefore needed by corporate in these situations. Also, there are instances where displaying a chart with an expatriate at the top may not be prudent, if it is important for a local citizen to be shown as the head of an operation. Again, this information is needed, since successful management from a distance requires swift and accurate data to ensure that operations are being managed efficiently and within the basic policies. Information such as that shown in Table 8-2 should be considered for inclusion as an international basis for corporate's use.

Table 8-2. Potential Organizational Data Requirements

Organization structure of operating units:
    Reporting relationships of units
    Size in terms of sales, products, profitability, employees
    Physical location of plants/number of employees
    Planned output and employee levels required
    Historical production

Names and titles of key individuals in operating units:
    Organization chart data
    Positions (position control) — tie to succession planning data
    Requirements for position/duties of incumbent
    Development plans — tie to succession planning data
    Subordinates who report directly
    Goals and targets of incumbent

Critical planning issues:
    Stable production/service issues
    New initiatives planned/ramp-ups needed
    Key positions and vulnerabilities — tie to succession plan data
    Gaps, shortfalls expected
    Planned organizational moves
    Goals and targets of key units
    Political and economic climate

Relationships with suppliers, joint ventures, co-sponsors:
    Key individuals/targets for hire
    Structure of third-party organizations' relationships to affiliates
    Possible mergers, acquisitions, divestitures

HR plans and policies:
    Benefit schemes/social insurance
    Compensation levels/grades
    Training and development issues/needs
    Key policies which may need revamping
    Transfer and movement plans (intra- or intercountry).

Administration of Expatriates

Multinational organizations that rely on large numbers of expatriate employees—U.S. citizens assigned abroad or non-U.S. employees working in this country, usually on tours scheduled to last a year or more or to coincide with the duration of a project—have special needs for HR management and systems support. Costs of such assignments can be three or four times that of identical assignments in the home country, and the "failure rate" of expatriates—the percentage who return home for one reason or another before completing their scheduled tours—is legendary. The extra complexities of human resource management of expatriates include the selection and preparation of those suited to work aboard for extended periods (sometimes limited to those suited to work in a given country or culture); relocation of the expatriate (and sometimes whole families); compensation and living expenses abroad; the general "strangeness" of many overseas environments for employees, including both living environments and new organizational structures; and the reentry of returning expatriates into the home organization. And when expatriate assignments are part of management development programs, as they frequently are in global organizations requiring managerial skills and talents throughout the world, international movement of managers and succession planning issues come to the fore.

In addition, management-level expatriates—as opposed to work teams or groups transported en masse to complete a project—sometimes must work "alone"—as the only company employee, compared to home environments where lines of authority and organizational structure were more clearly defined and staff help is available. Characteristics such as self-sufficiency, an adventurous spirit, adaptability to change, and entrepreneurial behavior are often more important abroad.

Because so much of the data required to manage expatriates is unique to assignments, and not covered in the domestic HRIS, a separate system or module for expatriate administration is usually in order for any organization with more than a few hundred employees overseas. This system will carry data about domestic candidates for overseas assignments—going well beyond the usual skills inventory information such as foreign language proficiency or willingness to relocate—as well as unique information about overseas jobs and their incumbents. In global succession plans, the information carried may be even more elaborate than that suggested below, to account for international movement and development of managers.

Unique data in an expatriate HR system usually includes a number of differently calculated compensation increments, beginning with a base increment for all overseas assignments that applies to all employees willing to leave home, perhaps family, and familiar surroundings.

Second, "hardship allowances" may be added for assignments in developing nations, where political unrest may add stress, or where cultural acclimation may be a problem. These allowances take into account the reality that assignments in London, Geneva, Rome, or Paris are usually more attractive than those in Southeast Asia or the Middle East.

Third, cost-of-living allowances may be factored in where there are major differences in everyday expenses, as there are between Cleveland and Tokyo.

Fourth, a tax equalization allowance may be paid to cover any difference between taxes paid by the expatriate to foreign governments and what the expatriate would have paid in the United States.

Fifth, expense payments to cover additional costs that might be incurred because of local customs or the foreign environment—such as club memberships, use of an automobile, or private education for family members—need to be accounted for in some situations.

Information will also be collected about the family situation, such as number of children and their schooling arrangements. Also, number of visits to the home country and data about sponsor working situations could be maintained.

Potential reassignment information will be very important, since one of the perennial problems in expatriate administration is where to place people upon completion of their tours. Are they having problems with their relocation and have to return early? Can they be extended? Can we ship them to a third country? Any data the HRIS can carry to help in this area is welcome.

Future Issues in International Human Resource Management

The only thing certain about the future of international human resource management is that it is here to stay, as multinational organizations continue to expand their overseas operations, telecommunications and other technology continues to shrink the world, and more and more organizations—U.S.-based or otherwise—move beyond traditional national borders to become "global."

Many of the new HR issues will follow the lead of business, economic, and social changes that are already upon us: the demise of the Hong Kong territory as we know it after 1997; the emerging European Community (EC) becoming more unified each year; continuing change in the developing countries; new political and governmental institutions redefining free enterprise in many nations; and economic changes including runaway inflation in some areas. All of these changes will affect multinational organizations and their employees abroad.

In general, the challenge for human resources and HR systems for the multinational workforce will continue to be the development of country- or region-specific policies, procedures, and programs at the local level that are shaped and guided by "global" business aims and HR practices that support the multinational business.

International changes such as those now underway in the European Community, for example, include new pension liabilities that each multinational will be facing as it enters the EC arena; employee rights, especially regarding plant closings, shutdowns, and layoffs; environmental concerns, especially throughout eastern and southern Europe with its aging infrastructure, and problems with water supply, quality of air, and safety standards; and job rights and conduct with respect to work practices. These issues are still emerging, and of course will take a great degree of watching. For instance, European work councils, which have been in place for many years in Germany and other highly industrialized nations, will now be mandated for an EC-wide multinational firm which employs at least 1000 people within the community. Economic reports will be required, and work councils meeting with management proposals are likely to have a significant impact on the workforce. These and other regulations will require a new method of participative management with government and employee work groups.

Another interesting sidelight in the international arena is the growth of privatization in the former Soviet Union and other Eastern Block countries. Beginning in 1988, certain Russian citizens were permitted to establish personal pension accounts. Employed men and women between the ages of 30 and 60 could participate in the system, paying premiums through payroll deductions. With this money they could buy into an annuity which grows in value roughly equivalently with the state social security pensions in Russia, which are payable at age 60 for men and 55 for women with a minimum of five years participation. The continued movement and shift of these types of plans will mean, from a systems standpoint, that a more common type of system architecture needs to be setup. Continued differences in plan design as well as hardware/software differences, though, will make it hard to implement pension systems on a worldwide basis in the foreseeable future.

The events in the eastern countries will mean more opportunities for U.S. companies but put a higher premium on plan flexibility. The newly unified EC market is equal in size or greater than that of the

United States. However, because of various problems of the member states, e.g. Denmark, full cohesion or "harmonization" will not take place for some years. For American multinational corporations it does mean stronger European competition, and increases the need for efficient operations, low-cost production, simplified organizational structures, and coherent marketing approaches. Cultural prejudices will be difficult for American firms to overcome.

This stronger European economic community will eventually be not only larger than the U.S. economy, but will naturally have a market preference for purchasing goods from European firms. For many multinationals, this means that a toehold or an operations base in the EC is absolutely essential. One fear is that the past protectionism of European countries will grow with unification, as the EC tries to keep out North American and Japanese firms, and even European firms from countries which have not joined the EC. Carried to extremes, the "European fortress" mentality will become more imposing than it is now.

Multinationals doing business in Europe must also be aware of Eastern Bloc countries which are now emerging from years of communist control and domination by the Soviet Union. There is abundant cheap labor in these countries; they are very close to the EC community in terms of distance; their own domestic markets have a good potential for being developed, and might well receive some preferential treatment from the EC because of the "fortress Europe" mentality. If full integration of these Eastern Bloc countries takes place, the EC as it evolves will be even larger in size and more difficult for North American multinationals to penetrate.

North American firms doing business with the European Community will of course have to deal with employment terms and conditions very unlike those of North America. Although these are changing and becoming more like U.S. plans, there are many social security-type provisions and social charges that are now imposed upon employers. These plans have very high payout ratios for individual employees who achieve pensioner status. Payouts reach as much as 75 percent of final average earnings in Spain and Italy, for instance, whereas in the more developed northern countries such as the U.K. and Germany, payout ratios are in the neighborhood of 40 to 45 percent, much closer to those of North American plans.

Another consideration is the "borderless" view of workers in the EC, and the implications of this view. With freer movement of people expected among the various countries, there may well be a greater shift to capital accumulation plans in the future, since enhanced portability of pensions will provide workers a much more mobile status. This mobility has been brought about in large part due to the changes in the social security rights of migrant workers, i.e., workers outside their home country. These rights have been agreed to by member nations in the EC, and basically guarantee that migrating workers will enjoy the same rights as local nationals. The new regulations apply to most state-sponsored social security schemes, including sickness, disability, old age, unemployment, and family and allowance programs. The general principles behind these coordination schemes, not quite "harmonization" yet, is that a migrant worker will be subject to only one law at a time—the law of the member state where he or she is working within the EC—not that of the home country. Individuals covered by the regulations are entitled to receive a pension benefit prorated to reflect length of local service from the EC country of employment. The payment of the pension for the migrant will be calculated by determining the member state where the worker qualified for benefits. That state will need to pay the higher of the actual pension due under the local scheme for the period of residence or coverage the worker spent there or the theoretical pension to which the worker would have been entitled had he or she completed all service in that country—prorated, of course, to reflect actual local service. These regulations—along with others such as a common passport—will permit a much greater degree of freedom of the human resources within the EC. This shift of labor will enable EC companies to compete more effectively in the marketplace, but will stretch pension calculation and HRIS record-keeping capability as more complex sets of requirements are brought about during EC harmonization.

PART 3

Making the Vision Work

Principles and Practices of Strategic HRIS Management

9
The HRIS Organization

In the early days of HRIS, before the microprocessor revolution of the 1980s and the advent of advanced languages that permit wide user access, distributed processing, and other user-friendly technological advances, the "ideal" structure of the HRIS management organization was virtually dictated. In the mainframe environment of the 1960s and 1970s, the technical skills required to enter data, produce program reports, retrieve information, perform edits, and otherwise manage human resource systems mandated the establishment of a centralized HRIS management organization, often called a human resource information center (HRIC), staffed by technically skilled data systems professionals who served as "middlemen" between the system and its users. Data was sent on paper forms to the HRIC, all processing occurred there, and when a user needed information or a new report, a request was put in to this staff organization. In many cases, given the level of technology at the time and the demands being made on HRIC organizations by expanding, multifunctional human resource departments, requests for data and reports often joined a queue of requests, to be fulfilled days or weeks later.

While centralized management of a HRIS had (and continues to have) certain advantages for some organizations, the premicrocomputer technical environment presented a number of insurmountable obstacles to optimal HRIS use and operating efficiency. Not only were HRIC staffers burdened with time-consuming data-entry procedures, updates, edits, and processing, but the management users of HRIS data—those for whom this "access" systems was originally installed—had virtually no unobstructed access to the data and reports needed to improve the quality of their work. If you needed more than the standard reports churned out in predesigned formats at scheduled intervals, you had to explain your needs to systems specialists and get in the queue. This arrangement, while an improvement over the need to deal with the MIS group directly, still set up barriers to access.

The microcomputer and easier-to-use technology changed all that. On-line systems, micro-based systems that could be downloaded from a mainframe, standalone PC-based systems, networks, and other HRIS configurations added up to one thing for HRIS users in terms of access: freedom from the "middlemen" of the HRIC. Everything from data entry and edits to processing and user-defined reports could be done at the local level, wherever a user with minimal computer skills had access to a microcomputer.

While the decentralization of computer use has obviated the need for a centralized staff organization to enter, process, and retrieve all HRIS data, a need usually remains for some level of HRIS management in an "oversight" capacity. Whatever the HRIS configuration, issues such as the quality and consistency of corporatewide data, privacy and security, maintenance, training, and other organizationwide issues usually need to be addressed at an organizational level that oversees individual users and functions, to prevent the fragmentation of the HRIS into multiple systems that speak in a babel of voices and operate inefficiently.

The typical objectives of HRIS management are shown in Figure 9-1, and the usual activities associated with meeting these objectives are shown in Figure 9-2. The questions, and the focus of the remainder of

- Deploy and manage systems and practices according to organizational and legal standards.

- Consulting—to provide data, technology, and systems solutions to line managers and other users.

- Gather information about the organization's overall human resources—past, present, and future—and the context in which they work.

- Plan for future information requirements and technology deployment throughout the corporation.

- Establish standards, policies, and procedures needed to carry out the HRIS mission, and assure compliance, governance, and oversight.

- Assist with introduction of organizational change.

Figure 9-1. Typical objectives of the HRIS management function.

In designing a HRIS management organization, most if not all of the following HRIS management activities need to be accounted for, as well as others—such as the collection of competitive and external data—that grow out of organization-specific HRIS missions. Decisions about "where" these activities should be performed, as discussed in the text, depend on the overall mission of HRIS recognizing the sometimes overlapping role of IS, organizational structure and information requirements, and the needs of specific functions.

Data Collection and Entry

- Defining needed data and edits
- Collecting data from users
- Entering data into the system (mainly table changes and notes)
- Maintaining accuracy of databases

System Development and Enhancements

- Defining user needs
- Developing specifications/prototypes
- Determining priorities
- Developing new programs and systems
- Installating new features and modules
- Testing new features
- Converting to new modules
- Evaluating vendors

Operations (Shared with IS)

- System operation
- System scheduling
- Table maintenance
- Answering users' questions
- Running recurring jobs

Administration

- Setting standards and introducing company rules
- Determining access and security privileges
- Producing documentation
- Structuring database elements

Figure 9-2. Activities of HRIS management. (*Continued*)

Retrieval

- Producing models, displays, reports, and analyses
- Designing new queries, modules, and reports
- Analyzing trends
- Generating user data sets

Research and Development

- Evaluating vendors
- Ordering hardware/software
- Instructing users
- Solving problems
- Testing new technology and determining how it can be used

Consulting/Assisting with Organizational Change

- Meeting with users
- Defining problems (diagnosis)
- Generating solutions
- Determining alternative courses of action
- Reengineering processes
- Utilizing methodologies (WFA, AA, etc.)

Figure 9-2. (*Continued*)

this chapter, are where and how these essential activities will be performed in the organization. The answers to these questions—actually, a number of answers in most cases—varies among different organizations, usually depending on (1) the mission of the HRIS in the organization, (2) organizational structure and information requirements, and (3) the needs and constraints of specific HR functions using the HRIS. At the end of this chapter a model organizational structure for HRIS management is presented (see Figure 9-4), which may apply to large, multifunctional HR departments and which incorporates a high level of procedural efficiency. The model, however, is not necessarily ideal for all organizations. In fact, one of the worst mistakes HRIS developers can make in devising a means of managing a system is to "force-fit" a predetermined management structure on an existing organization. Rather, when a HRIS management organization is being designed or restructured, company-specific answers to the questions raised in the following sections should dictate its structure, responsibilities, staffing evels, and the specific activities it performs or manages in an oversight apacity.

The HRIS Mission

The HRIS management organization, whether it consists of a single person or a HRIC staff of dozens, is essentially a staff organization. As such, HRIS management organizations often come under the close scrutiny of those responsible for corporate reorganizations, just as do the staff functions of finance, MIS, legal, research and development, marketing, and other areas where decentralization and local autonomy show promise of improved or more efficient operations. But before deciding that decentralization is in itself a good idea for HRIS management, the first and perhaps most important question to be answered is "What is the mission of the HRIS?" or sometimes "What *should be* the mission of the HRIS?"

The HRIS management objectives shown in Figure 9-1 are typical goals, and to some extent each of these generalized objectives should guide the structure and mission of the management organization. But the actual design of a new or restructured HRIS management organization will require a more detailed analysis of the role of technology in the organization, and this begins with the identification of the HRIS mission, or core reason for being. This mission may have one or more main components and numerous subobjectives, with priorities set by a process such as the identification of critical success factors described in Chapter 6.

Following are some examples of what a HRIS mission might be, with discussions of what each might mean in terms of HRIS management organization.

Uniform Consistent HR Policy and Information Through Standards

When HR consistency of plans and policies is the overriding issue in HRIS management, centralized administration of the database, data quality, data collection procedures, updates, and any on-line processing is normally considered essential. Uniformity and standards is a complex subject, including not only the accuracy and consistency of the data but its timeliness, its relevance to organizational management needs, interpretation and definition, protection from natural or human disasters, and the prescriptions of HRIS privacy policy. In all of these areas, the proliferation of microcomputer users in the organization should probably not dictate distribution of this key HRIS management function. This is particularly true when ensuring the quality of "core data" is a shared responsibility between data owners and the HRIS team. Core data, data elements used throughout the organization in various applications (such as organization codes, names, locations, salary grades, etc., and their definitions), may be too important to leave to the potentially uneven data management of numerous users in a decentralized environment. Setting the standards should be a corporate responsibility, but accuracy and quality must be primarily a local duty.

When setting data standards and measurements is the central HRIS mission, however, this does not preclude decentralization of all of the HRIS management activities shown in Figure 9-2. For example, data entry and local edit clearance can and should be performed at the local level whenever possible, especially for applications with unique data elements, such as a performance appraisal system. Rather, the overriding need for data standards means that a form of centralized management organization is needed to establish and administer constant checks on data quality, privacy guidelines, security codes and passwords, periodic audits, and other measures necessary to assure continuing data quality. (See Chapter 11 for more on achieving data accuracy and quality.)

Strategic Planning

Another HRIS mission that implies a need for some level of centralization of HRIS management is the use of HRIS in strategic planning. When data carried in the HRIS database is critical to the development of plans and business moves essential to the long-term survival and success of the organization, a staff organization that assures the currency and dependability of this data may be needed.

In addition, strategic planning typically requires data from external sources, information on environmental issues that is not normally collected by local users or through function-specific applications. Demographic data, trends in the labor market, educational statistics, changes in the global economy, and similar data—everything from the price of oil to changes in the political climate—are types of information best collected and managed by a centralized staff. Together with internal data provided by local users and specific applications—such as projections of the number of experienced engineers who will be available within the company five years from now, based on data from a career management system—this strategic planning information provides the decision-support data needed to shape the organization of the future.

When strategic planning is a key mission of the HRIS, the HRIS staff organization can maintain databases on internal and external trends shaping business environment. Again, this role of a staff HRIS management organization does not preclude the decentralization of local or application-specific data entry, processing, and other HRIS uses, but rather supports a HRIS management configuration that includes a staff-level organization dedicated to planning.

Providing Information to Managers

Like data quality, the HRIS mission of providing information to managers can be a complex, multifaceted set of objectives. A HRIS, it should be remembered, is essentially an *access* system as opposed to a production system, but the ways in which managers and professionals in the organization gain access to its information are infinitely variable.

In general, managers get information from the HRIS database in one of two ways, one of which implies a centralized management organization and the other of which suggests the need for decentralization. The first type of access—historically the only way—is through standard reports and access screens and displays, such as monthly headcount data, benefits statements, EEO updates, and so on. This type of data is best supplied by a staff organization and requires a team to be on hand to produce such reports on a recurring basis. The second method, letting users access the system directly or generate their own reports, suggests a new role for the HRIS team: to develop tools and a support structure that will enable users to be self-sufficient.

Therefore, one of the most important and worthwhile objectives of decentralizing computing power in HRIS organizations over the years has been the goal of putting the ability to create and run analytical reports in the hands of functional users themselves. This ability represents what may be the most sophisticated, advanced use of the HRIS from a management perspective, because it provides analytical power to users, which means more than mere information. An advanced system helps users with background data and context information needed to examine trends, relationships, and other factors managers wish to examine in search of insights that can be used to improve human resource management.

Analytical reports and displays devised by users, often called ad-hoc retrievals to distinguish them from the regular reports churned out on schedule by the HRIS, are typically one-time analyses designed to test a hypothesis, identify the nature and extent of a relationship, or provide other statistical evidence to support (or refute) a view about the impacts of human resource policies and programs in the organization. By definition, these reports are not available from the HRIS in the normal course of operations; they are also, as a rule, "dreamed up" by functional users rather than HRIS managers, created because the user is seeking answers or knowledge specific to a functional issue. Examples might include:

- An analysis that shows the relationship between sources of employees—different employment agencies, college recruiters, employment office walk-ins, employee referrals, etc.—and turnover, confirming or refuting a manager's hunch that college recruiters are creating false expectations among prospective employees

- An analysis that identifies performance appraisal ratings by the sex (or other variable, such as age or length of service) of appraisers and appraisees, to identify possible bias

- An analysis linking historical changes in the rate of inflation to average retirement age, to see whether or not a relationship exists, and what it might mean given strategic planning's estimate that inflation will escalate sharply in the next five years

- "What-if" analyses of all kinds, projecting the probable impact of a range of variables on other factors, such as the cost savings of subcontracting a particular function, the budget impact of a new merit pay structure, or staffing changes necessitated by a possible merger or acquisition.

The HRIS team must then shift from a production shop to a datamodeling group, developing multipurpose analyses and protocols which many users can access and tailor to their own needs.

Organization Structure and Information Requirements

Once the mission of the HRIS has been clarified established and agreed upon by senior management and all interested parties, the factors that help determine the most effective approach to HRIS management are found in two related areas:

- The nature of the organizational structure being served by the HRIS, which may turn out to be the overriding issue in determining whether centralized or decentralized HRIS functions are most effective

- Information requirements and flows required by HRIS users, which include not only the types of information carried by the HRIS but issues such as where data comes from and where it is used—issues that relate to the structure of the organization being served by the system

Too often, companies introducing new technology such as a HRIS organize around the technology they bought or developed instead of using the technology to achieve a more effective organization. The full benfits of the automation of data and procedures are more likely to merge when systems are brought to bear on organizationally effective tructures, rather than imposed on procedures to create a new, only echnically efficient structure. The "should be" state, as discussed in hapter 5, needs to be recognized.

For example, a company using an applicant tracking system to create database of all job applicants for EEO reporting and other purposes an either establish separate systems at all employment locations in a decentralized environment or can submit data on-line to a centralized system. Which will work best for the organization? If many or most of the different local organizations are engaged in dissimilar lines of business, nd have their own job descriptions, employment requirements, and olicies (and perhaps their own EEO plans), the apparently "more effiient" structure of an on-line or networked applicant-tracking system nay not be effective. Different job codes, unique requirements, and ther variables may defy usability when consolidated in a single database.

The most natural configuration for HRIS management organizations n companies having numerous lines of business, applications, or localies with unique data and data requirements, and other dissimilar IRIS-related characteristics, is usually a decentralized mode. Yet data hat can be commonly defined can be made part of a centralized or core" database. And the centralization of HRIS core data—names, ompensation, organization codes, locations, etc.—does not necessarily nean that all the activities associated with this data need to be perormed centrally. Data entry and updates, for example, can be made at he local level; reporting can be done at the staff level. Also, the trend to mpowerment and extension of the HRIS to the line manager and emloyee will put new demands on the HRIS team which should be conidered.

And although the most important determinants of HRIS organizaional structure—the HRIS mission, corporate structure, etc.—are nique to each organization, some of the general principles that apply o all or most human resource systems, as discussed in Chapter 3, deerve consideration. For example, as a general rule, it's a good idea to ollect data early and edit locally (Principle 5.1). Both efficiency and ata quality benefit when a transaction or change is entered as close as possible to its source, in terms of both time and physical proximity. Thi principle, of course, suggests the desirability of decentralized data entr and local edits, when possible.

Organization Types

There are many ways of categorizing organizations by structural type any one of which may be relevant in coming to a decision about the most effective HRIS management organization. A company with 50(employees in a single location, for example, has different HRIS man agement needs than one with 150,000 employees throughout the world A hierarchical management structure may imply a different HRIS thai a horizontal or matrix-managed company. The categorization sug gested below, however, is valid in assessing how a HRIS managemen organization might be structured in most profit-making organizations and it is worth considering when creating or reorganizing this function Also, a company "running lean" cannot hope to have a HR organizatioi which is top-heavy: The culture would not permit it. As a service providing organization, the HRIS function can be structured to serve one or a combination of these organizational structures:

- *Geographic.* When the organization is separated into a number o geographic entities—local, regional, or by country—the same reason for this structure may apply to HRIS management. A HRIS manage ment organization for each geographic entity may be in a better po sition to deal with local regulations, labor market issues, cultural dif ferences relevant to HR, locally effective compensation, and so on This model could be appropriate where HR administration is also de livered locally.

- *Line of service.* Companies in more than one line of business—di versified into a number of industries or by product line—may requir(HR management practices and policies that vary greatly among sub sidiaries or business units. Skills requirements, pay packages, benefits and many other subjects of data in the HRIS that support human re source management can vary enormously between, for example, ; subsidiary doing genetic research and one retailing fast food. An(when customer-oriented information such as service measurements merit pay based on marketing data, or other customer satisfactioi indicia is carried in the HRIS, systems designed and operated specif ically for each main line of business may represent the optimal HRIS configuration.

- *Customer.* The customer organizational model is one in which the organization is structured to provide products or services to a certain type of customer or industry — say, retail clothing buyers or the banking industry. This model usually permits a high level of centralization of HR management and the HRIS organization, in the absence of major geographic differences among locations. And yet, many of the activities associated with HRIS management — data entry, processing, retrievals, etc. — can be performed at the local level and passed electronically to a staff organization.

Functional. In the functional organizational model, all employees who perform a like function — sales, engineering, manufacturing, and so on — are treated differently by human resource management, requiring different types of HR plans, support systems, and data. For example, a skills inventory database, showing employees' professional credentials, licenses, experience, training, and technical competencies, is obviously more important in engineering than in retail sales (unless the company is selling unique chemical compounds or other high-tech products or services). And the plans and programs in HR might also be different, thereby requiring different HR systems.

Organizational structures such as these do not preclude creation of a mixed" HRIS management structure, in which all payroll management r benefits administration is handled centrally, for example, and other IR functions are supported by local systems. Also, work can be divided long a staff or line basis, with some types of data or transactions handled in the field and others managed centrally.

nformation Requirements and Data 'lows

The overall configuration of a HRIS is (or should be) the result of a horough needs analysis preceding systems development or acquisition, n analysis that examines and documents all management and end-user equirements for data and automated processes (Chapter 4). One outome of this needs analysis is development of a *data plan,* a comprehensive listing of all information that will be used by the HRIS, where it omes from, where it goes, how it moves through the organization, and /here it is stored and maintained. This data model can also contain a reate/use/monitor analysis to highlight where information should best e stored. It should reflect the vision system in Chapter 5.

The organization-specific information requirements and data flows f a well-developed data plan can have an important bearing on the lacement of HRIS management activities. In most cases, these data requirements and flows emerge from the identification of the HRIS mission and organizational structure, and represent a "next step" in refining or sharpening the questions that need to be answered about HRIS management. For example:

- If the HRIS mission is primarily to administer benefits, should the HRIS management organization be located in the benefits department?

- If each division or business unit has its own unique data requirements, with no real core data or core functions because of different HR programs and policies, environmental factors, or job requirements, the collection and management of this data should probably be handled in each business unit.

- When the mission of the HRIS is to put data and analytical power in the hands of users and managers throughout the organization, the technology of distributed or local processing and report writing may be indicated, but a HRIS management organization may be necessary at the staff level to set standards and to provide corporatewide training and user support.

- Specific HR functions with application-specific data requirements may be standardized corporatewide, with sources of data and users at numerous locations. This implies a need for local data processing capabilities for this application, along with staff centralization of basic personnel or core data—commending itself to a mix of centralized and decentralized HRIS management.

The development of optimal data flows in the organization typically starts with the identification of who, or what function, should be responsible for originating a required piece of information. Data originators are also data "owners," i.e., those responsible for assuring that the data is collected in a timely manner, that it remains accurate, and that it is changed when necessary. Because of their responsibility to assure the accuracy and relevance of the data they "own," data originators are usually people or functions who best understand what the data element is and what it will be used for: e.g., benefits administrators for benefits data, EEO specialists for protected class categories, employees themselves for résumé information.

The next step in establishing data flows is to determine who needs the data, when, and by what means of HRIS access. Is the data element one that is only used locally, or does it need to be part of the central database? Is it application-specific, such as a table of management development courses in a succession planning system, or will it be used in a number of applications, such as a person's job title?

When is data needed, and why? For example, many HRIS organizations in recent years have decided to bring the data entry and processing associated with new hires into the HR department or to move it to line organizations, taking it away from its traditional home in payroll. Through interfaces, systems integration, or the functional integration of payroll work with HR, these organizations have developed a HRIS organizational structure in which the data "owners" are identified as the people in HR who understand benefits regulation, administer cafeteria plans and other payroll-affecting programs, and *need* new hire data before the first check is cut for a new employee.

Functional and Process Views Affecting HRIS Management Alignment

One way to appreciate the growth of the human resource management role in business over the past two decades is to make two lists, one showing the functions or types of work performed by the "personnel department" and another showing the range of functions that might be found in today's expanded human resource management organization. The old personnel department was usually responsible for hiring procedures, administration of a standard benefits package, some record keeping, and termination paperwork; today, the functional diversity and growth of the HR department presents a different picture, one suggested by the list of potential functional specialties in human resources in Figure 9-3. Each of these more or less specialized functions — and others that may be added in the years ahead — requires some level of specialized staff expertise, unique procedures, function-specific information requirements, and sometimes even its own information technology. And just as the HR department has become a diverse collection of specialized functions, the systems that support human resource management have become numerous and specialized in many organizations.

In fact, the proliferation of specialized HR functions and systems that support these functions has led, in many organizations, to a dysfunctional fragmentation of the HRIS — which has become not one but many systems — as well as an unfortunate dispersal of HRIS management responsibility. Subsystems that run EEO data don't communicate with the career development system; the skills inventory system is not linked to HR planning; succession planning uses different job descriptions than those found in the core database; and so on.

Today's technology can resolve the technical issues involved in systems integration. As discussed in Chapter 2, the evolution of HRIS technology — still continuing — has created an environment where virtually any HRIS technical configuration is possible, and issues such as

In large organizations today, each of the following functions is potentially a separate specialization handled by its own work group and supported by the HRIS:

- Applicant tracking
- College recruitment
- Payroll
- Benefits administration
  Savings plans
  Insurance plans
  Pensions
- Training
- Career development
- Performance appraisal
- Salary administration
- HR planning
- Labor relations
- EEO/AAP
- Compensation
- Financial planning
- Employee assistance programs
- Position control
- Job analysis
- Time and attendance
- Health and safety
- Environmental scanning
- Succession planning
- Résumé retrieval
- Job posting
- Attitude surveys
- Quality-of-worklife programs
- Skills inventories
- Salary surveys
- Outplacement

Figure 9-3. Potential human resource functions.

- Employee communications
- International HR
- Executive compensation
- Labor distribution
- Tuition reimbursement
- Quality improvement programs
- Productivity programs
- Retirement planning
- Relocation
- Awards programs
- Potential assessment
- Testing
- Other regulatory compliance (ADA, COBRA, ADEA, etc.)

Figure 9-3. (Continued)

ntersystems communications no longer present obstacles to HRIS developers.

Still, technology alone cannot "homogenize" human resource management, which requires an increasingly diverse and specialized array of skills, professional competencies, and function-specific data and processes to support different types of work. And because the structure of the HRIS management organization should follow the structure of the organization using the HRIS, the placement of some or all of the HRIS activities in support of the functions shown in Figure 9-3 should in some cases be influenced by the nature and extent of the activities actually performed in the specialized functions. Thus, for each of the functions shown in Figure 9-3 that represents a major area of work in the human resource department, HRIS managers responsible for establishing the location and type of HRIS support should undertake an analysis of the function's activities and tasks to see whether a horizontal view, one based on processes, might be better. The review should include the following considerations:

- The volume of work supported by systems, always a first consider ation in technology management

- The mission of the function and its congruence with the overall HRIS function

- The number and extent of "customers," such as line managers, othe functions, employees, and where they are located

- Timing and through-put requirements, or when and how often worl needs to be accomplished, reports completed, etc.;

- The autonomy of the function, including its reporting relationship interrelationships with other functions, uniqueness in terms of dat requirements and automated procedures, or professional specializa tion

- Staffing issues, including the technical competency of existing staff training issues, turnover, and projections based on career develop ment or forecasting outcomes

- Applicability of companywide HR policies and practices — For exam ple, is this a "bastard" organization with rules of its own, like som high-tech R&D organizations?

- Requirements for accuracy, consistency, and the reliability of output such as payroll processing requires

- Legal and regulatory requirements unique to the function, such a the tax laws applicable to qualified benefits plans

- The relationship of this function to other functions — For example, i the now separate payroll processing department is heavily dependen on benefits processing and calculations, perhaps a merged organiza tion is in order.

These issues will help define the level and types of HRIS manage ment activity that can or should be performed at the functional level, b a benefits organization, the EEO function, HR planning, or anothe specialized work group. They do not necessarily dictate an overall con figuration for the HRIS, however. Data collection and edits for demo graphic data can be performed by the EEO function, for example, anc uploaded to a centralized HRIS for processing, storage, and retrieval.

Specialization and Outsourcing

At times, the level of specialized skills and knowledge required to per form a human resource function effectively — and the staff resource needed to do the work — are such that the most effective approach i "outsourcing." The use of service bureaus or third-party administrators (TPAs) to handle payroll, benefits administration, and such technically complex functions as pension administration has long been a viable, highly cost-effective solution for organizations seeking an alternative to internal staff buildup or the need to develop and maintain specialized expertise in-house.

Outside firms that specialize in certain human resource functions can bring both economies and functional quality to HR administration. The economies come from the fact that these companies specialize in this function, utilizing expert staffers, technology, and other resources to perform a specialized job. Anyone who has ever compared the internal versus external costs of claims processing—handling all medical insurance claims, verifing claims, checking the usual and customary rates, etc.— can appreciate the economies achievable through outsourcing.

Even more important, especially in an environment increasingly burdened by regulatory requirements and the need for high levels of quality and consistency, administrative specialists in areas such as benefits and compensation already have the staff expertise, procedures, and technology needed to assure compliance and quality of the function. Since this is what the company does, the outside administrator also has in place legislative and regulatory monitoring procedures—whose cost is likely to be spread out over a number of clients—to assure cost-effective planning for inevitable change and up-to-date response to new legal requirements.

Specialization and Common Administration

Finally, two of the organizational effectiveness principles discussed in Chapter 3—should be considered in designing functional structure. They are:

- *Centralize specialization* (Principle 2.3), so that whenever possible the specialized skills and knowledge needed to perform a function professionally can be leveraged and used throughout the organization; and

- *Create a common administration instead of organizational mimicry,* (Principle 2.5), which warns against unnecessary "clone organizations" at local levels that mimic centralized staff functions.

When the administration of a function is centralized or outsourced, it should be remembered, it does not necessarily follow that the function itself—the day-to-day use of data and procedures associated with benefits or some other function—must also be centralized. Technological HRIS configurations such as distributed access, on-line systems, networks, and other ways of bringing data and procedures to potentially global work locations remain possible, as discussed in Chapter 2.

A Model HRIS Management Organization and Alternative Structures

A model HRIS organization would accommodate the wide number of users and constituents that a shifting business demands. That is, it would be adaptable to selective centralization for those items that require centralization, while enabling users and smaller units to float free of encumbrances. User access and data entry would be locally provided for within the HRIS itself, so that user support and training would not be required at the local level to the extent it might be today.

The HRIS management organization would be consulting oriented (see Chapter 13), and would have technology planning, reengineering, and data analysis as key objectives. Also, standards, governance, and oversight would be high on the list of objectives. An outline of such a model HRIS organization is shown in Figure 9-4.

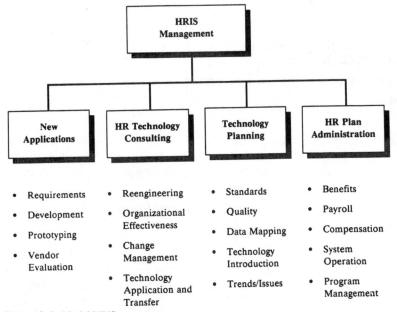

Figure 9-4. Model HRIS organization.

One of the hallmarks of this organization is that it would handle all of the HR, payroll and benefits administration, and technology issues in a given geographic area—defined here as North America, or a given country in an international arena—for all organizational units with common plans. There should be no need for duplicate units where there are common HR plans within a politically defined boundary. The days of separate HR and payroll units should be over. The issues between the HR, payroll, and benefits groups are so intertwined that it is virtually impossible to separate them. Therefore a common approach to handling HR data issues is a model HRIS organization goal.

10

The User
as a Primary
Element

User testing of all parts of an HRIS-in-development—not just to see if it works, but to participate in changes or development of features that will make the system more effective—is one of the most valuable aspects of HR systems development. If the purpose of technology is to improve the effectiveness and ease the burden of organizational work, it follows that those who use the technology to perform work are in many ways the most important participants in development.

The advent of packaged systems and HRIS modules, more rapid development schedules using such tools as computer-assisted systems engineering prototyping methodologies, new relational database systems, and architectures that allow applications to be developed on low-cost micro platforms, more powerful knowledge base systems and retrieval tools, and other new technologies have changed forever the HRIS development landscape in which users were considered a "menace" to on-time completion of the project. More important, the project team can now take advantage of the positive contributions users can make to HRIS effectiveness, because the technology permits the team to respond to users' needs and wants without disastrous effects on the development schedule.

In the days when human resource systems were built largely from scratch—developed internally by project teams heavily dependent on MIS or IS systems designers, specification writers, and programmers—user testing typically occurred at the end of the development process. Because of the technical requirements of HRIS development and the fact that the system was not sufficiently "presentable" until the end of the cycle, typical user interaction with a HRIS project followed a sequence such as this:

1. Needs analysis, in which users were heavily involved, as the project team sought to identify all user needs and requirements that would be met by the new system

2. Specifications and design, conducted by systems people without user involvement

3. Actual development (coding), carried out without user input

4. Systems testing, to be sure of the technical soundness of the system, conducted by IS staffers without user input

5. Final conversion, including user testing of the virtually completed HRIS.

This sequence, in which most HRIS development work and time (which was carried out by the systems organization) went into the specifications, design, and development stages, typically left very little time or opportunity for actual user involvement in the main building phases of the HRIS. In effect, users were asked what they wanted at the needs analysis stage, the project team went away and built it, and a year or so later the users were presented with a system for testing. The results, too often, were users saying "That's not what we meant at all," or "Why couldn't we also have this?"

Early and ongoing user involvement and testing in the development stages requires a systematic, planned approach that becomes an integral part of the project cycle. The methodology and types of tests recommended here work well for large systems involving numerous components—the most difficult type of system to test effectively—and suggest an approach that should serve developers of smaller systems as well. At the end of this chapter, a nontraditional view of the role of user training in today's technological environment will be presented—a view that suggests that including more and new methods of training development and administration in the HRIS can have important, useful effects on HR systems development.

Involving Users in the Development Cycle

Faster development cycles and more flexible software now permit user testing to be performed on parts or modules of the system, during a 10- to 20-day period immediately following the development of each user process or system module. During that time, users decide whether to accept or reject the process or module, and make suggestions for possible improvements. Essentially, they get to answer the question, "Is this what you want?"—often by responding, "It's close, but it would be better if it worked in the following fashion."

A planned, detailed approach to user testing can include each user transaction and option in a work process and require user evaluation of all results. These results are recorded for review by the systems developers. Without a detailed, comprehensive plan, certain problems or anomalies may be overlooked in testing. Further, as discussed below, the tests performed should be sufficiently comprehensive to assure that the new process is what the user desires.

Types of HRIS Testing

Several different types of data and systems testing should be performed.

First, individual transactions should be entered that involve the processes and functions of the populations and system constituents—employees, applicants, beneficiaries, plan options, etc.—including both correct and incorrect situations. These transactions will be data values, dates, and code sets for any and all fields in the system. Combinations and sets of transactions designed to test the logic will be entered.

Another set of tests should include selected operational portions of the system as they apply to a process or module. Such processes include end-of-the-month, end-of-the-year, file load/unload features and data transmission, and linkages with other systems such as word processing, payroll, financial, and external systems. Complex examples of combinations of transactions or scenarios can be constructed to reflect the user environment.

A third type of test should be made on the system's construction and security, both from an intrusion standpoint, to test the risks from outside entry and on a "robustness" basis, including system backup and recovery capabilities.

Fourth, every display, report, and system output should be reviewed and tested for content and accuracy. Audit trails, transaction logging systems reports, as well as normal reports will be tested. For example, users should ensure that data entered and edited through the screen is not corrupted or changed in any fashion as it flows through the modules, unless it is changed in conformance with user instructions.

Fifth, volume and "stress" testing should be performed to ascertain the system's performance characteristics under normal conditions and those of heavy loading.

User involvement in all aspects of this testing is critical, since users provide the quality control and certification of the final product. Without conducting some or all of the testing themselves, users will not fully understand the system, nor will they be certain when they accept the system from the developers that it will perform according to specifications.

User testing should address the completeness and quality of the data; that is, is the data all there and is it correct? Are the files, the database, and the reports essentially accurate with respect to the data entered? Did the edits screen out erroneous and incomplete data? Are the logic rules correct? Were they applied in the proper sequence?

Another aspect of testing is to see whether the work processes as they have been reengineered (Chapter 5) are correct. For example, were all the functions performed in a new-hire or salary-change process as the user envisions? Were all the month-end or weekly processes completed? Were the appropriate help commands and panels presented?

Lastly, is the system operating correctly from a speed and performance standpoint as well as from a work flow and esthetics point of view? Does it respond fast enough? How does it perform with five people on the LAN? With 15? What about 50 at one time? Remember, the user base will eventually include both supervisors and employees.

Testing Plans

Because the nature and objectives of each type of test will vary, each will have a different methodology associated with it. Tests of individual data transactions, such as a transaction constructed to simulate a certain type of benefit calculation or payout option, would be handled quite differently from a test of the payroll print function. In the first case, individual data is entered via the main terminal; in the second, data is not entered but is printed in a controlled, secure computer room. So the method of testing may be different for each component of the system.

For each module, there should be an overall plan for testing, which should consist of at least the following components:

- A schedule for the test, with dates and milestones
- A test specifications approach and unit test plans
- Test participants
- Responsibilities of each participant
- A test data construction plan
- Test review procedures
- Acceptance criteria procedure

Testing itself is conducted only after the plan has been circulated and approved.

The testing plan for each module should outline the major tasks and responsibilities of those involved. An example is shown in Table 10-1.

Each test should first be conducted separately and repeated separately, and then conducted in conjunction with other modules as they are approved. Linkage of unproven modules and testing of joined modules should not be attempted until they have been tested and accepted as separate units.

The test plan should specify the testing schedule, with actual dates that the testing should begin, milestones in the 10- to 20-day time period, and sequence of testing processes.

Testing Dimensions

User training should include testing each module, user function, and work process for at least the following dimensions:

- *Accuracy.* Is the data entered and accepted/rejected accurately, i.e., according to the edit rules?

- *Completeness.* Can all the components and elements of the HRIS be accessed and updated?

- *Authorization.* Is data only viewed or is it also changed and altered? Is access to both data and functions properly authorized and controlled according to the rules?

- *Reconstruction.* Can all files and procedures be interrupted and recovered properly?

- *Integrity.* Does the data, once stored, remain accurate, or is it corrupted? Are reports correct?

- *Security.* Is the system protected from intrusion or disaster?

Table 10-1. Module Testing Plan

Task	Responsibility
Receipt of module from developer	IS
Installation of module on computer	IS
Issuance of module test plan	Project manager
Development of module test specifications	User/project manager
Creation of test data	User
Actual test (may be multiple tests)	User
Review and evaluation of test result	User/project manager/IS
Notification of evaluation to developer	Project manager

- *Processing.*   Do the various jobs, programs, and processing cycles — e.g., end-of-month reporting — run through to completion accurately? Is the system navigation pathed correctly?

- *Responsiveness.*   Is the system sufficiently responsive to user needs to provide adequate service levels? Do reports, screens, panels, ad-hoc report generators, and displays respond?

- *Compliance.*   Are the processes in accordance with the specifications, plans, personnel policies, and with legal rulings and regulations?

- *Connectivity.*   Does each module work with the appropriate interfaces and with other modules?

- *Satisfaction.*   Does the module meet the user's desired level of satisfaction?

Errors and omissions should be documented and reviewed with the project manager and system developer for discussion and resolution. Problems, especially critical ones uncovered in the testing phase, should be noted; these will have to be corrected by the developer and resubmitted to the testing team for retesting. The testing iteration will then begin again with new dates established.

Programming Assistance

The first area where information systems assistance may be required is to establish separate test data sets and modules. In order to test fully and to control the test properly, it is usually recommended that each user or user group have its own test area in the computer. These separate areas are for retention of a database of test cases, which can be applied to each module and each function of the system. These versions and test data sets must be kept separate from other testers, usually in test libraries, so that results of each unit test can be properly recorded, examined, and evaluated, and not overwritten or destroyed by other users. Often, the logic needed to test fully is an involved process. With a common database, there is risk that another user could alter the data, its structure, tables, etc., while you are conducting the testing, thereby changing or destroying your test.

It is suggested that multiple versions be loaded in a library with test files and disk areas for each module, along with test data sets for each user.

Another need for programming during the testing process is to generate sufficient volumes of information. It is often very difficult to produce a large number of transactions on an immediate basis to produce a valid stress and volume test. Therefore, a program that reformats data from an existing file might be a strategy for testing response time with a full database. Another might be to computer-generate or copy sufficient dummy records to accomplish the same end. In either case, where thousands of records are needed, programming may well be the answer.

Actual Testing—Let the Users Have at the System

During testing, the users should work through the list of tests of functions and processes they have outlined in their test specifications. For example, if the updating of basic data is being tested, the testing must provide the answer to the fundamental question, "Is the data written correctly to all records and files?" However, other questions need to be addressed as well: Are duplicates getting created? Does the correct data go into other records as well? Is it fully accepted, or only partially? Are the reports correct? Are calculations on the data handled properly?

The first attempt to discover errors is usually to try to put "bad" data into the system, with the purpose of getting at the easier edits and trying to "crash" the system. Following free-format testing, when users enter virtually anything into the system and generate lots of transactions, a more disciplined approach is called for.

The testing specifications, developed by the user ahead of time, control the types and extent of the testing for each unit and function. Tests for accepting good data, rejecting good data, accepting bad data, rejecting bad data, etc., are conducted. Isolation of each error or omission found is essential, with screen number, data contents, files and contents, printouts of screens, and test examples documented for each problem encountered.

In an on-line interactive system, it is often difficult to duplicate the exact system environment, so detailed documentation will expedite the process.

A useful strategy where there are sufficient users is to use a different focus. Each user tests for as many of the test dimensions as are applicable for that module. For example, all modules usually have data-entry capability and, therefore, this feature can be tested for accuracy, completeness, and authorization. However, not all modules may have a processing component. In addition, the project manager and the IS organization also conduct tests. Each user is expected to conduct tests independently and to deliver to the project manager the test results, documentation, and an overall evaluation of findings. Periodic audits of the test process should be conducted by the project manager. A goal could be to have an initial evaluation of the testing about halfway through the testing period. An example of the testing specifications for a new hire/rehire process is shown in Figure 10-1.

Another user testing scenario is shown in Figure 10-2, which indicates how to test HRIS logic among modules.

Another, more traditional set of checks to ensure data logic is shown in Figure 10-3.

Training for HRIS Users

User involvement in tests of the system as it is being developed not only assures that the completed system will be ready for the users, but that the users will be ready for the system. Each work simulation, test exercise, user interview, and report on the results of user testing provides opportunities to begin training users in new procedures and other aspects of the HRIS-in-development; further, user testing provides the project team with opportunities to begin work in these important areas:

- Development of a modularized training program that provides appropriate training to various HRIS constituencies, addressing the different needs of different users in the organization
- Planning and development of appropriate formats and media for training and documentation, which may include on-line help, performance-support technology, or computer-based training that becomes part of the HRIS being developed
- User testing of initial training programs, to assure the training's effectiveness, identify problems in advance, and evaluate the need for systems or work process changes that should be made to the HRIS before it is turned over to users or incorporated into user training programs

This last objective of training development—to change the work itself (another example of reengineering) when it becomes clear that such changes will be more cost-efficient or effective than trying to devise training adequate to user needs—may be the most important reason why the HRIS training effort should begin early in the development process, while systems developers still have choices about HRIS features and characteristics. For example, if a given procedure for executing a transaction is unusually complicated or difficult to learn, perhaps a system change could simplify or eliminate the procedure. Or help screens could be added to this part of the program to guide the user through the steps.

In all of these areas, however, the early development of training and

- Test if new hire (NH) process will create a record for a new hire, i.e., an employee not currently or previously employed (as determined by the presence or absence of a record on the database).

- Determine if all NH employee data elements can be utilized and accept/reject information.

- Determine if all NH employee edits are in accordance with specifications for all changes.

- Determine if NH employee data can be deleted by normal usage.

- Test to see if a rehired employee (RH) can be entered as a NH.

- Test to transfer data in from applicant module (if that module has been developed)

- Test to see if employee status is calculated correctly.

- Test to see if work history is calculated correctly.

- Determine if mandatory fields can/cannot be bypassed.

- Print an employee's profile immediately upon creation of record.

- Test to see if a NH can be put in as a RH.

- Test to activate old information and have the new information merge with it correctly, not destroying the "old" information in the process.

- Determine if date sequence logic is working correctly, i.e., cannot have rehire date earlier than previous hire information.

- Test to see if an employee can be employed by two or more divisions/units concurrently.

- Determine if status code stays active and if employee can be paid if employee is active with at least one unit.

- Test to see if work history is tracking each unit correctly.

- Check posting of data common to both units to see if combinations of specific and common data can be displayed and printed correctly.

- Determine if access to one unit's data can be denied while permitting access to the other.

Figure 10-1. Sample user testing: new hire/rehire process.

- Test inconsistencies in hire, transfer, rehire, and death sequences.
- Terminate a death case; rehire death case.
- Rehire an active employee; terminate a terminated employee.
- Test applicant file with change of status in employee module.
- Put an applicant into a pay status in the employee file; terminate and rehire.
- Examine calculated fields to see if changes to one component affect another.
- Examine each form of user to ensure presence of data in system and that access to modules (security) cannot be breached in any module.
- Process pay changes, job changes to inactive employees.
- Test all service calculations — start/stop dates — to ensure soundness of logic or eligibility dates and premium calculations based on dates.
- Test retroactivity and logic of status, pay, and effective dates.

Figure 10-2. Sample user testing: logic sequence.

- New hire under age 16.
- New hire over age 75.
- Rehire without key data fields.
- Termination without forwarding address.
- New hire without pay status, salary, DOB, race/sex, etc.
- New hire with invalid date, i.e., future date.
- Acceptance of new hire with past dates of job and benefit service?
- New hire with salary change dates equal to hire date.

Figure 10-3. Sample user testing: data ranges and edits.

documentation, including testing on users or user-group representatives, offers key advantages in the ultimate effectiveness of a HRIS. One of the most important of these is the simple reality of most project-basis work in organizations: tasks put off to the end of a project, until apparently more pressing deadlines have been met, typically get short shrift from systems developers. Toward the end of a long, difficult project, some members of the team are thinking about their next assignment; others have already left; and both the enthusiasm and expertise that has achieved other implementation deadlines may be in short supply.

Audience-Specific Training

The HRIS user community is not monolithic in its training requirements. Not only do user needs vary according to functions such as benefits administration or affirmative action planning, but senior managers have different needs than mid-level analysts, support personnel, or employees generally.

Effective training development takes these differences into account, and creates different course content for users with different needs. When training and documentation are being considered at the same time as user testing is being performed, these different needs can be identified and planned for by the project team. One important requirement of user testing that should be borne in mind when training needs are being identified is to be sure that the "users" involved are truly "users," or truly representative of those who will eventually be using the HRIS. If the skills levels of those involved in user testing are significantly higher than those of the eventual users, important training needs may be underestimated or overlooked.

Training developed in audience-specific modules takes into account what specific types of users need to know, tailors training to work-related issues, and makes training more effective by eliminating surplus instruction that is irrelevant to particular users' needs.

Utilizing the Appropriate Training Technology

One of the most important reasons for identifying training needs and getting an early start on training and documentation is that choices about how to integrate training with the HRIS can be made during development, without going back and revising the system or adding training programs as an overlay to an existing system. These choices may represent cost-effective solutions to training needs, such as the addition of explanatory help screens within procedures, or may represent a totally new approach to systems architecture, such as a decision to switch to a graphical user interface (GUI) technology that effectively translates all screens and data from various systems to common screen formats, and where split-screens can be used to pull up the code set or help fields, and thus helps embed the training in the system itself.

The options available to systems designers in selecting formats and delivery mechanisms for HRIS training are theoretically broad and varied. They include:

- Traditional instructor-led classroom training, such as hands-on training that teaches basic computer skills, how to use a retrieval tool, or how to write a report
- Computer-based training (CBT) tutorials, typically a set of disks that instructs individual users on a PC, provides simulated work exercises, tests proficiency as the user progresses, and provides records of results to training administrators
- Performance-support tools, programs that allow users to move back and forth between HRIS software and the computer's random access memory and knowledge-based links to look up information or instruction as needed
- User manuals and other written documentation
- One-on-one training, either formally delivered or provided by experienced supervisors as part of on-the-job training
- A range of computer-based training provided within the HRIS programs themselves, such as on-line help screens, reference guides, glossaries, and other instruction and information.

Moreover, the technologies that can be utilized with computer-based training formats provide further options. Voice-activated systems can make a performance-support tool respond to a spoken question or key word; CBT linked to interactive video can walk a trainee through a simulated interview with a job applicant; multimedia computers can add sound and video to computer-based training programs; teleconferencing reaches many people at once.

All of these formats for the delivery of user understanding and HRIS training—as well as others such as video presentations and telephone hookups—have pros and cons depending on the situation. Instructor-led training has advantages for certain subjects and training audiences, such as entry-level personnel who are new to computer use. Performance-support tools that help users locate information quickly may be optimal for telephone response to inquiries; CBT has advantages when user turnover is high or when users are located at many dispersed locations; and so on. When user training is developed during systems design, and not added on once the technical configuration and HRIS procedures have been made final, HRIS developers have more freedom to select technology appropriate to users' needs.

Early "Testing" of User Training Can Change the Work Itself

Another reason for developing initial training during systems development, and testing the effectiveness of this training on representative users, is the opportunities this approach can provide for changing the system or work processes themselves, even beyond the users' stated "should-be" case. At times, systems developers can identify bottlenecks or troublesome procedures in advance, and address these issues through systems design.

For example, a certain set of screens used in an on-line performance-appraisal system may appear to designers to be self-explanatory, telling the supervisor how to enter ratings, select developmental activities appropriate to the appraisee's needs, and so on. But supervisors, when asked to use these screens without written documentation that explains what ratings mean, appear to need additional training. For one thing, appraisers do this only once a year; for another, many are managers who don't use computers in their regular work. User tests followed by trials of different training mechanisms to correct this training shortfall can inform a systems decision that will resolve the problem, perhaps through additional screens that carry user documentation.

In summary, new advances in computer design and development make it imperative that the user community become involved early and often in the system shake-down process, in order that they may help shape the work to their expectations.

PART 4

Cost-Justifying the Vision

11
Achieving Data Accuracy

Introduction: Why Is Data Accuracy Important?

One of the most important topics of HRIS management, and one that becomes increasingly pressing with the growing decentralization of systems that creates users in any of a dozen or more separate functions, many locations, with varying skills, and possibly in countries throughout the world, is data accuracy. Once the sole responsibility of a human resource information center (HRIC) or similarly centralized HRIS administrative organization, data accuracy in a decentralized environment usually requires a totally new approach, one that is guided by two essential principles.

First, when information is created, processed, and used by decentralized users, responsibility for its accuracy should be as close as possible to the users themselves. This is more efficient—avoiding back-and-forth transactions and data checks—and more likely to produce accurate data: Who knows course codes better than the training department, protected class codes better than EEO, or employees' home addresses better than the employees themselves? One reason for decentralization has always been to move data closer to its source, making data originators "owners" of that data and responsible for its accuracy. As discussed below, this has presented problems affecting accuracy, but the problems are surmountable.

Second, accuracy in decentralized environments requires that a number of systematic and procedural features be built into the systems, and monitored through sampling and other techniques. Those include edits, data verification programs, data standardization, design principles, and the use of measurements. Each is discussed in this chapter, along with the need for "accuracy management" coordinators at some level in the organization.

The importance of data accuracy cannot be overstressed, and it is important on a number of levels.

First, there is a functional necessity for accurate HRIS data, most notably in relation to payroll, compensation, benefits, and health and safety. Payroll check processing and financial reporting should not be 98 percent accurate, a rate that could cost a large company millions during the year. Reports filed with regulatory agencies, if inaccurate, may make the company subject to fines. A line manager or recruitment officer who hires a person with the wrong skills or who has not had safety training has created a costly problem, and so on.

Second, inaccurate data needs to be reconciled, corrected, validated, or "made right" at some point, especially if the bad data is costing the organization time or money. The amount or level of data accuracy you start with has a direct bearing on how much more time and money will be spent finding and correcting mistakes. As discussed later, some types of bad data are much harder to find and correct than others, which means that those who must wade through voluminous errors have a harder time focusing on the most hard-to-find mistakes.

The third reason is "soft," but no less important. People throughout the organization — from top management through users and employees — need to have confidence in the accuracy of HRIS data. Accuracy is one of the strongest "marketing" themes an HRIS can have, and the lack of it can doom future budget requests in advance. For those who would extend the reach of HRIS to a broader user community, or assure that all new applications are appropriately linked with the core HRIS, perceptions that the database is inaccurate represent a major obstacle. The same is true of employees generally, especially concerning personal information. If employees sense that data in their personnel records may be wrong, they will be much more likely to want to review such data — and less likely to believe in the system when they are passed over for a promotion or when a new benefits deduction is calculated. The HR department will end up answering questions in person that the system was designed to answer electronically.

In a very real sense, accuracy begets accuracy in a HRIS, as those working with quality issues know. Data entered correctly in the first place is easier to keep accurate; users accustomed to working with accurate data, like potential litterbugs on a spotless street, are more conscientious; validity checks are easier to handle when errors are few; and senior management is more likely to provide the resources needed to maintain data accuracy if the HRIS has earned their respect as a reliable provider of information.

Moving Data to Users: Problems and Solutions

Decentralization often presents HRIS management with a dilemma regarding accuracy. On the one hand, we *want* decentralized users to be responsible for accuracy; on the other, the user community is often its own worst enemy when it comes to data accuracy.

Accuracy studies in decentralized environments have yielded problems such as the following:

- Users have "other jobs" than HRIS administration; as part-time HRIS users, they cannot give data accuracy the time it deserves.
- Their supervisors frequently do not understand the importance of accuracy, or themselves have "other jobs" competing for their time and attention.
- Users do not retain the skills learned when they started, or lose written documentation explaining procedures, carrying data definitions, and other supporting documentation.
- Users have a high turnover rate, and newcomers lack training or their predecessors' attitude about the importance of accuracy.
- Users hired for their computer skills, such as word processing specialists, do not understand the functions they support, negating a chief advantage of "data ownership" at the functional level.
- Users with functional skills do not have the systems knowledge needed to select the right data elements, code sets, or follow complex procedures.

Despite all this "bad news" from studies and our own experience with users' attention to data accuracy, none of this vitiates the principle that most HRIS data should "belong" to users, who should originate it and assure its accuracy. The dilemma, of course, is that we cannot change the basic fact of organizational life that most users have other jobs that preclude their spending the time and attention needed on data administration. Further, most users in multifunctional human resource organizations do not originate all of the data they use: Managers in salary administration do not create performance appraisal or time and attendance data, for example; these come from the line organizations. The

HR managers would appreciate accuracy controls that would assure that data they accept from other sources is correct.

In decentralized environments, therefore, a combination of approaches is usually necessary to achieve optimal data accuracy. The first approach is the development of a conceptual model that puts data in the hands of users, but that assures some level of data administration and user training in a HRIS management organization. The second approach involves a series of key programs and systems attributes that assure continuing data accuracy in a HRIS, whether it is decentralized or not.

A Decentralized Model with Centralized Accuracy Control

The model we propose has several parts, as illustrated in Figure 11-1. The employee as inputter is shown at the upper left of the model. The system permits employee access to the system to perform several key functions, such as inquiring about their own data, status, and accuracy; initiating or updating selected functions, such as names, addresses, and the like; and enrolling in medical plans, changing investment directions, and so on. The system also permits this employee – under proper usage constraints and security provisions – to access open jobs for which he or she might be qualified. This also extends to training programs. It becomes the employee's responsibility to verify the data on the system, and if an error is detected then the system permits the appropriate change to be made. The HR system transmits that change either directly into the system, if no further approval is required, or routes it to the supervisor or responsible HR function for further approval and review.

The line manager or supervisor is shown at the lower left of Figure 11-1. This manager can access the system and review certain employee transactions or changes, schedule work, assign employees to training, perform salary administration, and do appraisals. With the employees' participation, the manager might lay out selected employee development plans.

A series of measurements statistics and control information is also available to line supervisors. These might cover productivity, headcount control, budget variances, and other topics, in charts and statistical reports. Managers can see their own organization data and records of the employees under them. Under certain circumstances, they can also see the records of other employees in the company. For instance, they may

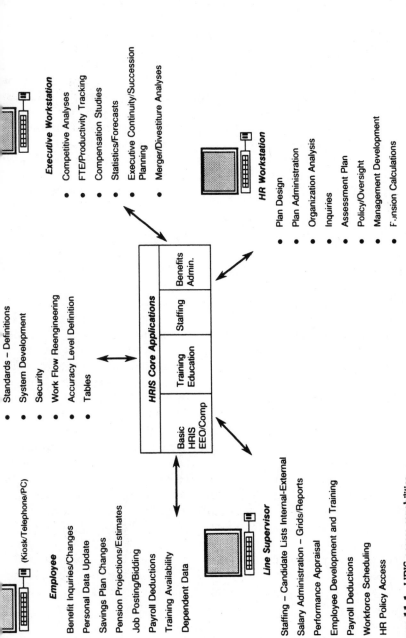

Figure 11-1. HRIS access capabilities.

Employee (Kiosk/Telephone/PC)
- Benefit Inquiries/Changes
- Personal Data Update
- Savings Plan Changes
- Pension Projections/Estimates
- Job Posting/Bidding
- Payroll Deductions
- Training Availability
- Dependent Data

Executive Workstation
- Competitive Analyses
- FTE/Productivity Tracking
- Compensation Studies
- Statistics/Forecasts
- Executive Continuity/Succession Planning
- Merger/Divestiture Analyses

HR Workstation
- Plan Design
- Plan Administration
- Organization Analysis
- Inquiries
- Assessment Plan
- Policy/Oversight
- Management Development
- Pension Calculations

HRIS Core Applications

Basic HRIS EEO/Comp	Training Education	Staffing	Benefits Admin.

- Standards – Definitions
- System Development
- Security
- Work Flow Reengineering
- Accuracy Level Definition
- Tables

Line Supervisor
- Staffing – Candidate Lists Internal-External
- Salary Administration – Grids/Reports
- Performance Appraisal
- Employee Development and Training
- Payroll Deductions
- Workforce Scheduling
- HR Policy Access

225

be able to view the file of an employee who has bid on a job under this particular supervisor's control.

On the right-hand side of the model are the various user groups, such as senior management and executives, and normal HR functional experts who act as policy setters and provide oversight.

At the top of the model, the HR technology team is responsible for maintaining the overall HRIS structure, handling systemwide administration and standards, and introducing new technologies.

Each of the HR groups must play an ongoing functional responsibility role in this model. For instance, the employment department, the benefits department, salary administration, EEO, etc., must work with the HR technology team to define the code sets, process rules, data standards, and definitional groupings for the entire, corporatewide HR system.

Further, the technology team must coordinate and manage all changes to the systems, and help implement new releases to the system. For example, in past years, if a new sucession planning and development program were to be introduced, the functional HR group responsible for that area would more than likely send a package of material to the various line functions explaining what levels of employees needed to be coded, how forms were to be filled out, how the people were to be appraised and judged as to their future potential, development, experiences, and so forth. In the new environment, with the new systems in place, the electronic equivalent of that paper distribution process must be implemented. Therefore, the functional user and the HR technology team must jointly develop the screens, panels, queries, edits, and data contents of the process. Of equal importance is how to communicate to the line organizations and how to maintain the accuracy levels of the data. Training users in the use of the system falls to the HR technology team.

In order to administer the system effectively, it is suggested that each line organization have a designated coordinator with whom the HR technology team can work on a day-to-day basis. These contacts are a vital communication link for the organizational knowledge that will be transferred in systems implementations. These coordination points are extremely important, for example, in order to achieve uniform implementation of the process rules and data sets. In a sense, they become the local trainer and system interpreter for the users at their locations. And they represent a local contact to ensure that the data accuracy is sufficient.

There are several options as to where to place these implementation points or coordinators. It depends on whether the controlling HRIS ad-

ninistration is in the human resource department, the systems depart-
nent, or has been fully delegated to the line functions. Another ques-
ion is whether or not these units should be located in a centralized
livisional organization, or out in the line functions themselves. It is usu-
lly recommended that these coordinators be matrixed to a centralized
rganizational responsibility, in order to develop effective extension of
IR policy making and personnel matters. That way you can achieve
nore consistent policy making and interpretation of the various func-
ional components of the system.

Components of an Accurate HR System—Sampling Plans and Data Interception

everal major components should be addressed in a HRIS data accu-
acy program, most of which apply to centralized as well as decentral-
zed systems. In a decentralized environment, however, the effective in-
orporation of most of these parts into the overall data accuracy
rogram is even more important than it would be if all data were en-
ered, updated, and processed by a centralized technology.

It should be stressed that the overriding concern of a data accuracy
rogram is to prevent errors from occurring in the first place. If data is
ncorrect within the borders of the system, it is obviously much harder
o correct. Even when data resides in more than one database and one
latabase is considered "correct," a conscientious data verification and
learance program means that all discrepancies must be explained and
econciled. Either way, errors that find their way into the system can
epresent the most time-consuming and expensive problem of systems
dministration. It's much easier to design systems and procedures that
eep them out in the first place.

An effective HRIS data accuracy program should include at least the
ollowing characteristics.

- Comprehensive local data edits
- Standardization of codes, process rules, and data content
- Measurements based on statistical sampling
- Data verification programs
- Built-in design and administrative controls

Comprehensive Local Data Edits

During the systems specifications stage of HRIS development, each data element is given "edit requirements" that are designed to prevent the incorrect entry or use of data. These are systematic barriers to errors, and in well-designed systems they incorporate error messages and help screens that not only prevent mistakes but tell the user how to get it right. Data should be subject to these edits at the earliest point they are detected by the system. See (Chapter 3, Principle 5.1.)

There are several types of systems edits, the most common being (1) simple code or content checks, (2) range validation, (3) table checks, and (4) relational edits.

The most basic HRIS edits check the size and type of data—such as the code for a work location—or the data content, such as the code for male or female (all other codes are errors).

Range validation edits check to assure that data falls within an allowable range—e.g., that a person's salary is within the range specified by the person's salary grade, or that a merit pay increase falls within the allowable limits under the salary increase guide.

Table checks validate data against tabular data—such as skills codes, job numbers, or other organizational data that applies to whole categories of jobs or people—to assure that a code carried in the HRIS database means what it should mean.

Relational edits, sometimes referred to as "in context" checks, are often the most expensive but frequently the most effective type of edit; they require access to data outside the borders of the system or application. For example, if an employee is asking for an insurance plan that includes family coverage for six dependents, a relational edit would check payroll's W-2 data to verify that the employee has six dependents. An extension of this type of edit goes deeper into the record. For example, if a person is requesting enrollment in a certain training course requiring prerequisites, the edit could check to see of the person has satisfied these requirements. These edits can be difficult to develop, because to be true edits they must prevent incorrect data entry. As noted earlier, the first priority of a data accuracy program should be the prevention of errors before they enter the system.

Over the years, and especially today with the growth of decentralized systems and new emphasis on user access and distributed processing, there has emerged an ambivalence about the need for "tight" edits and a certain amount of leeway in data accuracy. At times, the absence of good source documentation or a user's lack of knowledge about what is on the database can prevent the user from entering or changing data. Stringent edits can prevent many users from using the system at all, or

educe the productivity of other users who need outside help to do their
obs.

For some kinds of data and in some applications, 100 percent data
ccuracy may be less important than users' ability to perform their jobs
rithout delay. Information about where a 50-year-old manager went to
igh school is surely less critical than her contribution to the 401(k) sav-
1gs plan. In other cases, supplementary programs—such as a set of
uick-hire screens that get a person on the payroll before all required
ata is available—may be appropriate. At times, some level of compro-
1ise may be necessary to balance functionality and accuracy.

tandardization of Codes and Data
ontent

)ne of the key issues in HRIS data accuracy has always been the stan-
ardization of data element definitions. Every item of information, each
f hundreds of different data elements, including codes, must have its
wn standard definition—what it means, how it is expressed, and its
omponents when it is an element made up of various components. For
xample, if the data field requires a home address, there must be a stan-
ard, uniform way of entering state designations, as well as variations
uch as apartment numbers or addresses that should read "c/o" (care of)
omeone besides the employee. If post office box numbers are used,
iat too must be defined and spelled out in a data dictionary and com-
iunicated to users entering new data.

The basic reason why this standardization has always been an issue in
IRIS data specification writing and use is the infinite variability of peo-
le and jobs. Further, very little information about living human beings
 permanent, and organizational change affecting work and workers is
constant. At least one entertainment company, for example, has a
eld for "previous sex code," as well as current sex code.

Even the most apparently immutable, clear-cut data elements can
resent problems of data accuracy if not uniformly defined and stan-
ardized for all users and applications. A person's name, for example,
ould be entered as John Doe, John A. Doe, J. A. Doe, Jack Doe, John
ndrew Doe, and J. Andrew Doe (or you can call him "Johnny"), all in
ifferent application-specific files, or by different users entering data.
Vhich name is accurate? (In this case, the name on the person's social
ecurity card is probably the correct entry, given the need for accurate
ix filings.)

In many applications, of course, data elements such as names, home
ddresses, and organizational information such as job titles are down-

loaded from a core system, to assure that all users follow standard formats, definitions, and data field contents. In some applications—such as in an applicant-tracking or employment system where numerous users at many locations are entering "new" data on job applicants—this may not be easy. In these cases, an alternative is to write standardized help screens that all users can call up when entering or changing an item of data. The screens might include such features as:

- An error message when an entry is incorrect
- A template or mask showing the correct format or structure
- A list of applicable codes or rules for usage, with any needed explanation (or a message referring the user to a written manual of codes)

Of course, standardization of data elements and codes needs to be worked out with users, usually in the systems specifications stage of development. The same criteria of functional necessity that goes into all other systems development decisions should determine data definitions. For example, the need for accurate tax reporting to the IRS and other government agencies mandates the "correct" spelling of a person's name.

Without standardization, systematic validity checks that compare data against a base of "known accurate" data are of course impossible and decentralized control through the HRIS cannot be achieved.

Measurements Based on Statistical Sampling

Periodic data verification programs—whether they consist of data matching programs, sequential analysis of "what happens" in a given transaction or activity, spot checks, or periodic reviews of data by users—should be an integral part of data management. The pros and cons of these different types of programs, each designed to clear errors in a HRIS database and related systems, are discussed in the next section.

Before developing the data verification plan, however, the HRIS technology team or HRIS management organization needs to have a way of measuring the ongoing accuracy of the HR system and its component parts. Measurements of accuracy are essential in order to set priorities in the development of data verification programs. They tell the technology team, for example, that data coming from one field location is only 95 percent accurate when all other locations have a 99 percent accuracy rate; or that social security numbers companywide are 99.9 percent accurate while EEO "protected class" designations are only 85 percent accurate. Policy decisions based on the functional necessity

or accuracy, perhaps stated in a performance standard, can then guide
he allocation of resources to be deployed in data verification programs.

Given the amount of data in most fully developed HR systems, and all
f the different events and transactions that occur involving data, the
ask of developing a procedure that measures the accuracy of all or even
parts of the database can be a formidable one. Many records can be au-
omatically checked in audits that compare one database against an-
ther; but, as discussed in the section on data verification, this process
las its limitations, beginning with the fact that much research may be
equired to establish which of two data elements that do not match is
accurate."

A sampling technique developed at AT&T in the 1970s, when the
Bell System Personnel Data System included data generated in over 25
lifferent operating companies with varying levels of accuracy, offers
ignificant advantages as a model with which to measure data accuracy.
Instead of measuring all transactions, AT&T developed a plan that as-
esses the accuracy of a statistically significant number of data elements — such as 8 percent of all job function codes in an organization.
Using the statistical sample and an employee code index, users in the
organization being measured were the judges of whether a piece of in-
ormation was incorrect. An error might be a mistake in coding, an er-
or in transmission, data that had not been updated, or any other type
of error.

The number of errors was then placed over the total number of in-
oming transactions in the sample and an error rate established. For example, all documents generating change to the job function code
ormed the base, and the number of errors found became the error
ate. This data was then judged to ascertain whether the error rate was
beyond the performance standard.

Data Verification Programs

One essential component of an effective data accuracy plan is an ongo-
ng program that periodically checks the accuracy and validity of all
data elements or sets of elements. This may be done once a year, quar-
erly, or more frequently for certain highly critical sets of data elements,
such as payroll-related data, but it should be a matter of HRIS policy
that all data elements are checked in a scheduled program of some
kind, and then cleared.

The "systems approach" to data verification is to run a program that
matches elements from one database against another, which automatically flags discrepancies. This approach at first seems easiest, because it
simply cascades databases against one another and churns out a list of

possible errors, items that do not match. The difficulties with this method emerge when it comes to clearing these possible errors: Who verifies that the information in one database is correct, how did the wrong data get into the database, and what can be done to prevent this from happening again?

The identification of discrepancies in a database matching program is usually just the first step in a long, laborious process that needs to be coordinated by a HRIS management organization, and will ultimately involve originators of data in several places, supervisors, users, managers responsible for affected functions, and sometimes employees themselves. Research is involved because a discrepancy alone does not tell the HRIS accuracy investigators which—if either—nonmatching data element is correct. Also, some errors are easier to clear than others. If a person's name is carried two different ways—as J. A. Doe and John Doe—it's easy to check the social security name and use that. If the company has undergone a phased-in reorganization that changed numerous job titles and job descriptions over a period of time, finding out "who did what when" may be considerably more complex, time consuming, and expensive.

The other problem with matching databases is that not all data elements are truly comparable, and those that are may be limited in number. If a payroll database is run against HR's, for example, length-of-service calculations may be somewhat different—one driven by a benefits plan, the other by an anniversary date. In any case, there are usually only a dozen or so "common" data elements in separately developed payroll and HR systems, which may leave hundreds of items unchecked.

While database matching will always have its place in a data verification program—especially in large organizations, and for critical data elements that need to be reviewed frequently in a cost-effective manner—other programs should usually be incorporated into the overall data verification effort. These range from scheduled programs that have users check their own data at least quarterly or once a year to methods of giving employees access to the data for periodic checking. Employee access to their own data—through printed reports they can take home, on-line screens checked at PCs on their desks or at kiosks, or voice-response systems utilizing telephone lines—can be a highly effective way of correcting errors.

Periodic accuracy checks can also be built into certain applications that use data, of course. In a performance appraisal system that calls for annual appraisals (and, in well-designed programs, more frequent reviews of employee progress), the first system output received by appraisers is often a screen or form for verification. Information such as ob titles, objectives, biographical data, and last year's rating can be checked by the user at the source, before actual use.

Other types of data verification that have a role in a data accuracy program, but that do not replace scheduled, periodic analysis and error clearance, include spot checking with data subjects and sequential analysis of selected work flows or processes. Both offer opportunities to cost-effectively identify and correct localized data accuracy problems, and when this informal method of checking for errors produces results that warrant a major data accuracy program, spot checks are a decision-support tool.

A spot check of data subjects can be as easy as making a phone call to find out if Jane Doe received her scheduled merit pay increase in her last paycheck, or a call to the Cleveland office manager to confirm headcount. Selecting data and events at random, the HRIS technology team is simply ascertaining that what the HRIS says is true is actually true, by going to the real world for confirmation.

Sequential analysis examines the steps or flow of data in selected transactions. What happens when a new hire is entered? Or, within that process, what happens in background checks of new hires? This is a form of work-flow analysis as discussed in Chapter 5, with the focus here on the accuracy of data.

Built-In Design and Administrative Controls

In addition to the above components, an effective data accuracy program often stems from HRIS design principles identified earlier in this book, and the work of a "coordinating infrastructure," part of the job of HRIS management in even the most decentralized systems.

The design principles that apply include the following:

- Extension of data entry, use, and responsibility to the lowest possible level, or to the level of the data "owners" who know most about its truth.

- The massive use of tables and table administration as a separate function

- Where possible, the elimination of reediting within the borders of the system

In addition, the HRIS management organization must take oversight responsibility for data accuracy, centralizing some tasks and providing data coordination points as needed.

12
Cost Justification Methodology and Model

Historically, human resource systems projects have been very difficult to cost-justify through cost/benefit analysis. As information and management support systems, they have usually one or both of two objectives: (1) to produce better, more accurate, more useful information for management to improve the quality of decision making; and (2) to deliver data and automated processes to payroll, benefits, and other functions to meet legal and corporate requirements.

The first of these objectives, and the specific benefits that derive from its accomplishment, depend to a great extent on the "strategic fit" of HRIS in the organization. How well will it help support critical success factors and other business goals, both in HR and in the organization generally? And in certain areas, such as the provision of decision-support data, how do you quantify the benefits of having data you never had before, such as job skills data that improves HR utilization, the effectiveness of training, or the ability to make decisions that improve product or service quality?

Regarding the second objective, the automation of functional requirements, some HRIS benefits are easier to quantify than others. Most HRIS cost justification in the past has focused on this area, often presenting "laundry lists" of benefits such as more efficient payroll processing, less time-consuming benefits administration, or less costly compliance with governmentally required reports. The employer's "risk" in not having a HRIS to provide data – the shortcomings of existing systems and procedures versus the benefits of a new HRIS—have usually been factored in. As discussed in Chapter 5, however, the most significant and compelling reasons for automating HR work are yet to be seen in most organizations, and will emerge from work-flow analysis and the reengineering of work *before* existing processes are automated.

Thus, the methodology for cost justification presented here is an all-encompassing one. It suggests an approach that identifies immediate costs, project development costs, and continuing operating costs of the HRIS; benefits estimation covers both tangible, direct benefits and intangible or indirect benefits. Then, a model for analyzing and presenting overall cost/benefits is presented, followed by a case study of cost justification for the hypothetical Alpha Company HRIS Project.

It is important to emphasize that HRIS cost justification *can* be done, in a credible, businesslike fashion, without relying on vague promises of improved efficiency or management quality. Moreover, it must be done by HR and HRIS managers seeking the major corporate resources that may be needed to support the kind of human resource information systems envisioned by this book. The approach discussed below, and exemplified in the case study of the Alpha Company, has three essential components, no one of which can be given anything less than comprehensive, realistic analysis before asking top management to invest in a new HRIS. They are:

- *Cost estimation,* covering the costs of HRIS development as well as the ongoing costs of operating, maintaining, and enhancing systems
- *Benefits evaluation,* determining the benefits, both tangible and intangible, to be derived from the new system
- *Cost/benefit model development,* which calculates a payback for the project and presents a formula for establishing return on investment (ROI) in the years after development.

Project Cost Estimation

The project team must estimate the cost of the new HRIS as precisely as possible. As it is very difficult to determine projected costs exactly, care must be taken to specify the borders of the system and what the project entails. For example, does project cost include the salaries and benefits of the users? The new software costs *and* hardware, or only the software? What about future modules and enhancements?

The estimating procedure must therefore include the definition of the project, its scope and boundaries, and what assumptions underlie the estimate — the daily or hourly charge rate, the cost of hardware, etc. And the team must estimate as precisely as possible the costs involved in both developing the initial HRIS and in maintaining and enhancing the system on an ongoing basis.

Project Development Costs

Estimating the costs of building the initial HRIS can be approached from several different perspectives, including (1) task estimating, (2) experience costing, and (3) external verification.

Task Estimating.   Task estimating is the most detailed approach, since it involves outlining each process involved in developing the HRIS and estimating the time (in work hours or days) and materials required to complete each task. Also, task estimates are needed for the entire project — which are often difficult to determine in advance. What is required is to make some assumptions regarding the size, scope, and systems development methodologies to be used in the HRIS project, and then to estimate an expected cost based on those assumptions. This will produce a basis, a standard, or a range of time and costs that might be used for each task in the system development cycle. A "degree of difficulty" could be established as well, since a more difficult task (one encountered for the first time, or a more technically complex task) may take more time than a relatively routine one and therefore cost more. Estimates of tasks are needed whether custom-developing a system or purchasing a product, since either approach involves human effort which needs to be costed out. Table 12-1 is an example of estimating the tasks involved in determining the scope of a HRIS. If the degree of difficulty were also to be estimated, a 20 to 50 percent range could be applied around the task, depending on the actual process and how management feels about the team's ability to perform against the expected (standard) estimate. This technique is useful in that routine tasks and those more near at hand are easier to estimate than those that are not done as frequently, or that are some months or years in the future. For example, a $25,000 task could be estimated at a range of $20,000–$30,000, with a 20 percent variance rather than an absolute $25,000. A wider spread can also be used if the team is less certain of eventual costs.

The task estimation process is based on the premise that each and every task is priced. This may be almost impossible for the entire HRIS project, since the cost of specific technologies which the team will employ are not always known in advance. For example, if prototyping and

Table 12-1. Example of Estimating Time to Determine HRIS Scope

Task	Estimate of Days
Initial draft of HRIS processes	3
Review with corporate users	3
Meetings with project team and analysis	10
Secondary draft; meeting with advisory team	4
Re-review/adjustments	10
Analysis of impact of technology	10
Presentation to steering committee	2
Documentation and final report	8
Total number of days	50
Total cost at $500/day	$25,000

CASE tools are utilized or specific software products are chosen for their system enablers, the task times will be reduced. If a fully customized approach is deemed to be best, the precise list of tasks obviously will be different than if a package-modification approach is adopted. And even for similar tasks, the time to complete a task will vary.

When this approach is used each area—i.e., labor, test time, quality checking, documentation, and processing costs—are all estimated. In addition, initial data load, data collection, and conversion costs must be included if at all possible.

Experience Costing. Experience costing relies on the past experience of the development team and asks questions such as these: "What in-house systems (or other development group) projects were similar to this? What projects using the same user definition and team approach would be about the same in terms of time and effort? What did those projects cost over what period of time? Did they use the same or a different system development approach? If a truly similar project cannot be found, is there one that is only slightly different from which an estimate can be made?"

The cost estimate in this approach most likely will not extend to a task-by-task identification and costing exercise. But if an estimate can be developed based on comparable experience, it will be helpful. Thus, this estimating process is predicated on the belief that the output which can be obtained from the same development organization under similar circumstances will be equivalent, since the same group in the same company will be doing the work.

External Verification. As a benchmarking process, it is often valuable to find out what similar projects cost other major American firms. The method of external verification should not be used exclusively, since even companies in the same industry are rarely alike. However, experienced systems developers do come to know that, where well-run organizations are concerned, using similar technologies, with a first-class team involved under good guidance and leadership, parallels can be drawn. Therefore, as an estimating tool, it is helpful to find what other companies are doing and have experienced in this regard. Care must be taken to find companies whose projects are as similar to the team's as possible, including the same functionality and software products.

Some categories of HRIS development and implementation costs are shown in Figure 12-1.

Development

- New systems' definition, scope, boundaries—requirements and specification
- Vendor evaluation process
- New software purchase/development
- Modification and initial development costs of purchased software
- Project team salaries and expenses
- Consultant expenses
- Hardware purchase or upgrades to existing hardware including DASD, networks, PCs, telecommunications
- New forms and supplies development
- System development tools (prototype, CASE)
- Programmers and analysts (custom and/or purchased software)
- Advisory participants/steering committee.

Implementation

- Testing-systems and user acceptance
- Initial data collection
- Conversion programming
- Training and documentation
- Training of users
- Communications
- Parallel processing costs
- New forms and procedures.

Figure 12-1. Categories of HRIS development and implementation.

Ongoing/Recurring Costs

Ongoing costs are similar to start-up costs, but with an added emphasis on steady-state operation. The system's impact on the user population must also be considered. In calculating ongoing costs, the current cost components which are external to or independent of the user, and the cost components that are related to the user, must be determined.

External-to-the-User Cost Components. Ongoing software, hardware, programming, and maintenance costs to support the system are typical external cost components. Other components might include outside charges for third-party expenditures, service bureaus, forms, training costs, and other cost items which apply to all users, such as management, documentation, rental, and depreciation.

By identifying both current and projected future costs for each component, a reasonable estimate of the net impact can be derived. Because of rapid changes in technology, a new HRIS based on packaged software (versus a custom-developed system) may have lower ongoing external costs, since the vendor may include extensive support in the annual maintenance agreement.

User Costs. The reason for estimating user costs separately is that new systems applications in HR invariably affect the time users spend on HR activities. Normally, the time users spend on many repetitive tasks will be reduced under the new system, or eliminated altogether if work-flow analysis and a reengineering approach were used. Estimates of the time currently spent on a given work activity must be gathered if the system affects that activity. These estimates can be obtained by measuring samples of work directly, using consultants or others trained in work-flow analysis, or activity-analysis techniques. As explained in Chapter 5, this process must precede development of the new system, or user costs may not in fact be lower.

The two sets of ongoing costs then comprise the expected costs in the postimplementation environment. These have to be compared to the existing costs to maintain and support the current environment. For example, suppose that the employment function today has approximately these annual costs in these categories:

Employment interviews and staff (four employees)	$260,000
Computerized systems expense	50,000

Forms, records, supplies, telephone	20,000
Outside agency fees (30 hires @ $20,000)	600,000
Space, overhead, temporaries	40,000
	$970,000

By reengineering the processes, thereby altering the staffing work, and installing certain on-line employment systems with new features and controls, the users and the team believe that the steady-state operation would be changed to the following, primarily through better internal placement procedures and reduction of outside agency fees:

Employment interviews and staff (four employees)	$300,000
Computerized systems expense	20,000
Forms, records, supplies, telephone	20,000
Outside agency fees (25 hires at $20,000)	500,000
Space, overhead, temporaries	30,000
	$870,000

The expected costs would drop by $100,000 per year in this example.

Evaluation of Project Benefits

Expected HRIS project benefits can be separated into two major types, either tangible or intangible. The tangible or direct benefits can be substantial and easily quantified. However, the indirect and intangible benefits can be just as important to the company, though much less easy to quantify. The two major types are explained below.

Tangible Benefits

The quantifiable, known areas where there will be direct savings or increased revenue to an organization as a result of the specific project or new system are direct, or tangible benefits. Each human resources function will have a number of areas where costs could be reduced through automation, and the project team and users should be able to construct the new system to penetrate deeply enough into work activities (through reengineering) to be able to reduce such costs.

Some examples of direct benefits include:

- Total displacement of staff (e.g., elimination of staff needed for specific processes)
- Partial displacement of staff (productivity increase), most frequently evidenced by a reduction in time spent on a function or activity
- Reductions in operating costs of currently installed computer systems
- Reduction or elimination of outside services or costs
- More effective operation of a function
- Improved data quality and accuracy (when demonstrable)
- Quicker response to management or employee queries (when demonstrable)
- Avoidance of the cost of building a different system
- Reduction in hardware and software costs
- Reduced overtime, clerical expenses, contractor payments
- Reduced space requirements, telephone charges, mailing costs

Any area where costs can be demonstrably reduced can be considered a tangible benefit. Also, quality and service improvements can often be treated as tangible benefits. However, the intent is not just to bring computerization to an area, but to change the work sufficiently to produce a real saving. Therefore "tangible" generally implies direct savings that can be given a dollar value.

When business reengineering methodologies are used, there is a vast source of potential savings, most of which can be counted as direct savings because work hours are saved. The process of reengineering normally produces a more streamlined, efficient process, which can be translated into tangible savings.

For example, a given process which today is heavily paper-intensive, with little effective automation, and which has duplicate or triplicate human checkers, coders, and reviewers, can be altered to be more efficient. The resulting savings are then captured in the cost/benefit analysis as either tangible savings if they fall into one of the above categories, or intangible (see below) if they are more qualitative in nature. In our experience, as much as 75 percent of the work normally associated with human resources administration can be improved or eliminated outright. These savings are attainable with properly deployed HRIS modules and related technologies (voice and touch systems, scanners, etc.). Because of the need for work changes and organizational realignments, the early HRIS projects focused more on the database and information retrieval aspects of the systems. Now, however, cost and efficiency imperatives are overwhelming, and management is insisting on significant cost savings. The good news is that in most companies the tangible savings that can be identified are more than sufficient to generate a very favorable return on investment (ROI) for the HRIS project.

Huge savings can be achieved by eliminating unnecessary steps such as duplicate handling by HR, finance, supervisors, and the like. The new HRIS can and should perform the checks, controls, and balances that heretofore people had to perform. New knowledge-based tables, rules, processes, and procedures will further help eliminate low-end work for the HR and finance groups, and provide uniformity across the organization. The result is not only "people savings" due to less paper and form handling, but also a more consistent interpretation of policy and procedures.

Cost avoidance can generally be considered a one-time tangible benefit, as an offset to systems development costs, but only if it was a real budgeted item which definitely would have been an incurred cost.

Intangible Benefits

The intangible benefits of the HRIS are the most difficult of all to quantify. The first reaction of successful HRIS project managers to the phrase "intangible benefits" should be skepticism. Intangibility implies that a benefit cannot be measured, that no quantitative yardstick can be applied that shows one way of doing something is better than another way, and this should be seen as a challenge to the cost/benefit analyst seeking concrete rationales for HRIS investment levels. Many benefits of automation will indeed turn out to be intangible, but some that may seem so are merely difficult to measure in themselves, and require a broader, sometimes more "strategic" approach.

For example, the benefits derived from an employee benefits communications system that improves employees' understanding and appreciation of their benefits may, at first look, appear largely intangible. But what impact can the system be expected to have on morale-related factors such as unwanted turnover, hiring costs, and productivity? And if the benefits communication system supports a flexible benefits program that in itself reduces costs, such as one that includes less costly health maintenance organization (HMO) insurance coverage or other choices that have been designed to reduce or control benefits costs to the organization, more than employee morale may be involved, and benefits may be measurable.

A second reason that HRIS project managers should be skeptical about intangible benefits is that top management is likely to view these benefits with a skepticism of its own. Even when they are listed as "indirect" benefits, items such as "improved employee morale" seem like gratuitous throw-ins in a listing of benefits. Management may doubt the credibility of the entire document if it appears to be "padded" with superfluous, unsubstantiated benefits.

Thus, a project team conducting cost/benefit analysis should first attempt to relate intangible, indirect benefits to quantifiable data, before deciding whether or not to list one of these hard-to-measure items as unmeasurable. For example:

- The benefits of training are frequently hard to measure as cost savings or productivity improvements, especially when it is white-collar training for jobs without productivity measurements. But a system that not only tracks training and helps administer the function, but also incorporates new data on the *results* of training, such as new productivity measurements or competitive data, provides benefits that can be measured.

- The accuracy of information collected during the employment process—from previous employers to home address—may not seem critical to the employment process itself. Reference checks and address verification can be done later, once the applicant has been tentatively selected. But at what cost?

- A succession planning system that is basically designed to assure the continuity of leadership at the top may cover only 1 or 2 percent of the management population. But if it is integrated with an overall management development program, it can serve as a force to reduce turnover, inspire improved performance, and prepare managers for positions at *all* levels, thus multiplying benefits.

Indirect or intangible benefits of automation are often measurable in terms of employee morale (as determined by attitude surveys), hiring costs, turnover data, or performance measurements. At times, estimates of savings or other benefits can be made on the basis of competitive information: What happened to employment costs at the Ajax Company when they ran a help-wanted ad for systems analysts to work on a technically advanced, highly challenging new system? At other times, company-specific problems or conditions that are currently costing

- Faster and more accurate information on payroll and benefits administration, at corporate, business unit, other levels
- Improved new-hire information flow for faster placement of new employees
- Comprehensive data on workforce throughout the organization
- More accurate management information for decisions on deployment
- Reduced litigation costs, with the availability of more complete, accurate data
- Faster turnaround time on medical claims payments
- More accurate information on promotions and transfers
- Complete training information, including data on results
- More up-to-date, detailed data on medical insurance costs
- Faster response times on management and employee inquiries
- Reduced turnover among technical professionals seeking state-of-the-art work experience

Figure 12-2. Examples of indrect or intangible benefits.

more than they should may provide the basis for a dollars-and-cents benefit estimate. For example, exit interviews in a company experiencing expensive turnover rates among systems analysts may reveal that most are leaving because current technology is "behind the times," and is neither interesting nor professionally rewarding.

In putting a dollar value on apparently indirect benefits, however, the project team should be sure to qualify these items as "potential" benefits, supported by as much documented evidence as possible, and always estimate on the low side. A range, rather than a specific dollar amount that pretends to predict an exact outcome, is usually a good idea. Following are a few examples of how some intangible benefits of automation, such as those shown in Figure 12-2, might be estimated in cost/benefit analysis.

1. Improved new-hire information flow, which results in faster placements of new employees
   - Average orientation period or waiting time between new hire and work assignment with existing method: 5 days
   - Average payroll cost per day of waiting time: $200
   - Estimated reduction of waiting time per employee: 2–4 days

- Estimated new hires in year: 80–100 employees
- Potential savings in payroll costs incurred before new hires are productively employed: $32,000–$80,000

2. Avoidance of the cost of building or acquiring a separate system
   - Cost of system A, developed internally: $450,000
   - Cost of system B, a package: $300,000
   - Cost of system C, a heavily modified package: $400,000
   - Potential savings in avoided costs: $300,000–$450,000

The expected value of these types of intangible benefits can be quantified through the use of either probability weights or the pessimistic, "most certain" method outlined below. Also, benefits of systems integration should not be overlooked and should be estimated. Multiple systems with redundant data, each with separate maintenance teams and update cycles in different user areas, are expensive, and should be brought under common management when possible.

Support for the strategic direction of both the company and the HR department are also objectives which have intangible benefits. Also, there are benefits in obtaining competitive intelligence, enabling the personnel department and users to gain access to new and more relevant data sets regarding competitors' costs. It is impossible to include all the categories of intangible benefits, since they vary widely from company to company, but there are usually a great number of them.

A useful approach in estimating the value of intangible benefits is to discount the overall project team estimate to a more conservative number, since the management team will view the intangible benefits with as much skepticism as the HRIS manager does. Therefore, each number representing the potential dollar value of intangible savings could be reduced to a fraction of its estimated value if the team wishes to present more realistic or achievable benefits to management. For instance, if an intangible benefit of $100,000 was projected, the team could discount that to 50 percent or even 25 percent of the original number. In a sense, the project team is telling management that they too understand that these savings are "soft," but a certain percentage of them are real and obtainable and therefore should be counted.

The Cost/Benefit Model

The general formula for the computation of HRIS cost/benefits (CB) can be represented as:

$$CB = (D - A) + [(B_1 - C_1) + (B_2 - C_2) + (B_3 - C_3) + (B_4 - C_4) +$$

$$(B_5 - C_5)]$$

where: D = initial development costs (as explained above)
  A = cost avoidance
  B_1 = benefits from the project in year 1 after development
  C_1 = ongoing costs associated with the project in year 1
  B_2 = benefits from the project in year 2 after development
  C_2 = ongoing costs associated with the project in year 2, etc.

The cost/benefit can then be examined using present-value analysis and a return on investment computed. Return on investment involves a subjective evaluation of the amount of gain or reduction in cost obtained from the use of capital. Since the HRIS will involve an initial outlay of funds to develop, and its use will extend over at least a five-year period, then it is proper to analyze the returns on a future basis. This analysis therefore involves a return on investment (ROI) approach. The simple formula for determining the ROI is cost savings (C) divided by investment (I), or:

$$ROI = C/I$$

However, the simple formula can be examined on a time value basis as well, since we need to relate the investment over its life, e.g., five years. Therefore the present value (PV) of the ROI (or a benefit) is discounted to allow for the fact that our investment in the HRIS is using capital which could be earning a rate of return elsewhere. The PV formula allows the team to utilize differing PV percentages depending on interest and inflation rates. The example shown below assumes a 10 percent discount rate where the PV for the first year would take the benefit derived (cost saved) for the first year and divide it by 1.1 ($1 × 1.10). The second year the formula would call for the cost savings to be divided by a further 10 percent reduction in its value, or $1 × (1.10 × 1.10) = 1.21; and so on. The formula then for a 10 percent discount is:

$$PV = \frac{\text{Savings in initial year}}{1.0} + \frac{\text{Savings in first year}}{1.10} + \frac{\text{Savings in second year}}{1.21}$$

$$+ \frac{\text{Savings in third year}}{1.331} + \frac{\text{Savings in fourth year}}{1.464} + \frac{\text{Savings in fifth year}}{1.61}$$

Refinements in the calculation can be made to handle ongoing development expenses by including these in recurring costs. That is, if the HRIS development project will span two or three years, then a decision has to be made on how long the initial development cycle will be: one year, two years, or longer. Any residual HRIS development costs beyond that initial time period will then be included in the yearly cost figures.

The cost avoidance (*A*) offset against the initial development costs represents any planned-for or in-progress projects which will not be completed, or budgeted expense items which will not be incurred if the HRIS is built and alleviates the need for duplicative systems development.

If users have no information to the contrary, then all benefits and costs are typically assumed to occur at the beginning of a time period. The average working life of a well-designed system should be between 10 and 15 years. Therefore, using a 5-year benefits analysis as the ROI period of time should be more than conservative. In other words, benefits begin in the first year postimplementation, and extend for at least 5 years from that point. Care should be taken to include only those benefits and costs related to the project under review within this time frame.

An Example

To illustrate the use of the formulas and to show the time value of money, let us assume that there is a project which will cost $100,000 to develop, with an annual operating cost of $10,000. This project is expected to provide benefits equal to $5,000 the first year; $20,000 the second year; $30,000 the third year; $50,000 the fourth year; and $100,000 the fifth year. There is no initial cost avoidance.

Using the formula for cost/benefit, we get the following values (in thousands of dollars):

$$CB = (-100 + 0) + [(5 - 10) + (20 - 10) + (30 - 10) + (50 - 10) +$$

$$(100 - 10)]$$

$$= (-100) + (155)$$

$$= \$55,000$$

Then return on investment = cost/investment (per-year basis):

$$ROI = \frac{C}{I}$$

$$= \frac{\$55,000}{5}$$

$$= \frac{\$11,000}{\$100,000} = 11\% \text{ return on investment}$$

Using the present-value formula, however, with a 10 percent discount rate, we get a very different result (almost breakeven), again in thousands of dollars:

$$PV = \left(\frac{-100}{1.000}\right) + \left(\frac{-5}{1.100} + \frac{+10}{1.210} + \frac{20}{1.331} + \frac{+40}{1.464} + \frac{+90}{1.40}\right)$$

$$= -\$100,000 + \$101,967$$

$$= \$1,967$$

Case Study

The Alpha Company HRIS Project

I. Project Development Cost Estimates
   A. *Overview.* As it is extremely difficult to estimate costs for the entire project before the size, scope, and functions of the system have been determined, it has been suggested that the project be divided into two phases. This will permit management to ascertain the project's scope and payback as the work proceeds. It will also allow major funding to be allocated after the first phase, thereby limiting the risk of significant up-front investment before the project has been specified in greater detail. Therefore, two estimates are to be presented: one, for Phase I (5 percent of the total cost); and two, for Phase II (95 percent of the total cost). The phases are explained below.
   B. *Phase I Cost Estimates.*
      1. *Objective.* To determine the scope, user functionality, and development direction of the HRIS CORE modules defined as a basic set of HRIS functionalities, e.g., compensation, employee records, and payroll transactions, which will be standard for all business units to meet local Alpha unit and corporate/group-level user needs for HR data.
      2. *Duration.* The project will take a total of six months, beginning as soon as possible. The six months is to be divided into two periods, one period of three to four months of project team work, followed by a second period of one to two months of cost/benefit analysis and management review.
      3. *Activities.*
         a. Determine the scope and timing of the project, by user modules and in terms of deliverables for the CORE HRIS functions.

    b. Produce a functional specification and user requirements statement for the inputs, edits, processes, outputs, and displays to be delivered in the CORE detail needed on the first set of deliverables.

    c. Outline the functionalities for the CORE modules that are not in the first set of deliverables.

    d. Reengineer the major data flow and HR processes involved in the first deliverables.

    e. Conduct a vendor evaluation to determine the applicability of commercial software.

    f. Determine local unit interface needs.

    g. Build a data dictionary for elements for the CORE.

    h. Prototype major functionalities for user acceptance.

    i. Determine the specific hardware, software, and telecommunications environment.

    j. Hold steering committee presentations.

    k. Develop initial data codes for key common codes.

    l. Produce a more detailed cost/benefit analysis and list development tasks for the remainder of the project.

    m. Outline implementation and conversion activities.

4. *Approach.* The work will be performed in a Joint Application Development JAD project team environment where IS works closely with the users with participation from Alpha business operations, corporate, and other units on a voluntary basis. Consultant support will be provided for guidance and assistance. Guidance on functions will be supplied by advisory representatives from all Alpha units. The entire project team will report to a senior-level steering committee composed of corporate and business-unit HR and IS vice presidents. Methodologies will include direct user and management interviewing, systems review, HR process reengineering, data flow diagraming, data modeling and prototyping, prioritization, cost/benefit analysis, and user-team trade-offs. Acceptance of users will be required before project proceeds. Alpha's new purchase/merger with Beta Company's needs can be factored in through the integration teams.

5. *Staffing.* Costs for the CORE project team's salary and expenses will be charged to the project. The team will consist of seven to nine full-time equivalent (FTE) participants as follows (see Table 12-2 for costs):

    a. One project director

    b. Two representatives from the HR user areas of the major business units

    c. Two representatives from corporate and/or other business units

    d. Two representatives from information systems

    e. Five consultants

Table 12-2. Staff Costs (in thousands of dollars)

Category	Number of individuals	Cost per month per individual	Total cost per month	Total cost over 6 months
Project team	7	$6	$42	$252
Consultants	5	$6	$30	180
Total				$432

6. *Other costs.*
   a. *Advisory team.* An advisory team comprised of a representative from each of the major Alpha business units at the HR and IS director level plus corporate HR functional representation will participate throughout the duration of Phase I on a part-time basis. In estimating costs, it is assumed that the advisory group will attend approximately two meetings per month for eight months and include an average of four to six representatives. The project will assume travel and living expenses for this team. Time charges will be absorbed by the unit.
   b. *Support.* Case, data dictionary costs, etc.: $30,000–$50,000.
   c. *Clerical/space.* Word processing, photocopying, desk space, PC usage: $25,000–$35,000.
   d. *Travel and living expenses.* (Assumes Chicago, Illinois, Project Team location plus field trips.)
      (1) New York, New Jersey-based corporate and consultants: 20 trips @ $1,200/trip × 4 = $96,000.
      (2) Advisory group: 12 trips @ $1,200 × 4 = $57,600.
      (3) Information Systems: 20 trips @ $1,200 × 2 = $48,000.
      (4) Chicago-based team travel: $20,000.
      (5) Total travel/living expenses: $221,600.
7. *Summary.* Table 12-3 provides for a summary of Phase I costs.

Table 12-3. Phase I Cost Summary

Project team and consultants	$432,000
Clerical/space	30,000
Support tools	40,000
Travel and living expenses	221,600
Contingency	26,400
Total	$750,000

C. *Phase II Cost Estimates.*
 1. *Objective.* To design, build, test, and implement the CORE Alpha HRIS as specified, scoped, and sized in Phase I. It is assumed that the HRIS will be built in a modular fashion to permit easier development and implementable sets of deliverables.
 2. *Duration.* Major development will take from 12 to 24 months beginning after the end of Phase I, and extend (for minor enhancements) over the life of the system.
 3. *Activities.* (According to system development life cycle.)
    a. Design
    b. Development (in-house customized or commercial project purchase and modifications)
    c. Testing
    d. Pilot operation
    e. Installation (including local interfaces and conversion)
    f. Modification and enhancement
    g. Maintenance
 4. *Approach.*
    a. The work will be done in an integrated project team fashion, with users and developers interacting and sharing work activities. System enablers, CASE tools, screen printers, etc., will be employed to shorten the development cycle. Installation and roll-out of enhancements will take about two years after initial release.
    b. It is assumed that the project will supply the information needed by payroll and claims processing functions, and both improve the delivery of data to them as well as facilitate the reverse feed of data back to the line departments and other business units and employees where possible. However, no significant impact is expected on the payroll or administrative claims processing functions themselves.
    c. There will be no impact on time and attendance data.
    d. Provision will be made during the life of the project to handle conversion to a flexible benefits system, either by providing data to a third party for administration or within the Alpha HRIS if sufficient time and priorities permit.
    e. Central funding will handle development for the CORE modules by the central project. The logic will permit local add-ons and attachments/interfaces to be made at the unit level to satisfy local needs. The central project development group will make releases to the CORE modules only.
 5. *Staffing.* An original team of eight, plus contract IS programmers at times to supplement the CORE project team, and additional HR assistance to assist with specific legal, benefits, and compensation issues. Also, a HR standard coding team will be added. At the maximum level, a team of about 20 is assumed.
 6. Cost Assumptions.

    a. Project leader and CORE team required for three to four years maximum

    b. IS and project team gradually cut back in fourth year

    c. Terminal hardware mostly in place; utilization of mainframe for remote locations

    d. LANS and increased file/server capacity in targeted locations

    e. Wide area network in place

    f. Commercial purchase of some software to cut timeframes

    g. Data Base Management System (DBMS) of sufficient quality in place

    h. HR and users to handle most access and retrievals and supply assistance for common code set development

    i. Local Alpha units to be responsible for local programming of interfaces and non-CORE applications under standards set forth by the project team

    j. Increase in storage, e.g., Direct Access Storage Device (DASD)/mainframe capacity, at one or two central sites.

D. *Total project development costs.* Total project development cost estimates, for Phase I and Phase II, are summarized in Table 12-4.

E. *Ongoing Recurring System Cost Estimates.* It is assumed that the new Alpha HRIS will have approximately the same systems operating costs as today (estimated at $11.3 million), as increases in hardware costs will be offset by programmer-support decreases and improved efficiencies in the entire data-flow cycle from data capture through the payroll and benefits functions. Therefore, even though there will be a greater volume of data stored and processed, there will be a reduction in the number of repeat runs, fewer errors, less reconciliation, and fewer duplicative edits needed in the new system.

II. Project Benefits

A. *Tangible benefits.* Tangible savings will be realized in the decreased time and costs in HR administration due to work reengineering and interaction with the Alpha HRIS installation.

    1. Benefits will be derived from remapping all the major HR and payroll input/output processes, which are extremely time-consuming and labor-intensive throughout Alpha Corporation, and which have little or no automation support at this time. Processes and functions affected include the following:

        a. Employment

        b. New hire/rehire

        c. Transfer (change of job/organization)

        d. Termination

        e. Payroll withholding

        f. Retirement/death

        g. To/from leave of absence

        h. Enrollment in benefits (flexible or nonflexible)

        i. Training

        j. Staffing (job posting, interviewing, etc.)

        k. Wage and salary administration

Table 12-4. Total Project Development Costs Estimates: Phase I and Phase II (in thousands of current dollars)

Alpha HRIS module	Requirements reengineering design and development Year 1		Basic HRIS system and staffing comp, benefits, EEO Year 2		Basic HRIS Residual functionality and training Year 3	Basic HRIS residual training and safety Year 4
	Phase I	Design/build	Build/test	Test pilot	Install	Enhance
CORE						
Project team	$750	$ 750	$ 800	$ 800	$ 1,600	$ 500
Additional team		300	300	300	500	100
IS programming		300	600	600	1,200	600
Purchase/custom		700			300	
Hardware/DASD			300	100	400	
Testing/trial			200	200	200	100
Local						
Hardware				500	500	500
Local interface		200		500	1,000	
Subtotal	750	2,250	2,200	3,000	5,700	1,800
CORE costs	750	2,050	2,200	2,000	4,200	1,300
CORE costs cumulative	750	2,800	5,000	7,000	11,200	12,500
Total Projects						
Local costs		200		1,000	1,500	500
Cum. local costs		200	200	1,200	2,700	3,200
Overall total						
Cum. costs	750	3,000	5,200	8,200	13,900	15,700

*5% increase in salary and benefits have been estimated.

253

2. The project team has identified 2,580 HR full-time equivalents (FTEs) and have used 40 percent as an estimate of those involved in administration — conservative estimates for our model below. These percentages have also been substantiated as representative of what other large U.S. employers experience in the HR area. They do not include Beta Corporation or office services personnel such as cafeteria or building and security guards. By substituting technology and by changing the way the work is handled — i.e., eliminating steps, streamlining the processes, reducing tasks, and cutting out forms and records — the total costs of the administrative work will be reduced by 10 to 25 percent, depending on the HR application.

3. The average current-year cost of nonexempt employees in Alpha was $24,300 and of exempt employees was $47,300. A benefits and support loading of 25 percent was used.

3. *Savings model.* Table 12-5 depicts the tangible savings due to HRIS implementation. It includes those employees assigned to human resources, in all Alpha units (excluding Beta Corporation). It does not include building services, print shop, company store, guard services, and other office service areas. The actual impact of the savings will be more precisely defined in the next phase of the project, as will the modules to be developed in the CORE system.

    a. For our cost modeling we assume that the basic HRIS module savings will be available when the first CORE deliverable is actually installed (year 3) and the other modules, i.e., residual basic plus training and safety, will each be installed one year later. The availability of the tangible benefits over the next several years will then be as shown in Table 12-6.

    b. The cost benefits of the project are equal to the development cost less any one-time cost avoidance, *plus* the difference between the annual benefits and the annual costs for each of the next five years. Therefore,

$$CB = (-8.2) + [(8.68 - 5.7) + (10.54 - 1.8)$$
$$+ (12.82 - 0) + (13.47 - 0) + (14.14 - 0)]$$

$$= (-8.2) + [(2.98) + (8.74) + (12.82) + (13.47)$$
$$+ (14.14)]$$

$$= (-8.2) + (52.15)$$

$$= \$43.95 \text{ million}$$

Table 12-5. Alpha HRIS Project Impact Model Savings in HR-Related Work

HR functional area	HRIS module	(A) Functional employee distribution (%)	(B) Employee total	(C) No. involved in admin. (40%)*	(D) HRIS impact (%)	(E) Net savings (FTES)
HR, Comp., EEO, Benefits, Emp. Rel.	Basic Ben. Comp. Staffing	60	1,762	705	25	176
Training, staffing, education	Training	27	552	221	10	22
Safety, health	Safety	13	266	106	25	27
Total		100	2,580			225

Per Area	FTEs savings	Annual cost	Total annual savings
Basic HRIS	176	$42,600	$7.5 M
Training and education	22	53,000	1.17 M
Safety and health	27	51,100	1.38 M

Table 12-5. Alpha HRIS Project Impact Model (*Continued*)
HRIS Cost/Benefits
(FTE Savings Stream Including 5% Growth per Year)†

FTEs	Current year (baseline)	Project development		Post-HRIS implementation (millions of $)					
		Year 1	Year 2	Year 3	Year 4	Year 5	Year 6	Year 7
176	7.50	7.88	8.27	8.68	9.12	9.57	10.05	10.55
22	1.17	1.23	1.29	1.35	1.42	1.49	1.57	1.65
27	1.38	1.45	1.52	1.60	1.68	1.76	1.85	1.94
Annual tangible benefits				8.68	10.54	12.82	13.47	14.14
Cumulative tangible benefits				8.68	19.22	32.04	45.51	59.65

*Estimating technology impact.
†Benefits are inside boxes.

Table 12-6. Cumulative Benefits

		($ millions)				
		Annual			Cumulative	
Year	Module	Cost	Benefit	Net	Benefit	Benefit – Cost
1 and 2	Development	8.2	0	– 8.2	0	– 8.2
3	Basic HRIS	5.7	8.68	2.98	8.68	– 5.22
4	Training and staffing module + HRIS	1.8	10.54	8.74	19.22	3.52
5	Safety + training + HRIS	0	12.82	12.82	32.04	16.34
6	All modules	0	13.47	13.47	45.51	29.81
7	All modules	0	14.14	14.14	59.65	43.95

Using the present-value formula and a 10 percent discount rate,

$$PV = \frac{-8.2}{1.00} + \frac{(2.98)}{1.10} + \frac{(8.74)}{1.210} + \frac{(12.82)}{1.331}$$

$$+ \frac{(13.47)}{1.464} + \frac{(14.14)}{1.61}$$

$$= -8.2 + (2.71) + (7.22) + (9.63) + (9.20) + (8.78)$$

$$= -8.2 + 37.54$$

$$= \$29.34 \text{ M}$$

4. *Alternative plan.* An alternative development plan under which only the CORE HRIS will be built would cost $8.2 million plus $4.2 million additional development in year 3 and year 4. It would yield a net present value of $23.83 million through year 2.

B. *Intangible benefits.* The upgrading and improvement of the Alpha HRIS, including revamping of the information processes which support the human resources functions, will result in many benefits for the organization and its employees over and above those which result in direct dollar savings. These are categorized into several areas.

- *Coverage.* The effect that the systems will have on the work it-self and the numbers of functions which will be included in the new processes
- *Quality.* The improvements of accuracy, timeliness, and reliability due to better editing and delivery of information to end users and, by extension, an increased level of service by the HR departments
- *Risk.* The level of exposure that the Alpha units face in the day-to-day conduct of its business, ranging from EPA, EEO, OSHA, and various other government regulations to the failure of systems and related computer processing components
- *Support.* How the Alpha HRIS will assist management with decision making to meet its corporate mission, the various HR goals, assist the line supervisor in handling the workforce, and satisfy the employee's need for information
- *Fit.* How the new system will conform to the organization's quest for integrated operations, synergy between business units, and managerial direction and style

1. *Coverage.* The Alpha HRIS is expected to assist with the following areas of human resource processing and significantly upgrade the depth of penetration of technology in many ways. Some examples are provided regarding the basic and staffing modules.

   a. Basic HRIS modules
   - On-line employee setup, enrollment, and change processing with local editing and improved screens—alleviating the need for paper transit time
   - Direct access to more employee data by supervisors, managers, and HR personnel
   - Single front-end to payroll, benefits, and HR systems
   - Expanded use of interactive systems to create a more user-friendly environment
   - More complete historical information on employees
   - More integrated systems environment, thereby reducing the number of systems to be supported
   - Expanded collection of data elements to provide a more complete set of employee and organization data

   b. Staffing module
   - Integrated process, better controlled, originating at point of requisition and involving employees and applicants
   - Work experience data relevant to the job carried in the system
   - Standard job briefs on-line, which provide better information for employees to learn about open positions

- Automatic screening of applicants against open/future positions
- Better tracking and statistics in the hiring process

2. *Quality.* The quality of the information in the system, and the service level of the units the data supports, will be increased. Benefits will be derived from the following improvements.
   a. *Accuracy.* The information itself will improve in terms of its relation to the event to which it is related. Tighter edits, imposed locally, will preclude many variances now found in the data and often detected only long after the event. Data sharing and employee access will also help.
   b. *Reliability.* The information will be more consistent over time because of better standards of usage and more disciplined administration. Policy enforcement on several items will be needed to achieve full benefit.
   c. *Timeliness.* Data will be more readily available to the user, due to restructured work processes and on-line data systems.
   d. *Accessibility.* The Alpha HRIS will provide more open access to the data, under proper controls, thereby alleviating proper records and lengthy reports.

3. *Risk.* The Alpha HRIS will reduce the exposure that the business now faces by providing a greater degree of consistency of employee treatment with respect to policy interpretation, access to jobs, and record keeping. Improved audit trails, certification of licenses, and training will ensure safer plant operations and better supervisory assignments to critical jobs. In addition, by altering and reengineering the employment and selection processes, with improved data monitoring, a more uniform system will be installed. Also, better security and privacy of information will be available due to newer and more secure networks and database administration systems. These internal controls will also assist in better systems with lower risk of adverse-impact lawsuits and discrimination cases filed, since there will be improved early-warning detection capabilities.

4. *Support.* Providing senior management with better and more accurate data for health-care cost containment, productivity ratios, number of people to be trained, relative staff size, and similar such uses are all examples of the support the new system will provide. There are literally hundreds if not thousands of reasons that managers will access the system, and the ease of use of the systems will permit these analyses to be made much more efficiently.
   a. One major area which the HRIS will greatly aid will be organization analysis in order to create work groups which will meet customer needs in a more effective manner. This includes providing managers with information with which to

analyze work group size, type of work performed, number of management levels, productivity, and service indices, and to help create more efficient, integrated organizations for the future.

b. Another area which will have a priority will be to facilitate the entire payroll, benefits, and compensation processes and to permit new forms of nontraditional pay and benefits to be implemented throughout Alpha Corporation in a more timely manner.

c. In the newly designed system, better employee communications vehicles will be featured, thereby assisting with faster response to employee questions and allowing a more diverse workforce to be supported in a cost-effective manner.

5. *Fit.*   Better adapting technology to fit the managerial style and needs of the business is another intangible benefit. The assistance that the system will provide will help management with achieving the proper roles and responsibility shifts consistent with the vision of supervisory empowerment. The human resources function will be able to shift their emphasis from a heavy orientation on administration to one of consulting with line management on business issues—thus becoming more a strategic partner.

PART 5

Where Do We
Go from Here?

13

Characteristics of the New HRIS Manager

Creating and Managing Successful Systems

If the human resource system of the future will be different from that of the past — and it will be — it stands to reason that the managers of tomorrow's systems will also need to be different. This chapter examines some of the key traits that HRIS managers of the future will need to have to be successful, both as agents of change, driving the transformation of HR work through technology, and as managers of the HRIS of the future.

It should be noted that the "HRIS manager" referred to in this chapter does not necessarily have that title in the organization. Many who manage HR systems today, especially in organizations where the HRIS function is already highly valued, are vice presidents or directors of human resources. Others covered by our definition of HRIS manager are the men and women responsible for overall systems development, project team leaders, and those responsible for systems supporting specific applications, such as benefits or management development.

An Organizational Focus: Understanding the Business

The people who lead HR and HRIS in the organization should be businesspeople first of all, and then HR professionals and HR systems people. This has been said many times in many ways, but it remains an elusive goal in many organizations, or is given only lip service by HR people who see the sense of it but feel unable to take the time or do the work needed to understand all there is to know about the organization.

As part of a support function, HRIS people need to understand what it is the role supports. Earlier chapters in this book on business analysis and the identification of critical success factors (Chapters 4 and 6) present a methodology for understanding the business.

An important perspective for HRIS managers seeking to understand the company better is to remember that the HRIS organization does not serve individual people, departments, business units, or even those who approve its budgets. The first responsibility of HRIS is to serve the organization as a whole, which requires an understanding of the overall mission, products or services, ways of marketing, resource allocation, financial measurements, how products or services are created, and so on. This is a tall order, obviously, but it will be an increasingly vital component of the successful HRIS manager's repertoire in the years ahead.

To the extent that a HRIS manager thinks of himself or herself as a "systems professional" or "HR manager," he or she will always be "responsive" rather than a "pro-active" member of the management team. And as long as this is the case, the HRIS manager probably *will* be "too busy" to learn about the business as fully as is necessary.

As a practical matter, one reason so many HRIS managers fail to focus first on the overall business of the organization has to do with their provenance. Many, whether their background has been in systems or in human resources, have grown in their careers by serving others, but not necessarily the organization as a whole. At first they may have served others in the HRIS organization or MIS; later they perhaps helped functional specialists develop applications; and at some point they were "keepers of the data," filling requests from departments or individual users. At no time, as a rule, did they ask the business-related reasons why they served. It was not their job, then; but it will be from now on.

Participant in Strategic Planning

Involvement in long-range strategic planning, either as a source of information to support existing corporate strategic planning or, when long-range planning is missing or ineffective, as a leader in bringing the long view to the attention of top management, will be an increasingly essential activity of successful HRIS managers of the future.

There are several reasons why HR and specifically HRIS managers should be key participants in the long-range planning process. First, and most important in organizations whose future success depends on the skills and talents of employees, HR planning *is* strategic planning. For example:

- If the ability of the company to diversify into a new business requires X levels of qualified chemical engineers within 10 years, it is the HR department's job to plan and carry out ways of obtaining these engineers
- If new technology is being introduced over the next 5 or 10 years that will eliminate some jobs, require new skills for others, and create a need for new organizational structures, planning for the impacts of new technology is clearly a HR job.
- The future direction of benefits costs, including the cost of administering benefits, depends not only on long-range plans for changes enacted by the company; factors including demographic trends, the political-regulatory climate, economic trends (such as the rate of inflation and its impact on retirement), and other "environmental" issues need to be factored in, and many of these issues are essentially HR planning issues.
- In scores of other scenarios presented by strategic planners as "the organizational future," the internal and external availability of the human resources needed to reach objectives, their costs, their training and development needs, how their jobs will change, and other needed information is the basic "meat" of HR and the systems that support HR.

The fully developed HRIS of the future will have, it is hoped, not only data on people and jobs within the organization, but will also incorporate or have links to whatever external or environmental data planners need to develop strategies for achieving long-range goals. This information could include, for example:

- Employee data, plan data, and financial statistics regarding the industry and competitors
- Census Bureau data on population shifts, demographic changes in the population (race, sex, age), and so on
- Labor Department data on workforce changes, from demographic trends nationally to regional or local changes in labor markets, as well as data about industry employment patterns
- Education Department information about trends in educational attainment levels, types of degrees, basic skills levels, etc.

- Economic projections for the nation as a whole, for regions, or for specific industries
- Information from other countries about the economic, demographic, social, legislative, and other issues relevant to HR planning
- Trends in medical statistics, political changes affecting the regulatory environment, natural resources availability, and a host of other subjects that may have a bearing on the company's future success

Why don't more HRIS organizations collect, analyze, and present internal and external strategic information? Sadly, they are rarely asked. American organizations in general—run by pragmatic managers who focus on quarterly financial results and planning horizons that rarely exceed one to three years—have never put the same faith in long-range planning as some of their global competitors. When things happen in the business environment that could have been projected in an alternative strategic planning scenario—such as the oil shortage of the 1970s or new benefits regulation—American companies have frequently been unprepared to respond competitively. Worse, organizations that have had ineffective strategic planning functions that failed to predict environmental changes saw that strategic planning could be "wrong," and decided it wasn't worth the effort. The baby went out with the bath water.

When top management doesn't ask for the long-range view of changes that could have a bearing on organizational success, it's up to the HRIS manager acting with the HR planner or perhaps as the HR planner to lead in this effort. The future belongs to those who anticipate and plan for it, and this is a natural role for HRIS managers of the future.

The New Meaning of "Quality"

One of the most important roles of successful HRIS managers of the past has always been the maintenance of quality data, a concept that includes not only data accuracy but its timeliness, security, and usefulness to the management functions supported by the system. This role will continue to be critical as long as data is the chief product of a HRIS, but today and in the years ahead, successful HRIS managers will in many cases be those who help or lead efforts to improve quality corporatewide, especially in areas within the logical purview of the human resource department. In this context, work quality is different from the reengineering work outlined in Chapter 5. This discussion aims at improving the level of HR service as managers using reengineering methods.

The emergence of quality control managers in American organizations in the late 1980s and early 1990s — managers with overall responsibility for developing and implementing "total quality" programs based on the concepts of W. Edwards Deming, the American consultant who helped Japanese manufacturers focus on quality after World War II — was driven largely by perceptions that American products and services lacked the quality needed to compete in world markets, or even against foreign companies selling in the United States. Companies that adopted total quality programs, such as Ford, Motorola, TRW, Xerox, and others, usually recognized that quality is not one thing, such as the reduction of product defects through improved inspection procedures at the end of the production line. Rather, it was generally agreed, quality improvement needed to become part of the fabric of the organization, suffusing employee attitudes and work habits throughout the organization, from office administration and customer relations to R&D, the shipping department, and all other functions needed to achieve corporate objectives.

From the start, however, many quality improvement programs have been hampered by a lack of measurements of quality in some of the new areas covered by these total quality programs. It is one thing to count product defects or returns from dissatisfied customers; it is something else to measure customer satisfaction with services, or how well a supervisor is managing her staff. And on another level, many of the new quality experts insisted that quality improvement should not be measured by the absence of negatives such as product defects alone, but should also include positive factors such as an improvement in customer service resulting from an employee suggestion.

Increasingly, the idea of total quality improvement has focused on the quality of teams, people working together to achieve common goals. As Dr. Deming and others had been saying all along, most organizational work is not accomplished by individuals working alone, but by interdependent functions. A sales representative who comes back from the field with a client problem needs to be able to work with technical staffers to solve the problem, for example. And the growing use of project teams and task forces to work on specific projects — such as organizational restructuring or HRIS development — further focused attention on teamwork.

What does the HRIS manager have to offer in this quality-conscious environment? Today, a great deal; in the years ahead, a massive contribution limited only by the HRIS manager's creativity, analytical prowess, and ability to persuade management that the HRIS database can be a vital tool in improving quality throughout the organization.

Examples of working with others in HR include the use of skills inventory data to create optimal "manning packages" for projects, and productivity and quality measurements that track and assess the success of differently constituted project teams; new quality objectives in managers' performance appraisal criteria, such as the results of employee attitude surveys or time spent communicating the company's substance abuse policies; or an "automated suggestion box" that lets employees use an interactive system to communicate their ideas for quality improvement to supervisors and management — and get an appropriate response on-line or through a personalized letter.

Because HRIS managers already have the data in many cases, and because they are (or should be) capable of creating new data about people and jobs, they are in an ideal position to participate in or lead new quality improvement programs. Statistical techniques and analytical capabilities, when possessed by HRIS managers of the future, will make these managers leaders in the quest for quality.

Reengineering and reshaping the work with work-flow analysis and activity analysis will greatly improve HR service and effectiveness. HRIS managers must be able to lead their clients through these processes.

The quality of HRIS products and services already being provided cannot be neglected, however, even as HRIS managers of the future set their sights on a larger role. The accuracy and integrity of information, timeliness, usefulness to users, and systems features such as security and ease of use, all require ongoing vigilance and management control.

Collegial Work Group Environment

Increasingly, human resource systems managers — indeed, almost all managers working in areas that require professional expertise and contributions from a range of business disciplines and skills — are being asked to work in collegial relationships with others. Easy-going working relationships where information and ideas flow freely, where subordinates feel like trusted partners, where all parties are respected for their contributions — these produce a climate that optimizes productivity and innovation in "knowledge jobs."

This climate, in marked contrast to bureaucratic, heavily structured hierarchies managed by authoritarian, sometimes autocratic bosses, is especially critical for successful HRIS managers of the future. A collegial approach to work is based on more than just democracy or some idea of equality; it assumes, instead, that all participants in a project or members of a work group indeed have something to offer, or they wouldn't be there. And in most HRIS work, the range and diversity of skills and knowledge that must be managed by successful HRIS managers is hardly matched in any other part of the organization.

The different categories of specialization required in HRIS work today go well beyond the familiar dichotomy that puts the "techies" on one side and HR people on the other, a distinction that has never been totally sharp in a field of multidisciplinary HRIS professionals. Today's HRIS work, like the human resource functions it supports, may require the skills and talents of people and functions as diverse as word processing specialists and pension actuaries, as numerous and widely scattered as there are business units and departments, and as culturally different as a Philadelphia lawyer and a Pakistani plant manager.

The skills needed by successful HRIS managers to create and foster collegial work environments are both analytical and matters of management style. The analytical component comes in picking the right people to work together or with a work group, deciding who does what, and in creating a team framework that ignores traditional boundaries, chains of command, and the prerogatives of managers over employees. The management style must be one that instills trust among colleagues, respect for the contributions of others, and an atmosphere that encourages teamwork in the pursuit of common goals. Most of the best and brightest workers in an organization, whether they're receptionists or R&D directors, respond to this style when working in groups.

A Builder of Relationships

The successful HRIS manager of the future will also be capable of building strong, mutually respectful relationships with others, especially in an extended HRIS that assumes a broader role in the organization than mere HR and payroll record keeping. Building on the collegial atmosphere of the HRIS, managers will need to accept the reality that their work is heavily dependent on open lines of communications and productive relationships with a range of constituencies: top management, line managers, HR finance, legal staff, HR customers, informative users, suppliers, technical professionals, and line employees.

Practicing a style that some call "management by walking around," successful HRIS managers will increasingly be those who can stay abreast of current priorities and problems, anticipate emerging needs, and let all with whom they do business know that they are willing to listen and respond to their concerns. At the same time, constant communications provide regular opportunities to be an agent of change within the organization, building alliances for programs and projects that will improve organizational effectiveness through the application of technology.

Casual conversations and a friendly attitude are no substitutes for work analysis, in-depth interviews, or disciplined study of the business and its operations, of course. But the knowledge and skills developed by successful HRIS managers can only be fully utilized with constant communications with all with whom they do business, and effective communications is often a matter of "being there" as a trusted colleague when people have something to communicate.

International Focus

As discussed in Chapter 8, it will be a rare company that is not in some sense "international" in the years ahead. Even those without overseas employees will have markets abroad, business partners in other countries, and—certainly—competitors. Increasingly, managers in all functions will need an international focus, and the skills and knowledge needed to deal with relevant cultures, languages, political environments, economies, and other regional and national differences.

In the future, HR and HRIS managers will be asked to plan for and address issues such as recruitment problems in Italy, compensation plan design in a French unit, or payroll processing in Taiwan. Depending on the extent of the organization's globalization, the HRIS manager of the future may be responsible for automating the full gamut of HR programs and policies now handled domestically—but with a whole new set of rules, constraints, and opportunities that might be different in a dozen different countries.

Marketing Orientation

The resources needed to improve organizational effectiveness through the application of technology are never infinite, but are part of a "pie" that the HRIS competes with other organizational function to enlarge or slice more advantageously. This means that HRIS managers in the future organization will need to be effective in marketing the HRIS to senior management.

HRIS marketing is something many managers have been reluctant to do in the past. Some misunderstand it as "hype," overly zealous selling of the type that has caused problems in the past, when expectations were raised beyond systems' ability to deliver. Others feel simply that those in the executive offices should understand the value of their function; they're the ones responsible for budgets, let them worry about dollars while we get on with our jobs.

Unfortunately, this is not the way it usually works. Management must be convinced of the bottom-line value of new projects (as well as existing operations), and HRIS managers need to speak their language to compete successfully with other functions. The type of cost justification recommended in Chapter 12, when based on the business and work analysis stressed throughout this book, is a critical tool for future HRIS managers seeking the resources they need to change the organization.

Adaptable to Change

Successful HRIS managers in the future will be able to lead change, changes in the way people work, how information is moved, the development of new technology, and so on. At the same time, however, many other business changes requiring adaptability and quick responsiveness will be imposed from without, and successful HRIS managers will need to be flexible, willing to change with the times, and open to innovation and improvement.

New technology, new management structures, changing business objectives, and changes in the business environment may require HRIS managers to walk away from pet projects, or discontinue an effort that has cost a great deal of time, money, and individual commitment. Companies with longer-term planning horizons or a more stable customer base, such as utilities or energy firms, may be less affected by changing customer requirements. Some change is always inevitable, however, and managers who are unable to adapt to it cannot expect to succeed.

Self-Contained, Individual Contributor

One of the clearest, yet most widely misunderstood, phenomena of the "professionalization" of management is that it is no longer enough to be a boss; increasingly, professionals who manage must also be self-contained, individual contributors, capable of understanding—or even doing—the work they manage. This requirement of today's professional manager is frequently misunderstood by old-school managers who believe that it runs counter to the art of delegating, theories about how to motivate others, and other traditional management concepts—most of which focus on ways of getting others to do the work while you keep a clean desk.

These skills will always be important to some degree. But managers in today's more professional business environment—and especially managers of a technology such as HRIS—need a more detailed, comprehensive, analytical understanding of the work itself than ever before, and in smaller companies and units it is imperative.

This does not imply that the successful HRIS manager of the future will need to be everywhere at once, overseeing activities from programming to benefits plan design. On the contrary, the continuing specialization of HR—the need for experts in the legal arena, outside firms that understand pension plan administration, and so on—makes this approach a virtual impossibility. It does mean, however, that successful HRIS managers will need to spend more time analyzing and understanding organizational work of all kinds, the available technology, business objectives, user needs, and other issues that have little or nothing to do with traditional ideas of leadership. True leaders in this field will be those who earn respect for their professional knowledge, and who know the work itself.

An Entrepreneurial Approach

One of the hallmarks of the future will be the ability to be self-driven, with the ability to strike out in new areas and develop new markets. Managers must make things happen, must be deal makers, and must act as brokers of change. A significant characteristic of this type of individual will be the need for a research and development mentality—always trying new software, new methods of delivering information to the end user, and willing to invest time, energy, and financial resources in coming up with new and untried solutions. Being tied to the past and processes that may have outgrown their usefulness will not be an advantage in the future.

A positive outlook on the future is also important. A "can do" attitude about the future is essential. Determination to succeed in the midst of chaos, across many barriers, will carry the HR technology team a long way.

Political savvy will also be needed. Entrepreneurs can be very lonely at times, and find themselves out on a limb, if they do not understand what senior management wants and know when to come forth with new initiatives—and when to stay put. Pushing for a new program at a time when budgets are tight may not be the best approach, and even entrepreneurs can get into trouble if they get too far ahead of the pack.

Cost Conscientious

An overriding concern will be the ability to keep costs within a proper framework. Managers who see themselves on a crusade or a mission—a management style that is sometimes needed—will get nowhere if they do not have the ability to project a cost-sensitive, cost-conscious attitude. There will never be quite enough resources available to accomplish all that such managers want. The ability to know when to ask for funds and when to retrench a bit and hold the line on current initiatives will be needed. Quite often, the ability to achieve desired results within budget constraints will define success.

As discussed in Chapter 12, the HR technology team can help generate significant cost reductions. However, the desired managerial trait that we're emphasizing here is being able to project a cost-conscious, "businesslike" attitude. This means projecting oneself as a member of the senior team on a continuing basis, and having an overall conservative style, not foolishly spending resources. Reusing systems, having a buy-versus-build bias, trying to get a bit more out of a particular program or piece of hardware, building around systems, leveraging particular products and services and reusing them if possible are all examples of being cost-sensitive.

HR Knowledgeable

Being well grounded in basic human resource management is essential. This includes knowing in some detail areas such as benefits, compensation, training, management development, organizational analysis, and the like. To be effective in one's chosen field, there is no substitute for competency in the core areas.

Among the basic areas of human resources management, it will also be essential to develop one or two specialties. A sound approach might be for the HR technology management team to develop cross-capabilities. For example, if one person becomes a benefits expert, another member of the team could concentrate on training or development, and develop expertise there. An interesting approach might be to develop or ensure that each HRIS staffer is knowledgeable about at least one of the more technical areas, such as benefits or compensation, as well one of the more behavioral-based areas, such as management development or training. This way a balance develops between the benefits/compensation functions and the development and training functions, and the HR technology group would have a foot in both camps.

A lack of functional HR knowledge puts one at a severe disadvantage in developing needs, priorities, or in consulting with line organizations. The main mission of the HR technology team is to translate the requirements for human resource management to the line organization and employees through the technical medium. Without functional knowledge, this mission will never be properly met.

In addition to human resources per se, one must also be aware of the particular HR plans and policies of the company. Because each corporate environment translates and develops policies for that environment, mere subject matter knowledge of HR will not be sufficient. One must know the particular nuances and interpretations of those policies over the years in order to put them in a proper historical context. These plans and policies will include rulings from committees and senior management in such areas as overtime, training and development, compensation, pay increases, and the like. Knowledge of human resources must extend from the academic and broader context to the reason for human resources plans in the first place, to specific rulings and interpretations as practiced in the corporate environment. In order to be successful, the HR technology team must be well versed about their "home field."

Technically Competent

In addition to being well grounded in human resources, HRIS managers must also be skilled in technology. In human resources work there are some specific technologies, mostly computer-based, which are essential. These include the classical HRIS activities of data specification, HRIS operation, retrieval, screen design, interfaces, and PC usage. In addition, some systems methodologies need to be considered. Some of the more important ones include systems design and development expertise. The system's life cycle—moving projects through the system from concept to design to development and then to installation—includes very important activities and technologies that must be managed. The HR manager must be familiar with these phases, how projects move ahead, how people work as a team, and when a particular project is in transition from one phase to the next, since different technologies in different phases will be more important than in today's environment, where we often get implementations "all at once" or through prototyping. Using CASE tools will often help. However the technology is chosen, it is important to know it to manage the project as it moves through its life cycle.

Another important technology that needs to be better understood, at least at a functional level, is networking, building networks from local area networks to wide area networks, and all of the different technical methodologies that are used in these networks. It is essential to understand and manage projects that implement such technology, and to be able to explain to users and to management how to employ network technology to achieve the desired systems environment. This also applies to distributed database concepts, corporation processing, technology, and open software systems.

Telecommunications awareness and knowledge are also essential, as most of the systems in the future will be employing and moving information over long distances. Switch digital services, analog/digital voice and traffic analysis, and data communications must be understood at least at a conceptual/user level.

Another technical competency is the ability to evaluate and choose vendors and software packages. Many if not most of the HR applications that will be developed will include the evaluation and purchase of commercial software. The specifics of how to move a project along to derive sufficient numbers of requirements in order to evaluate commercial software and applications, to eliminate from consideration any packages that do not meet requirements, and to follow through all the way to a contract will be essential. Often this will include a request for information (RFI) or a following document called a request for proposal (RFP). There will be hundreds if not thousands of vendor products available for purchase. Keeping aware of the most promising ones, and understanding the vendor evaluation process, is a needed attribute in this technical area.

Obviously, the use of knowledge-based systems will be one of the more important factors in making the HR function more effective in the future. Using such rule-based, "smart" systems to move the myriad of personnel procedures to automated state will be one of the major HRIS tasks in the years ahead.

Other emerging technologies to consider include more imaging, document management, voice response systems, video technology, pen-based systems, and others. And being able to blend all these technologies and to understand the importance of them and how to use them in a HR context is going to be more difficult in the years ahead.

Consulting Skills

One group of individual skills that will be most needed will be that of a consultant. Problem-solving skills, diagnostic skills, and the ability to guide clients through complex problems are examples of consulting skills that will be required.

The abilities to develop business plans and provide feedback will also be needed. Many of these skills can be learned either in a classroom or through direct observation. However, consulting roles are often best learned on the job, under the guidance of a mentor. Depending on the particular situation, there are certain basic consulting roles that need to be examined. The HR technology manager may act as an expert in a situation in which the client plays a fairly inactive role; or the client may do most of the directing; or the consultant and the client may work on the problem together. In other words, you're (1) an expert, or (2) a pair of hands, or (3) a partner. In any event, the expertise required will extend from very early conceptual work all the way through to specific interviewing, methodologies, and guidance. Some of the more important methodologies that the HR technology consultant should be able to utilize are:

- *Planning,* including the use of automated systems, PERT charts, Gantt charts, work breakdown charts, and other methodologies related to planning and assignment. Strategic planning and aligning HRIS projects with corporate goals will also be vital.

- *Evaluating,* or helping the client work through a series of complex problems and employing some data synthesis and evaluating some various options.

- *Cost justification,* helping the client work through the cost versus benefits and cost/resource analysis of a given approach.

- *Testing and trialing,* actually testing the new product to ensure that it meets the clients' specifications or using it in a pilot project.

- *Prioritization,* assisting management in determining what is the desired sequence of events and what is most important.

- *Activity analysis (technical impact analysis),* having a method to determine the work that people do and the various time frames and hours spent on that work within a given work group and the impact that technology has in that work.

- *Workflow analysis,* as discussed in Chapter 5, the ability to show the sequence of steps and tasks in performing work.

- *Installation/conversion,* being able to assist the client in coming up with a proper sequence of events to install a new or modified HR technology.

- *Performance audits,* knowing how to come into a given work group area and do an audit of current adequacy against the targets and missions of that group.

- *Data modeling,* the ability to analyze and show data relationships.

- *Project management,* being able to demonstrate to management or clients how projects large and small should be managed to achieve proper effectiveness. Utilizing computerized systems to help manage a complex project as a series of projects will often be necessary.

Summary

We have discussed the traits that the HRIS manager of the future must possess. These traits should be channeled into certain activities which will have a higher payback in the future than they might have had in the past. Again, they imply a transition from a more formal bureaucratic organizational state to a much more fluid and individually participative one.

In addition, much of the success of an individual will have to be laid at the feet of personality and style, and how fixed the adult personality is. In order to accomplish needed change, individuals work within an organizational framework, and the change must occur in both the organization and the individual. The structure of the job must change, compensation patterns must change, and management response to these changes will be watched to see whether the changes are accepted and endorsed.

We have seen that management tends to be conservative in responding to outside pressures, and will move forward with programs only when management is sure the programs will be acceptable within in the larger framework of cost effectiveness and positive results on the bottom line.

We have also seen that new work groups, self-directed work teams, and the other innovations are slow to take hold in many organizations. One reason is the very complex nature of compensation and benefit plans that may have to be dismantled, as well as organizational structures. However, we are convinced that as the technology grows and our ability to change the work increases, and as management style becomes more participative, the HR technology team will change its form dramatically. And its most successful leaders and managers will have all or most of the qualities outlined here.

14

The Future
of Human Resources
and the HRIS
That Will
Make It Possible

As we approach the third millennium, major changes seem certain in the role of human resources management and the technology that supports—and shapes—the management of people and organizational work. These changes will be much more profound than the sudden obsolescence of millions of forms that read "19_" on a date line, and will be driven by forces affecting business organizations generally, such as management decentralization, the need to do more with fewer people, customer focus, and listening to clients, as well as other economic, demographic, and technological changes affecting human resource management. In this chapter we will review some of the forces and trends that will continue to shape the HR role in the future, some likely characteristics of global organizations of the future, and some of the key concepts and goals of technological change in the years ahead. While none of this is inevitable for all organizations, each of these issues deserves consideration by HR and HRIS managers seeking to assure the corporate value of their functions into the third millennium and beyond.

Organizational Change: Decentralization and Downsizing

Because nothing predicts the immediate future as well as the immediate past, the first trends worth considering are today's most widespread organizational changes, the related trends of management decentralization and "downsizing" or reductions in force, especially the staff reductions that have taken place in centralized management organizations.

The decentralization of organizational management generally has been a response to competitive pressures that demonstrated the disadvantages of bureaucratic, relatively slow-moving organizations that do not respond well to changing conditions, locally discrete business environments, and other factors that mitigate against monolithic policies and centralized decision making. The meaning of "decentralization" has varied, but it covers a range of situations:

- Functional decentralization in vertically structured organizations, so that decision making that belongs at the production level stays there, that which should be with the distribution function stays there, the management of marketing is contained within this function, and so on. While all functions must be linked by the business plan in a vertically integrated organization, this type of decentralization recognizes that the day-to-day operations and functional goals of different units require decidedly different approaches, competencies, and management policies, and the decision-making autonomy to act on these discrete requirements remains intact and not defused. Some of this vertical orientation will shift to a more process driven view to support the customer. This will result in a horizontal structure in some companies.

- Geographic decentralization of management, putting decision making and other management activity at the local or regional level, closer to the customer.

- Line-of-business decentralization, in which management functions and policies previously centralized in a parent organization are now performed or developed by each subsidiary in a different line of business.

- Various forms of "political" or structural decentralization designed to put decision making and other management functions in the hands of work groups or individuals doing the work in order to be more customer oriented, nearer their markets and otherwise more effective — such as project teams, sales crews, research groups, or individuals expected to perform their job without previously enforced command and control.

- Selective centralization, where economies of scale or scarce resources require many users/customers to have access to the specialized skills of the few people who have them.

In all of these situations, the reader will be quick to recognize, the decentralization of previously centralized management functions is likely to be partial rather than total. There is a difference between autonomy and anarchy. Depending on the business of the organization and the type of management function, policy, or other previously centralized activity, decentralization of management roles is usually achieved only partially, after a process that includes analysis of both what *should* be decentralized and what *can* be decentralized. And in human resource management, the technology of human resource information systems has largely removed the obstacles inherent in the second part of this question.

For example, how decentralized does the organization want the employment process to be? Recognizing that each location has its own staffing needs, that local labor markets are the most cost-efficient source of employees for many jobs, and perhaps that hiring decisions need to be made quickly to respond to a volatile production schedule with sudden shifts in labor requirements, the organization may lean toward total decentralization of the employment process: Just tell headquarters who you've hired, after the fact. There are organizations and jobs for which this might be sufficient, but more often a company has standards, policies, regulatory compliance, financial controls, and a host of other interests in local employment decisions.

The technology of HRIS resolves such dilemmas. Organizationwide policies and procedures can be put on-line, incorporated in edits and systems documentation, while those parts of the employment process that should remain in the hands of local employment offices *can* be decentralized, through user-dedicated fields and other system features.

The basic reason why the technology of computers supports decentralization is that the newer systems permit diversity, variety, and virtually individualized treatment of information and transactions. This is more true every day, as the speed, power, and carrying capacity of computers continue to expand at phenomenal rates. The power of the PC, for example, doubled every two years in the 1980s; IBM estimates that a machine selling in 1991 for the same price as its 1981 model was 12 to 20 times faster, had 64 times more internal memory, and 500 times more disk storage. More expensive PCs are 100 times faster than the ones made in the early 1980s.

Along with this still-growing capacity for differentiation and diversity, technology has given managers the information and intelligence they need to make the right decisions—no matter where they are doing their managing. More, expert systems can *tell* the manager what the right decision should be, given a set of premises, rules, and specific conditions.

Meanwhile, what we are seeing now will continue. In an effort to remain competitive, U.S. companies have slimmed down and decentralized many of their operations. The aim has been to allow divisions to operate more profitably on their own, and to have the freedom to determine pricing, manufacturing, marketing, and distribution policies independently. Decentralized units are often able to hire new workers, set their own pay scales, and be responsible for development and employment continuity with less direction from corporate staffs. In many cases, the strategy has worked, and the divisions have become more profitable than in the past when they were part of a larger, more monolithic corporate environment.

It came as no shock that these smaller-sized, integrated-product-line, customer-oriented companies performed better than their larger, more bureaucratic, multiproduct former selves. The flexibility these new companies found helped them to shift more easily into and out of markets, move manufacturing sites, introduce or discontinue products, and regroup workforces. There are signs, however, that although this trend will continue, continued decentralization of functions will occur only as companies see further cost advantages in doing so. And recentralization may be occurring in certain situations. The pendulum may have swung out as far as it could and may be swinging back toward selective centralization.

The second major trend of recent years that will have a continuing impact on the future involves reductions in force. While trying to stay even with or ahead of the competition, many firms realized that profitability could be maintained only by reducing labor costs. As a result, many firms held the line on labor contract increases and eliminated many positions.

From an organizational perspective, a more significant target for savings became the high-priced middle manager or staff specialist, who was becoming increasingly expensive when compared with the value provided. The organization strived to become "leaner and meaner," employing fewer employees who would be more productive. We expect this trend to continue as self-directed work teams and self-managed work become a very profitable way of producing our goods and services. Information sharing and "smart" systems will permit ever-widening spans of control, often making traditional supervisory roles obsolete. The boss as coach or instructor will remain; the boss as work director will be rare.

In the 1980s and 1990s, the predominant cost-containment strategy that emerged examined the various staff functions to see if the roles and missions of, for example, finance, MIS, human resources, legal, and purchasing were appropriate. We expect that this type of examination will continue in the future, as companies prepare their annual budgets and review staff sizes. Organizations will continue to shrink, and staff groups and roles will be closely scrutinized. Unless a particular position or function is strategically oriented, vitally needed, and cost effective (all aspects of value added approach), it will be eliminated. Areas which are likely to survive are those which are highly technical, analytical, focused on the specific problems of a particular company, and cannot be easily obtained from others. If a service can be obtained from outside sources, it very likely will be. To survive, a staff function will have to be unique, and be able to demonstrate its value to the user and the buyer, since companies will still have to contain overhead expenses to maintain profitability. Global competition and a continued negative balance of payments will maintain their downward pressure on U.S. corporate profits and our own wages. The twin forces of low-cost labor in the emerging nations as well as the highly productive workforces of countries such as Japan and Germany make the need for productivity aims in U.S. corporations more important than ever if we are to continue to enjoy a fruitful economy and satisfying lifestyles.

Effects of Organizational Change

After examining these trends, clearer images of the companies and the human resources managers of the future begin to emerge. In terms of sales, the future company may be larger, but not by much. It will employ fewer full-time people. There will be a relatively large contingent workforce of contractors, part-timers, consultants, and rehires to enable the firm to expand and contract more easily. The company will consist of many small units, each economically and geographically situated to sustain the greatest competitive advantage. These highly decentralized units will do business on a global scale, with at least as many, if not more, manufacturing sites and sales offices overseas as in the United

States. More sales dollars will be generated by the international branches than by the domestic ones.

The company of the future will produce a wider variety of products than it does today, but it is likely to carry less inventory than today. Better information regarding customer buying habits, product life cycles, distribution patterns, inventory control systems (just-in-time and beyond), and more responsive purchasing and manufacturing systems will enable the company to improve turnaround on customer orders. Because of lower breakeven points and smaller production quantities, the future company will manufacture to order on short notice when that is economical.

The company will maintain strong advertising and sales campaigns, often globally oriented. These products will enjoy high customer loyalty, and sustained brand-name recognition. The company will care about its customers, spending money to let them know it and communicating with them to differentiate their company's products and price—performance advantages from those of the competition.

Effects on the Role of Human Resources

The central human resources function will have two primary areas and roles: (1) analyzing the business, providing leadership, and setting policy; and (2) providing cohesion and consistency in plan administration, primarily through technology. These roles will stem from the influences outlined above: Decentralization will push the programs themselves into the divisions, and technological advances will enable automation of administrative work and ensure low-cost delivery.

The central human resources group will continue to be valued for the overall direction and leadership it can provide for succession planning, senior management development, strategic planning, workforce deployment, compensation and benefits planning, equal employment and pay equity, ethics, and oversight. The local human resources manager will be poised to intervene in situations where skills in problem diagnosis, organizational effectiveness, and performance management are required.

The human resources groups will take a leadership position in both these roles, not merely react. The human resources function overall will lean toward purchasing programs and contracting activities out rather than building them from scratch or providing them themselves. It should be flexible and quick to abandon programs that prove ineffective. Few specialists will remain, since they tend to become obsolete.

From a policy standpoint, the human resources manager will issue guidelines (hopefully electronically) to line units that lay out what needs to be done, but not how to do it in detail. The systems will be able to direct or at least guide the user's actions. The last 4-inch-thick personnel procedures manual should have been published years ago.

The Role of Communications in Future Organizations

The company of the future will have a global, integrated telecommunications network, through which customer, supplier, financial, human resources, and interoffice messages will travel. Although highly sensitive, confidential company information will be transmitted through the system, complex security arrangements will assure that employees will be able to gain access (based on their need to know) to their own data as well as to some data on company operations. Employees will be able to access information regarding company performance, for example, its sales, account receivables, production volume, inventory, and similar information, on an up-to-date basis. Employees will be treated as shareowners, business partners, and members of management, because in reality they often will be all three in addition to being employees.

This network will permit employees, customers, and suppliers who need to gain access to it to do so very easily. Technological change will bring new production and staffing models to analyze utilities and resource use and productivity. Extension of networks that incorporate nonproprietary competitors' data, and information from outside service bureaus and data banks, will also be prevalent.

The integrated network will be accessible virtually anywhere in the world where the company does business and will link the end user by voice, video, imaging, and data to any other user or sets of users connected to the network. Teleconferencing, training sessions, sales presentations, product demonstrations, and similar activities will be handled via this network, extending the global reach of companies. Automatic translators will be available, helping to break the language barrier. Working at home will be easier and permitted for many individuals, but will still not be the norm because of the complex nature of much work, and the employees' psychological and social needs to work in a team setting and to interact with others. Data exchange and remote accessing and printing of documents will be easier and cheaper than in today's systems. Still, we can expect that the office of the future, though highly electronic and with imbedded imaging, will still have more paper than is desirable, because more information will be generated.

Communications and the Role of Human Resources

This same network will transport the administrative and record-keeping systems we now associate with the human resources and payroll functions. The ability to hire an employee; change a reporting relationship, benefits, and compensation rate; keep track of beneficiaries and dependents; and pay an employee will be contained in this shared system. This information will also be available to insurance carriers, banks, hospitals, doctors, government bodies, and others as needed. Data review and entry will be tightly controlled, with limited access to selected data fields. Work processes will have been reengineered and restructured, eliminating many inefficiencies. The system will contain information on production and marketing results, budgeting and forecasting data, competitor data when available, and links with national and international information banks. Statistics regarding the "health" of the workforce will be available to managers. This data will permit the organization to spot key trends in production, use of overtime, training hours, accidents, customer satisfaction levels, and worker attitudes. These indices will be predictors of the quality of the workforce and enable management to take early corrective action to ward off potential problems.

The system will also be tied into larger networks. For example, employee pension systems will automatically track pension credits and move them into the proper pension pools, which will be established by then on a national basis, enabling worker flexibility.

Effects on Applications and Users

These human resources systems will be built and maintained by the central human resource specialist group, but they will be administered locally by human resources representatives at the local level. This system of the future will have several audiences that will access it directly: senior management for the reports and statistics it needs to run the business; an outside constituency of those who need data, such as insurance carriers and actuaries; and the line unit itself, comprised of the employee, the manager, and the personnel representative.

An integral part of the system will be a series of policy interpretations and knowledge-based systems which will permit employees and management to obtain answers to particular work problems and situations arising from the work setting. Such items as conflict resolution, questions of pay for time not worked, access to company material, use of company equipment, assessment, training programs, career guidance, and more will be available on-line for those who need it, tailored to the work unit or location of the requester. These highly integrated systems will permit human resources departments to be related more directly to business and management problems than to administration.

Other expert systems and models projecting employees' retirement pay, options on future value of monies invested, opportunities for advancement in the home office or other work units on an international basis, including associated companies inside and outside the current corporate umbrella, will be part of the system. Employees will be encouraged to change their own data directly, making benefit choices, changing tax withholding, and revising personal information. Other human resources information data entry and analysis will be handled directly by the line unit or by managers in the field.

Systems Development Issues

The standard data portion of a human resource information system will be supported by those building and maintaining the central system, and local information will be supported by people in the field units who will fit and modify the central systems to the local unit's needs. The technical work should be similar to today's. Those who develop and implement the systems will have to contend with the same, and often even more, problems as we now encounter, such as changing corporate strategies, international challenges, culture clashes among users, learning and introducing new technologies, lack of resources, and not enough time. It's fairly clear that those difficulties will remain.

The underlying technologies will be highly user oriented, with voice activation and language adaption built into the product and database management systems which will be much easier to implement and change by the human resources team. The value-added part of the work, as today, will be in understanding of the work that has to be performed and in improving its fit to available technology. Advances in both hardware and software will continue to outpace the user's ability to digest and deploy them.

Advances in relational systems, knowledge-based systems, and systems development software will permit databases to contain and support as many different compensation, benefit, and career development plans and programs as there are employees. While this approach to human resource management may not be desirable in all companies—or even permitted by the tax codes and benefits regulations in some nations—it will enable extremely efficient administration. In many more situations than we care to admit, our inflexible payroll and HRIS systems and the underlying administrative infrastructure preclude dramatically new and different employer-employee relationships.

The company of the future will rely more on technology than it does today to reach its markets, deliver its products, and satisfy its customers. And, it is clear, human resources work will rely heavily on technology, because most of the management information and administrative processes remain to be automated. Professionals in the human resources end of that technology will play a major role in seeing that the transformation takes place.

The Challenge Ahead

Another benefit of these new technologies is that they will enable the human resources function to spend more time with its customers—the line manager and employees—on the activities that matter. The needs of these constituents have often been overlooked in the past because of the more pressing demands of meeting legislative and administrative plan requirements. By reshaping the human resources roles, we will help attain a closer fit with the business objectives by supporting the users' needs. In recent client engagements as well as outside surveys, it has become dramatically clear that the heavy administrative orientation of human resources work of the past is not what the customer wants the human resources function to be. Line managers generally rate administrative work as of low to intermediate importance, and unfortunately, also rate the quality of that service as below average to average. Line managers want the human resources function to be a more active business partner—to help with performance problems, training and development programs, and organizational issues.

To enable the human resources function to be more effective, the challenge of human resources management through the HRIS manager is to begin the reshaping work and carry it through in order to ensure the role is altered for the better. As this book has attempted to show, millions of dollars are being wasted in most corporations each year due to the misalignment of the HR systems and outdated and cumbersome human resources policies and procedures. By satisfying the customer's needs, the HRIS manager will meet the multiple objectives of helping realign the human resources work, increasing worker productivity, and cutting staff costs.

I believe the HRIS manager will have to lead the effort to reshape this work. In order to get on with this agenda, I suggest a three-point action program be adopted as follows:

1. Develop a representative cross-functional line management steering committee to assist with this program and help sort out the customer issues and focus the critical success factors, and to settle on an acceptable redefined HR business mission. The line managers are the clients and should help affirm the new responsibilities of the human resources function and understand where the "high touch" component and value-added nature of the function can best be maintained. They should, in the true sense of the word, "steer" the process.

2. Reengineer all major work processes (as outlined in Chapter 5) in order to develop the best ways to deliver these services, establish new organizational lines, generate cost savings, and help identify system requirements for the new technology. Nothing should be implemented until the processes have been reworked and aligned with the new mission.

3. Establish specific action plans (using the principles set forth in Chapter 3) to given senior management some achievable goals and targets to move the human resources function closer to is new mission. The line management steering committee should sponsor these plans and hold the HR management team accountable for their implementation. These action plans are needed, and they are needed now.

Will all this happen by the year 2000? Perhaps for some companies, but not for all. But if a company can achieve even some of these advantages, it will have a much greater chance of remaining profitable well into the third millenium.

Index

About the Author

Alfred J. Walker is a Principal with the New York City consulting firm of Towers Perrin. He specializes in the application of computer-based technology to human resource and management functions. His recent clients have included companies such as American Express, Coca-Cola, Dun & Bradstreet, Marriott, 3M, and Exxon. Before joining Towers Perrin, Mr. Walker directed human resources technology at AT&T for more than 17 years. Throughout his distinguished career, he has assisted more than 150 clients with their HRIS.

Recognized as a leading innovator in the human resources field, Mr. Walker is also a respected author and speaker. His prior books include *HRIS Development: A Project Team Guide to Building an Effective Personnel Information System.*